Supervision
of
Applied
Training

SUPERVISION OF APPLIED TRAINING

A Comparative Review

FOREWORD BY ALLEN E. IVEY

DEWAYNE J. KURPIUS,
RONALD D. BAKER,
and IRENE D. THOMAS

GP

GREENWOOD PRESS
Westport, Connecticut • London, England

Library of Congress Cataloging in Publication Data
Main entry under title:

Supervision of applied training.

Includes bibliographies and index.
1. Mental health—Study and teaching. 2. Social work education. I. Kurpius,
DeWayne J. II. Baker, Ronald D. III. Thomas, Irene D.
RA790.8.S94   658.31'24   76-28640
ISBN 0-8371-9288-9

Library of Congress Catalog Card Number: 76-28640
ISBN: 0-8371-9288-9

First published in 1977

Greenwood Press, Inc.
51 Riverside Avenue, Westport, Connecticut 06880

Printed in the United States of America

Contents

Figures

Tables

Foreword

Supervision in the helping services has too long been considered an art form reserved only for the master practitioner. This volume does much to explicate the process of supervision by carefully delineating the common denominators of quality supervision, examining alternative models of supervision, and providing a broad overview of the research.

The task of an effective supervisor is analogous to that of a master craftsperson. Both must (1) impart skills, knowledge, and wisdom and (2) *bring out* the trainee's inherent and natural skills so that he or she does not merely repeat what the master or others have done before. With effective supervision a craft or profession not only renews itself, but also has built-in processes which insure change and progress through the contributions of new and innovative individuals.

Kurpius, Thomas, and Baker have brought together an important statement on the supervision process. Although they cite the importance of a general theory or model of supervision, they carefully and wisely avoid making a definitive statement of what should be. Rather, by bringing together the diverse views of the authors of these chapters, they provide us with a foundation for an overarching view of the supervision process—its goals, methods, and outcomes. This foundation will be useful in fields as varied as education, social work, psychology, and medicine. In addition, paraprofessional and lay educational programs can profit from the insights of this work.

I am particularly taken with the concluding chapter, where the authors examine both the commonalities of supervisory approaches and the specific differences. The clear definition of the different models for supervision—the teaching, consultation, therapy, administrative, evaluation, and renewal models—provides a useful "map" of alternative supervisory styles. This map could well be imparted to students going through the supervisory process so that they will have some idea of what is happening to them. Too often beginning human service workers are thrown into a supervisory session expecting to be taught, but ending up, instead, with therapy or perhaps even evaluation. I do not mean to denigrate or support any special model, but rather to point out that those being supervised might profit more from the process if they had a clear understanding of the individual supervisor's purpose and style. Further, some individual supervisors do not know themselves what they are doing, and they could profit from the self-examination that the authors suggest.

My own belief is that the human service profession has been overly zealous in its pursuit of the "correct" model for supervision. All too often those who write about the process present us with definitive answers as to what is needed. Those committed to a competency-oriented approach sometimes lose sight of the purpose in their examination of the process, and those advocating an analytic/medical model may be so oriented toward "fitting" everything into a specific mold that they lose the larger situation within which they are working. Effective supervision lies somewhere between the minutia of the behavioral objectives model and the single-minded authoritarianism of traditional teaching/therapy models, although even rigid adherence to these models has value for some individuals.

The direction for the future will undoubtedly be determined by answering the question: "Which supervision method for which individual under what conditions at what time?" Just as our clientele differ, so do our supervisees. Some teachers- or therapists-intraining need therapy or group work in communication before they will benefit from any other type of supervision. Others may need structure; for them, a carefully systematized competency program or an instructional series would be the best way to begin supervision. Others may learn best by simply watching their own supervisor work. And just as there are "natural craftspeople," who function best when left to their own resources, there are "natural helpers," whom the supervisor should leave alone or perhaps even learn from. Determining the best route for the individual trainee is an important next step; it is practical both clinically and in research.

Speaking from my own experience, my high points as a supervisor have not come from my best lectures or case presentations. They have not come from the satisfaction that comes from having helped a student work through a "heavy" case. Although these are fine and important experiences, I remember particularly the special moments when I found myself learning *with* my supervisee and we became colleagues engaged in mutual exploration for the benefit of each other and humankind. This experience occurs frequently enough, for me and for others, to convince me that it is the heart of effective supervision. Yes, I and other supervisors have something to share and teach, but we are not fully mature until we recognize what we do not know. We must become participants in the search for meaning in our own lives, the supervisee's life, and the life of those whom he or she is helping.

I compliment all the authors in this valuable text. Psychiatric education does, indeed, provide the foundation for the supervision process, and social work has ably carried on this process. It is my impression, however, that counselor education has carried the supervision process farther and in a clearer manner than any other profession. The balance of theory, research, and clinical innovation in counselor education is a contribution to the entire helping field which has not yet been fully appreciated. In recent years there have been giant strides in supervision in teacher education, and the literature in the area could well provide new directions for psychiatry, psychology, social work, and counselor education.

The challenge for supervision in a future clouded by tight budgets, increasingly limited state certification and licensing systems, and an aging human services staff clearly lies in renewal and inservice supervision and training. Continuing education, special workshops, and new models of peer review are needed. The human services profession will be in a position to provide effective supervision and upgrading if there is a sense of the interconnections among teaching and psychiatric work, counselor education and social work, and the training of lay people and professionals. If, however, professionals choose to stay in their own narrow cubicles, there may be slow professional starvation for all.

In this volume, Kurpius, Thomas, and Baker bring us to a fuller awareness of the task before us. At first glance, some will wonder why articles with such a broad range of views are included. Yet it is this very diversity and breadth of vision that the helping profession needs at this time. We must thank these authors, individually and collectively, for bringing together such an effective array of work, theory, and research on the supervision process. May I suggest that the reader join these authors in the continuing search for a unified and unifying theory of helping. They have provided us with an important beginning and much stimulation. This book will occupy a central place in the thinking of all those who are seriously interested in the helping process.

Allen E. Ivey, Amherst, Mass., 1977

Preface

The importance of supervision in the training of teachers, counselors, psychiatrists, social workers, and clinical psychologists is marked by a considerable volume of literature as well as by a long tradition of practice. Despite the significant role of supervision in the preparation of professionals in these major human and social services, the rigor with which educators and trainers define the process, assess and evaluate the products, and conduct inquiry is remarkably weak. Inadvertently or not, writers in this field almost invariably cast supervision into a category unique into itself. In so doing, they mask the complexity of personal, interpersonal, learning, and communication variables. Even more important, when supervision is isolated as some unique process, it is removed from the mainstream of behavioral and social inquiry. This book is an attempt to explore critically a representative body of literature on supervision in the above fields. Each review chapter emphasizes similar topics, although the authors have presented them in their own styles and from the viewpoint of their own disciplines. These topics are the goals of supervision, models and theories, roles, techniques and methods, evaluation, research and historical trends. All of the reviews span a decade or more of the literature of the various fields.

They are intended to convey a representation of the conceptual and research literature; they are not exhaustive compilations of the total literature.

In the final chapter, we present an overview and comparison of significant issues that the contributing authors developed in their writings. We discuss each of the major themes mentioned above and provide a cross-referencing section so that interested readers can compare supervision topics across different fields.

The final portion of the concluding chapter contains some of our observations and views. We offer several models for conceptualizing the supervision of applied training. Our intent is not to prescribe *a* model, but to encourage educators and trainers to examine their individual and program practices, and to promote a basis for systematic evaluation and inquiry.

DeWayne J. Kurpius
Ronald D. Baker

Bloomington, Indiana
March 1977

Supervision
of
Applied
Training

Introduction

Psychiatry, counseling and psychotherapy, teaching, and social work—
practitioners in these fields all deliver a human service of one sort
or another to a client or group of clients. In that respect, they share
a number of interests and goals. The shared component in which
we are most interested is the training dimension, that is, the method
by which potential practitioners in these fields are trained to perform
their services. *Supervised applied training* is currently the dominant
mode for training professionals and renewing the skills of inservice
practitioners. With that in mind, we assumed that supervisors in
these fields might share many of the same challenges, problems,
and general goals. Yet few attempts have been made heretofore to
bring the body of knowledge implicit in the experience of prominent
trainers together with the research on applied training. Our primary
collective aim, then, is to provide a compact review of research and
literature published since 1960 which pertains to the training supervision of psychiatrists, counselors, teachers, and social workers.
Our secondary aim is to provide commentaries by prominent trainers
on the present and future state of the supervisory function within
their individual fields in order to encourage comparisons and patterns of possible influence. Finally, we have sought to fill some of

the gaps described by the reviewers/contributors by outlining a strong, data-based model for supervision which might serve the needs of any professional supervisor in any applied setting.

One of the things we discovered in compiling these reviews is that the traditional role of supervisor, which is assumed to be a constant, a reliable pivot in the training process, is subject to as many challenges as any other educational role. Traditionally the supervisor has been an autonomous figure who tends to answer to his own personal educational goals and philosophies rather than to a specific authority or an accepted model of supervision. As the arena for educational debates grows, however, the superior cannot escape the pressure to examine current issues. The move toward accountability, for example, demands that the supervisor be cognizant of whom he is most accountable to—his trainees, his trainees' clients, the target system (school, hospital, or agency), or his own sponsoring university. The trend toward accountability not only forces a redefinition of training roles and emphases, but it also increases the likelihood of collaboration among trainers with varying expertise. Rather than working in isolation, the supervisor may now be expected to form a working partnership with experienced practitioners at the training site and with training specialists in instructional media, for example. This movement, of course, raises the question of who will ultimately prevail over the training of initiates.

With educational movements, as with any movement, one finds the creation of "camps." The theoretical schism that our contributors point out, either explicitly or implicitly, is between the behaviorists and the mentalists. This schism is particularly evident in the supervisory styles reported in the articles on teacher and counselor education, for the issue of "what constitutes teaching" is called into question. But all of our writers are aware of the potential interplay between "systematized learning" and "learning by discovery" when they discuss the various supervisory models employed in their professions.

All our contributors accepted a definition of supervision as the conceptualization, implementation, control, and management of training in applied settings and conditions. We further agreed that in order for supervision to take place, a trainee or trainees must be working with clients (students, patients, or counselees) in preparation for future work with future clients. We found, additionally, that all the training specialists contributing to this review cited the increasing value placed on field-based training as opposed to classroom training. Their findings, both through personal experience and through the literature reviewed, support the movement toward earlier and more intensive field experiences for the trainee. Another area of agreement among our contributors is concern over the dearth of empirical studies measuring the effectiveness of supervisory techniques. It seems apparent that the number of theories for devising and evaluating training systems far exceeds the machinery developed for testing those theories. Our contributors sorely lament this state of affairs, but they are not surprised by it, considering the highly controversial issues related to empirical testing of educational performance.

Beyond these areas of agreement, there is considerable variation in practices, concerns, and goals among supervisors in these fields, according to the reports of our contributors. The supervisory arena, for example, is variously delimited with respect to the demands of different field settings. Clearly, the demands of a teaching hospital will differ from those of a public high school or social work agency. The hospital setting seems to impose more control on the training experience and forces a more direct client orientation than one finds in other field settings. Although the training hospital is not a clear analogue to other field settings, it has probably been most responsible for revealing the limitations of classroom training.

The question of who the client is seems to vary most according to goal identification; no less prominent a question is who the supervisor should be. Should he be a practicing professional or a university teacher? Should he play the role of consultant, therapist, resource person, critic, or traditional teacher (whatever that means)? Most of our writers supported the movement toward "increased ownership" by the trainee as a means of enlarging his or her experience. The literature reviewed tends to support the notion that the trainee in isolation with his supervisor and a small group of clients is becoming a model of the past. It is generally believed that trainees cannot realistically develop into practitioners prepared to meet complex and changing social needs unless they have input from their peers and experienced practitioners as well as from a large variety of clients. Hence we see the growth of the group practicum experience in counseling and social work and the rise of the school learning center as the preferred site for teacher training.

Related to the level of preparedness is the question of when supervised field training should take place—at the conclusion of course work, in conjunction with course work, or as a replacement for course work. Some of the writers report interest in promoting developmental stages of applied training and its supervision in order to "wean" the trainee satisfactorily.

The issues and questions just raised, then, seem to imply that despite the differing practices reported in the literature, the ultimate goals of supervision must be fairly uniform among the fields. After all, supervisors in the human services are all concerned with preparing and initiating professionals. However, as our writers point out, the absence of an overall conceptual framework of applied training necessarily creates a blurred image of the goals of that training and may be responsible for the lack of evaluative measures whereby trainees and supervisors are reviewed. We will see conceptual crosscurrents within each field as well as between the various fields. The major pivot might be called outcome orientation versus process orientation, that is, a difference in where priorities lie with respect to goals and means of evaluation. Is the priority on saving the client (pupil, patient, or counselee) or on developing the trainee to save later clients? The supervisor who steps in between the trainee and the trainee's client may be more interested in saving the client, the system, or his diagnosis than he is in developing the trainee. And in some situations, that is as it should be. The ultimate decisions about which goals are most defensible may be conditioned by the supervisor's intended relationship with his trainees, a matter which is given much attention in the following pages.

Our writers reluctantly agree that the ultimate aim of most supervisors is to socialize the trainee into the profession. But with that aim, there is a risk of perpetuating the stagnant parts of the system and blocking change where it is most needed. The article on "Renewal Training" by McGreevy and Rosengren aptly addresses this issue and urges the creation of a new supervisory level, a supervisor to oversee total systems changes.

Concerning this and other levels of supervision, a final question (which perhaps should be the first question) must be asked. Is supervision of applied training necessary? To phrase the question differently, what does the supervisor offer to the training process that could not be acquired in some other way, perhaps more effectively? Although it is not often asked of trainees, this question is in part answered by a report on trainees' perception of the supervisory function (see Brammer & Wassmer). Students clearly want supervision, but they are not sure of what type they want until the training period is over. Surely there is something to be learned from increased collaboration among all participants, and surely there are many insights to be borrowed from trainees and other practitioners.

We begin with a chapter on psychiatric training for several reasons. Recently there has been a rediscovery of the analogy between the medical professions and applied educational fields—mainly on the basis of similar training procedures and settings, the controlled granting of credentials, and so forth. Certain differences betwen the training of psychiatrists and the training of other human service professionals are worth consideration, for highlighting such differences may lead to mutual influence where overlap does, in fact, occur.

A primary goal of psychiatric trainers is the creation of a self-regulating, intrinsically motivated practitioner whose prime responsibility is to the patient. While educators and social workers, who also have clients, are struggling with the movement toward multiple accountability, psychiatrists remain clearly client oriented. The psychiatric training supervisor is relatively unconcerned with the trainee's position as a future representative of the profession. And once the trainee is a licensed psychiatrist, he can be far more independent than his counterparts in counseling and guidance, teaching, or social work who, now more than ever, are held accountable to parents, administrators, the community, training institutions, and the society at large, as well as to their immediate clients.

The implications of this differing orientation are particularly interesting when one considers goals, training controls, and the evident but slow changes that are taking place in training emphasis.

Psychiatric training supervisors, because of the traditionally clear direction of purpose, offer a counterpoint to other fields in their use of supervisory control. As we all know, the trainer in any applied field has a great deal of control over the future of the trainee, both as an evaluator and as an image-making role model. To what ends, to what purpose that control is exercised determines the orientation that a trainee will assume for himself. In the medical professions, the orientation has been toward outcome rather than process. In educational fields, the opposite orientation has been the rule. Although the goals of the other fields represented here are not as clearly defined or agreed upon, it appears from the articles that follow that these fields are moving slowly toward an outcome orientation which requires a firmer delineation of goals. On the other hand, psychiatric trainers (already more process oriented than other *medical* trainers) are moving increasingly toward process considerations in attaining their desired outcomes, already rather firmly fixed in client mental health. It appears, then, that the time is ripe for some collaboration among professions. In fact, Kagan and Werner point out that resident trainers who teach have been encouraged to learn instructional techniques from professional educators, and they report successful results from this movement.

You will note in the following articles that supervising the trainee is systematized to the degree that goals are recognized and identified. We believe that the trainers and the training fields represented here offer enough similarity, yet diversity, to suggest other broad perspectives on the applied training process. In order to enlarge your own perspective on applied training, we suggest that you pose questions while reading these pieces, questions which are particularly appropriate to the role with which you identify—trainer/professor, trainee/student, or field supervisor/administrator. For instance, what are your training goals? What kind of role do you wish to play in the process? What is your relationship with your colleagues in the training process? Which techniques or methodologies do you believe advance your learning? What is your stance on the relationship between process and outcome? What is your experiential reaction to the findings of the research reported here?

In the final chapter, the editors invite you to further investigate the supervisory process. To permit easy comparison among the fields and to generate inquiry across common issues, we first provide a topical summary. This summary is followed by an index with page references to the following eight topics which are, to varying degrees, discussed by all the contributors: goals of supervised training, models of supervised training, supervisory roles, supervisory skills, techniques of supervision, evaluation of supervisors, research issues, and historical trends. Only in this way could we make accessible to the reader the enormous bulk of information contained in each review article.

Our next summarizing attempt is a schematization and description of the three major and current approaches to supervision—teaching, consultation, and therapy—as they emerged from the literature reviewed. Our intention here is to uncover the underlying assumptions, goals, and practices and the probable outcomes inherent in each approach so that they can be more fully compared and evaluated.

Finally, we offer a challenge to supervisors in all related fields of human service, a challenge which we believe has merit for the planning of effective supervisory programs. *Planning* is the key word here since the literature on supervision reveals that little intentional planning has been built into supervisory models thus far. We present a planning model that neither ignores tradition nor is bound by it. Instead, what we propose is a highly dynamic conceptual model which is based on sound inquiry and evaluative procedures at every stage. These three discrete yet continuous stages are program preparation, implementation, and revision/renewal. In outlining the model based on these stages, we have included practical, data-based procedures and evaluative measures which can serve the ongoing needs of trainers in the human services. In addition, we would hope that such a model might encourage further research into the effectiveness of training procedures.

We believe, along with our reviewers, that it is time to improve the supervisory process, to make it more responsive to the ever-changing needs of clients, social institutions, and educational institutions. While some educators fear that the systematization of such an individualized training stage ultimately can be dehumanizing and impersonal, we believe that advanced planning and the regular review of a program's efficacy by its participants can only result in positive, purposeful change. We seek the kind of change that may bring training *processes* closer in line with desired *outcomes*. Planning for that eventuality will most likely contribute to rather than detract from the person-to-person spirit inherent in the human services professions.

Supervision in Psychiatric Education

NORMAN KAGAN AND ARNOLD WERNER

INTRODUCTION

Psychiatry occupies a unique position in medicine. A distant medical specialty concerned with the prevention and treatment of a defined set of disorders, its interests also extend to matters of health and illness of all people and to the development of certain skills and attitudes in all physicians. The field still lacks specific role functions, and psychiatrists follow divergent models. Some psychiatrists are reductionistic, with a heavy biologic emphasis; others are concerned primarily with broad social and cultural issues.

The field itself is in a state of transition. After the late nineteenth-century advances in systematic observation and classification, which coincided with the development of classical neuropathology, the early twentieth-century saw a very gradual interest growing in psychological theory. This interest accelerated with the growth of psychoanalysis, although in the 1930s somatic treatments for several illnesses were achieving new sophistication. Following World War II, psychoanalysis and psychodynamically oriented psychiatry experienced a growth spurt. Teaching and supervision in psychiatry seemed to have been concerned primarily with psychotherapy, particularly in a dyadic setting. A specific technique was elevated, and what had been tentative models in a previous era now became firm ones.

By the late 1950s, interest in social and cultural phenomena and their bearing on psychiatric illness began to increase. The 1960s saw this interest expressed clinically in community psychiatry. Training programs changed, and the emphasis on social issues resulted in psychiatrists becoming involved in areas far afield from traditional psychiatry. During the time that the community was being rediscovered, new medications which could alter the behavior of people with certain psychiatric disorders came into widespread use. More recently, biochemical advances and genetic studies offered new hope of understanding some aspects of schizophrenia and the affective disorders.

The transitional nature of the field was captured by Grinker (1964) in the whimsical title of his thoughtful and serious look at the field, "Psychiatry Rides Madly in All Directions." Today it appears to us that a little more direction and one hopes a little less madness are beginning to prevail. Questions are being asked, and studies are being conducted which may result in a more reliable, valid, and realistic approach to training and treatment and, in turn, to the integration of biological, psychological, and social factors in understanding man's behavior.

Initial attempts to deal with the expansion of information in many fields threatened a type of eclecticism that Clare (1972) terms "Reader's Digest psychiatry," with psychiatrists "regarded by their medical colleagues as intellectual and professional dilettantes, jacks of all subspecialties and masters of none [p. 754]." The complicated problem of providing an education in depth as well as breadth is being answered by attempts to formulate new theoretical frameworks to replace the strictly psychodynamic one (Abrams, 1969) and to be more specific about the components of a training program (Langee et al., 1972; Raskin, 1972; Reiser, 1972).

Critical reviews of past practices and future trends by Romano (1970) and West (1973) conclude that the basic biologic and behavioral sciences will be of increasing importance to the psychiatrist of the future. Kety (1974) addresses himself directly to the importance and validity of the medical model for psychiatry. He cites recent advances in psychiatric understanding and defines the scope and prominence of psychiatry and certain implications for training, including emphasis on the scientific method as applied to medicine.

Psychiatry now appears to be moving into the mainstream of medicine, for greater emphasis is being placed on understanding the biologic basis of illness. Educators and others are calling for psychiatrists to be of more assistance to their medical colleagues in the management of problems. Psychiatry also appears to be less possessive of certain skills. For example, psychotherapy, in the generic sense, is now accepted by psychiatry as being within the domain of many mental health professionals.

Psychiatrists and Non-Psychiatric Physicians

We can define a core set of psychiatric skills and functions which have persisted and will in all likelihood remain stable. Minimally, by the completion of training the psychiatrist is expected to be able to diagnose and treat a full range of mental disorders using a variety of modalities. Some treatment methods closely resemble traditional medical treatment and involve the use of pharmacologic agents; other methods involve psychotherapy and resemble the work of nonmedical mental health professionals. The psychiatrist is expected to work as a consultant in medical settings with patients suffering from physical illnesses and with the physicians and others who care for them. The psychiatrist is also expected to be able to function as a consultant in such nonmedical settings as schools and social agencies. Special skills acquired by psychiatrists who have chosen to act as agents of change or who are primarily involved in political or community activities are not generally included in formal training programs.

Medical practitioners other than psychiatrists also receive basic psychiatric training and do so for very valid reasons. Large numbers of patients who come to primary care physicians have psychologic problems either as their major complaint or as an important component of another health problem. The treatment dilemma posed by such patients has been immense. In those instances where the psychological basis of the disorder is not recognized, detrimental treatment may occur. Thus, while departments of psychiatry still train psychiatric specialists, they currently devote much of their time and resources to educating medical students, the majority of whom will be in fields other than psychiatry. The instruction of medical students and non-psychiatric physicians focuses only partially on teaching psychotherapeutic skills. For all physicians there is much to learn about skills which often derive from psychotherapy but which have broader applicability. Establishing the doctor-patient relationship, general interviewing and history taking, aiding and comforting the physically distressed, treating the terminally ill, and increasing patient adherence to a preventive program or a treatment regimen are examples of such skills.

Engel (1973) describes enduring attributes of medicine that cross time and social boundaries as well as specialty areas. These attributes include the complementarity of a need for help and a desire to provide service; the consistency of the transition from health to patienthood; the interpersonal nature of the encounter between the physician and his patient; clinical observation as the basis of data collection; analysis by reasoning, judgment, and decision making; and the social and interpersonal nature of the contract between the patient and physician. Of these attributes, the two dealing with the interpersonal nature of the doctor-patient encounter and contract very obviously relate to matters that psychiatry has been deeply concerned about both in its practice and in its teachings. An examination of the patient's need for help and the physician's desire to provide the help touches upon the development of the doctor-patient relationship. The transition from health to illness involves attention to a patient's awareness, perception, psychological state, and coping mechanisms, all areas addressed more by psychiatrists than by other physicians. Shakow (1972) discusses the importance of training in observation and specifies various types of observation—objective, participant, subjective, and self-observation. The ability to make observations and to use clinical reasoning and judgment depends as much upon the student's grasp of psychological matters as upon his possession of factual information. An analysis of these enduring attributes reveals that they are heavily dependent upon an education rich in the understanding of human behavior, an undertaking that traditionally has rested with departments of psychiatry.

Multidimensional Supervision

Just as the tasks performed by psychiatrists and non-psychiatric physicians involve a multiplicity of skills and talents, the supervision needed by psychiatric trainees is multidimensional. Nor is the role of supervisor unidimensional in nature. Unlike the trainee in teacher education or counselor education who is assigned a single supervisor during his period of internship, the psychiatric trainee (and the medical trainee) may have a series of supervisors with various specialties. These supervisors may be psychiatric social workers, clinical psychologists, or psychiatrists. They may be full-time faculty or affiliated people who have clinical rank. The latter group are often nonsalaried, nontenured professionals who serve as voluntary faculty. In the medical setting, such trainers consider it an honor to be asked to make a contribution to medical education.

One must also weigh the different learning needs of psychiatric residents and medical students. According to one study (Ables & Brandsma, 1973), these students prefer the general skills and knowledge acquired on psychiatric training rotations to the more highly specific subject matter usually included in resident training. Students also favored active participation and a set of experiences which seem to represent a more medically oriented approach to their training. Another study (Werkman, Landau, & Wakefield, 1973) shows that students look to people closer to their own peer group for supervision and that they are well supervised by residents.

Drawing on his long experience in working with non-psychiatric physicians, Kaufman (1971) argues that they need to have knowledge that is complete yet is within their own frame of reference. Specifically, he feels that

recognition of diagnostic categories is essential. Awareness of the complexities of personality functioning and interrelationships is important. Knowledge of the role of the patient-physician relationship and its utilization is part of the practice of medicine. There must also be the realization that the emotional problems with which the physician may be confronted are not neutral in terms of himself and that therefore capacity to perceive and handle them involves in most instances his own reaction to such problems [p. 610].

Each type of task to be performed by the psychiatrist or non-psychiatric physician requires a different kind of supervision. For instance, the diagnostic process appears to depend upon the practitioner's having a large mental library of cases against which to measure a case currently under examination. The work of Elstein, Kagan, and Shulman (1972) suggests that this library of cases resembles a set of paradigms which is added to with each new case. If their analogy is correct, the supervisory task in teaching the novice how to engage in diagnosis should consist of helping the student develop the critical capacities of observation and hypothesis generation which lead to the storage of valid information about human behavior. This process would be far more cognitive than simply learning psychotherapeutic skills. The success of some learning procedures might hinge upon structural rather than interpersonal matters. For instance, the trainee who is learning diagnosis and patient management ideally would benefit from the long-term follow-up of cases. When such follow-up is not available, the effectiveness of the learning situation can be diminished. This situation can result when the resident or student spends brief periods of time in various locations or does not have continuous responsibility for cases. However, if arrangements are made for the trainee to be notified whenever a patient reenters the health care system, he has the opportunity to correlate his early observations with later outcomes. Such a follow-up system is facilitated by computerized record-keeping systems rather than by specific supervisory techniques.

The area of psychotherapy supervision poses unique problems. Wide variations exist in the therapeutic strategies and goals of supervisors and departments. Psychotherapy supervision is not a known or standardized commodity. A wide range of psychotherapeutic approaches and activities are subsumed under the rubric of supervision, a point which is not specified often in the literature and which leads to confusion.

The lack of evaluation of psychotherapy supervision stems in part from the confusion over what kind of supervision is being done, with what kind of trainee, and for what purpose. Furthermore, the lack of adequate outcome studies involving patients in psychotherapy makes evaluating the supervisory role a more complicated problem since there is one more variable. We will, in a later section, look more closely at this matter.

In the following pages we will examine the current state of supervision in psychiatry, including the strategies and assumptions in psychotherapy supervision, supervision for the acquisition of specific skills, some of the technology being used in supervision, and the matter of evaluation.

ATTITUDES AND THEIR EXPRESSION IN PSYCHOTHERAPY

The matter of a trainee's development of certain attitudes necessary for therapeutic interaction is usually addressed indirectly through the supervisory process. However, there are examples of specially constructed experiences which aim at altering feelings and attitudes. In one of the very few studies based on systematic data collection and examining the relationship between clinical performance and personal traits, Liske, Ort, and Ford (1964) found that doctors rated highly by their colleagues in providing comprehensive care tended to define problems in ways which suggest a high level of objectivity and self-criticism while those rated less highly tended to define problems with respect to the patient's attributes and limitations. This startling difference in attitude on the part of the two groups of physicians suggests that "more effective clinical performance is associated with greater humanitarian concern and acceptance of responsibility [p. 79]." Conversely, the less effective physicians had impersonal relationships with their patients and yet expected recognition and attention from them. Such studies support the practice of constructing supervisory experiences to modify the attitudes and traits of medical students and residents in order to improve their medical performance.

Medical students' thoughts, attitudes, and behavior may be directly influenced by special experiences aimed at preventing dehumanization. In one project reported by Rubinstein and Levitt (1966), small groups of first year students were assigned to preceptors and met for group discussions of anxieties and the dehumanizing elements within the practice of medicine and for readings on subjects other than medicine. Attempting to increase "their capacity to respond sensitively to themselves and others [p. 287]," another group offered advanced medical students the opportunity to participate in a time-limited, goal-limited sensitivity group experience (Dashef, Espey, & Lazarus, 1974). As is typical of such groups, the participants themselves were the source of data.

Another approach to providing the students with attitude-altering supervision made use of small groups in which the members would role play a family affected by some distressing event. The "players" would then share with the rest of the group what it felt like to be so affected, and discussions would follow. The authors, Topham and Smith (1973), assumed that the students had the capacity to experience emotion and that their ability to empathize would be enhanced by experiencing the emotions of distressed people even in a simulated exercise.

Small group experiences were used in an attempt to modify the anxieties of second year students. Unlike the true sensitivity group in which the participants were the source of all data, these groups directly used clinical material and the reaction of the participants to the material (Cath, 1965). Concerned with a more selective group and working toward the specific goal of changing defensive reactions, Artiss and Levine (1973) conducted special seminars for oncology fellows dealing with the impact on the physician of severe illness, death, and dying. Concerning the approaches of providing supervision as problems arise and of working with problems at a slight distance, the authors observe that "if . . . the physician's anxiety is pointed out to him at the time of a crisis in patient management, it is likely that his anxiety will rise even higher [p. 1210]." From a supervisory point of view, the high anxiety level may result in the physician becoming arrogant and defensive to the point of transient disability.

Seeking an alternative means of coping with anxiety, Kagan (1973) has developed a series of filmed affect stimulation vignettes of a person confronting the trainee with threatening material. The supervisor helps the trainee deal with his reactions to the material. A modification of the basic technique makes use of variations in the trainee's physiologic parameters as a means of providing more feedback.

Although specific methodologies are not described for coping with the trainee's identity problems, such problems must be kept in mind by the supervisor (Tischler, 1972; Worby, 1970). Working with the trainee's identity problems, the supervisor is called upon to use psychotherapeutic skills; and this situation raises problems regarding the nature of the supervisor-supervisee relationship. Successful resolution of such problems enhances the trainee's functioning, but Halleck and Woods (1962) point out the potentially destructive forces that can result. Specifically, anxiety and guilt can be produced in the trainee when he is supervised in a fashion which highlights his inadequacies.

SKILLS AND THEIR USES
IN PSYCHOTHERAPY

Central and unique to the functioning of the psychiatrist and other physicians treating patients with emotional disorders are the skills of observation, diagnosis, pharmacologic and somatic treatment, and patient and ward management. The acquisition of skills in these areas begins early in medical school and continues throughout training. The beginning student learns how to make systematic observations and then learns how to use these observations to make diagnoses. The psychiatric resident often combines the diagnostic process with treatment management considerations. For the advanced resident, treatment and management often become primary considerations. Systematic methods of supervising beginning students as they learn to make observations and diagnoses are better developed at this time than are methods of supervising as they learn management or treatment, which more often follow an apprentice model.

Training the student in making observations begins with didactic experiences which may make use of filmed material, case presentations, demonstration interviews, and paper-and-pencil exercises. While acquiring the ability to make observations generally escapes supervision, in some schools students must write descriptions of demonstration interviews which are then evaluated. Once the student actually begins to interview patients, supervision by skilled teachers who are trained in teaching observation can be used to reinforce the didactic material learned earlier.

Differing from the usual concept of supervisory experiences are a variety of methods which make use of self-instruction. These self-instructional modes are not, strictly speaking, supervision, but they replace some traditional supervisory functions and permit the supervisor to be less of a tutor and more of an integrating influence. Suess (1973) has undertaken to teach freshman medical students psychodiagnosis and observation by using self-instructional programmed videotapes. He compared the self-instruction mode with traditional lecture material, and by using course testing, he found no difference in the gains made by the two groups of students.

A study by Miller and Tupin (1972) describes a method of teaching clinical psychopathology, emphasizing symptom recognition and diagnosis, which does not require direct supervision. The program is known as SAID (Systems Analysis Index for Diagnosis). Cline and Garrard (1973) evaluated SAID and found that students who took the complete course could make observations about and diagnose filmed patients better than students who took the course but did not attend the videotape feedback sessions. With live patients, the findings were not as clear. Interestingly, students rated the tutorial experience as better than the SAID approach, which in turn was rated as preferable to the live lecture approach. The tutorial experience most closely resembles what students expect of supervision, and the investigators' findings may suggest that some students prefer the personal contact inherent in such supervision. Such preferences, if they exist, must be weighed against the cost of personalized instruction.

In a highly refined course referred to as the Psychiatry Learning System or PLS, clinical medical students are taught using self-instruction techniques, interlocking videotapes and text, and extensive evaluation procedures. Preliminary studies have demonstrated the efficacy of the system in teaching cognitive material (see Randels, McCurdy, Powell, Kilpatrick, & Keeler, 1974). Their instructors, who are freed from lecturing, are now spending more time in clinical teaching.

Kilpatrick and Randels (1974) found a negative correlation between the performance on SAID tasks and the external locus of control, a high anxiety trait, and mood states of depression, anger, and confusion. They also report that "clinical performance and personality are not independent of method of instruction [p. 22]." They base their conclusions on different correlations between personality variables and outcome skills for a group which used PLS and a group which used traditional learning methods. These results would appear to support our earlier contention that different methods might be needed for some students, even in learning observational and diagnostic skills.

The classical means of supervising students in their clinical years involves the case presentation. In this model, the trainee evaluates a case and presents it to his supervisor and a group of peers. This presentation is often followed by the supervisor examining or interviewing the patient. Discussion follows. Emphasis is placed on the case and the supervisor's examination. Another approach shifts the focus to the student by having the student conduct an interview before the group of a patient he has not previously evaluated. The patient chosen has already been evaluated by another member of the group. The supervisor and the group then evaluate his technique and the data he has gathered. Discussion focuses on data gathering and hypothesis generation, but the supervisor has an opportunity to demonstrate specific skills to the students. This approach seeks to provide the student with needed skill supervision in areas which are usually not supervised, namely, data gathering, observation, and hypothesis generation.

The psychiatric resident must learn how to manage a variety of patient problems in a variety of settings. Much of his time is usually spent on inpatient units where the most severely ill patients are hospitalized. Inpatient units can be extraordinarily complex social systems, and the resident may have to manage this complexity. Usually calling upon his previous medical experience, the resident makes a variety of attempts to function within the unit's structure. Supervision in this setting appears to be dictated by the model set by the faculty member in charge of the unit. Sometimes a more senior resident supervises a less experienced resident, and there are others who may indirectly supervise the resident. For instance, the head nurse, unit social worker, or other permanent staff person may provide guidelines to the resident. There are few reports providing a systematic examination of learning in this setting. One can find descriptive material saying how it is done at one institution or another, but we do not know how transferable this information is.

Inpatient units do make use of ward meetings and staff meetings to review management decisions. Ward meetings typically involve the staff and patients and give all concerned with patient management an opportunity to observe and interact with all of the patients on the unit. Following the group meeting, the residents and staff members gather to discuss diagnoses and management, ward issues, and any staff conflicts (see Goldberg & Goodman, 1973). The beginning resident sees the more experienced members of the staff, including a senior psychiatrist, involved in decision making. Thus he has the opportunity to model the role of the more experienced psychiatrist.

The psychiatric trainee's activities in emergencies, consultation work, and community psychiatry call for specific skills and knowledge. The supervision of such trainees is usually on a one-to-one basis where some cases are presented to the supervisor while others are seen together (Kritzter & Langsley, 1967; McKegney, 1972; Pattison, 1972; Schwab et al., 1966). Supervision at this advanced level must permit a large degree of independent operation for the trainee, who will be working autonomously in a short time. Experience is crucial for learning, but experience without supervision can be detrimental.

Training and supervision in the use of psychopharmacologic agents poses problems related to the trainees' beliefs. Chien and Appleton (1970) have shown how a program of education coupled with adequate supervision in the form of discussion of the resident's cases during walking rounds conducted by the chief of the drug unit can influence drug usage. The educative and supervisory approaches were straightforward. Unique to this approach, however, was the testing of residents before and after the rotation. The residents divided themselves into two groups, the psychotherapeutically oriented and the eclectically oriented. After the course, 25 percent of each group were found to have changed their orientation. Both groups gained knowledge about drug usage. At the end of six months the increase was greater for the eclectic residents, although both groups began with the same knowledge. The authors stress the need to supervise first year residents' use of drugs.

Professional and graduate programs generally do not provide trainees with instruction or supervision in teaching. Medicine in general follows this pattern; yet advanced trainees and a substantial number of graduates of training programs have teaching responsibilities. Lazerson, Tufo, and Downey (1973) describe a unique program of supervised experience for first year residents in psychiatry who teach a course for undergraduate education majors. The residents, students, and supervisors evaluate the experience. The authors report benefits beyond learning how to teach. They believe that following the supervised teaching experience, "the residents retain a sensitivity and alertness to the teaching and learning dimensions throughout their residency and [gain] an additional capacity to conceptualize clinical problems in educational terms [p. 409]."

PSYCHOTHERAPY SUPERVISION

Psychotherapy as a generic term refers to the treatment of mental and emotional disorders through the therapist's relationship with the patient individually, in groups, or in families, primarily through the use of verbal and nonverbal communications. When carried out by physicians trained in psychiatric medicine, it includes ongoing medical diagnostic evaluation and may also include the use of drugs and other physical treatments (Frazier et al., 1975). In the generic sense, psychotherapy is carried out by psychologists, counselors, social workers, nurses, pastoral counselors, and others with special training. Psychotherapy supervision primarily concerns the psychiatric resident; this section will deal solely with supervision at the residency level.

Research in psychotherapy, regardless of the discipline, tends to refer to a similar body of literature. The problems of psychotherapy research in psychiatry are not essentially different from the problems of psychotherapy research in psychology, and supervision of the psychiatric trainee in generic psychotherapy may also be conducted by psychologists and other nonmedical psychotherapists. Likewise, the problems of supervision in psychotherapy are similar in various fields. Other sections of this work (see especially Brammer and Wassmer's observations in Article 2) address vital questions of supervision in psychotherapy which will not be reviewed here. Rather, we will primarily focus on assumptions and issues which lie behind the various methods of supervising in the psychiatric setting. In this way we hope to highlight approaches which might produce a more systematic understanding of problems in this area.

The centrality of psychotherapy to the psychiatrist's role is reflected in the immense amount of time, effort, and money spent in his training. From our personal experience and from the descriptions of programs in the literature, it appears that psychiatric residencies devote a great deal more time to direct supervision of trainees than do other mental health training programs. It is not unusual for a resident to have multiple supervisors for multiple tasks, including child work, group therapy, intensive psychotherapy, and general supervision.

Independent of the method of supervision is the fact that the trainee inevitably advances while being supervised. He grows more knowledgeable and skillful, he experiences a change in professional identity (more of a psychiatrist, less of a medical generalist), and he experiences an increase in self-awareness. Not all of these changes are due to supervision since didactic experiences, patient care experiences, personal life events, and many other variables influence the maturing process. In other words, a broad developmental sequence of events is occurring (Schuster, Sandt, & Thaler, 1972).

Supervision of the trainee implies certain risks. We previously referred to guilt being produced in the trainee, but there are also risks which involve ineffective or destructive activities by the trainee. Close contact with the supervisor inevitably produces modeling behaviors. When the modeling emulates the superficial behaviors and attributes of the supervisor, form often is transmitted at the expense of substance. This form of modeling is most apt to occur when the novice does not have an understanding of substance and when the supervisor fosters adoration. In other medical specialties, such emulation may be less hazardous since it may involve modeling highly specific and observable skills. Coming from a background in which modeling has been appropriate, the resident may be more vulnerable to continuing imitative behaviors even though they are no longer of value. Ornstein (1968) compares true understanding of the psychotherapeutic process to superficial imitation by using as an analogy the parable of the sorcerer's apprentice. He sees the problem as being compounded by the fact that what the trainee learns is rather quickly translated into actual patient care.

In writing about various evaluative aspects of supervision, Muslin and Thunblad (1974) identify four areas that need to be examined. These are: the observing and data gathering skills, the collating or formulating aspect (which may involve specific theoretical frameworks), the trainee's therapeutic responsiveness (which touches heavily on interpersonal skills), and the trainee's personal sensitivity. The authors discuss the degree to which the trainee accommodates to the supervisor's view of the therapeutic process and the degree to which evaluation depends upon such an accommodation. In their discussion of the personal sensitivity dimension, they explore the issue of modeling, noting that "the trainee learns to approach data with the supervisor's eyes, ears, and sensitivities. This *is* the learning mechanism involved, an attempt to approach the supervisor's cognitive and empathic styles [p. 168]." Answering the concern that this type of learning may only be superficial imitation, they observe that "ideally, the student takes from the supervisory process not only certain knowledge and understanding but certain partial identifications [p. 168]." One hopes that the student uses these identifications when they fit and does not when they are not appropriate. Monitoring the adoption of partial identifications takes place over a period of time.

"Problems about learning" and "learning problems" are phrases used by Eckstein and Wallerstein (1958) in their often-quoted work to designate the trainee's complex patterns of response in the supervisory setting and in the therapy setting. Problems about learning are the responses that are projected onto the supervisory session, while learning problems are those which emerge in work with patients. The supervisor must work with the trainee on issues involving any of the trainee's personal attributes which hinder his development as a therapist. In this sense, the task is similar to psychotherapy itself, but it has the important difference of being concerned primarily with the professional rather than the personal aspects of the trainee's life.

If the supervisory assumption is that learning problems are the substance of the supervisory experience, it would seem necessary to work with the trainee to see (or hear) what goes on between the patient and the trainee. Yet supervision often takes place with strictly verbal reports or careful notes generated by the resident. Such techniques must of necessity be dealing primarily with problems about learning. Muslin, Burstein, Gredo, and Sadow (1967) researched the hypothesis that

> on the basis of a therapist's *account* of a psychotherapeutic interview the supervisor will be able to arrive at a formulation of the status of the patient and of the patient-therapist interactions which will converge with the formulations arrived at by judges studying transcripts of the actual psychotherapeutic interview [p. 427].

Their findings did not support the hypothesis. Rather, the "results from this pilot study indicate that the supervisor and supervisory team of judges were unable to formulate the nature of the patient's current difficulties from the material offered during supervision [p. 430]."

Whatever occurs in discussing cases with trainees (and we believe that there is value in such activity) should not lead the supervisor to believe that the trainee's presentation will be congruent with his own observations or with those of a panel of experts. The good that derives from such supervisory experiences may relate much more to the resident's growth through contact with a mature and generous supervision. While different supervisors have different opinions related to the specific case. Thus the case under discussion may serve as a nonspecific stimulus for more general discussions of psychotherapy. The risk, of course, is that the student may systematically avoid certain critical but threatening themes.

Another assumption, which at the very least needs to be questioned, is that didactic approaches have little place in psychotherapy supervision. While different supervisors have different opinions about this matter, Goin and Kline (1974) observed supervision in an attempt to define qualities that identified outstanding supervisors, and they found that didactic exchanges were associated with superior supervision. The outstanding supervisors were those consistently rated so by residents. This method of selection has obvious limitatins, but as far as we can tell, it is as valid a means of selecting outstanding supervisors as any other practical method. The two outstanding supervisors were compared to a group of three who were considered good supervisors. Videotapes of the supervisory sessions were evaluated by the participants and by a separate group consisting of a psychologist and two psychiatrists. Sixteen types of supervisor statements were noted, and each was scored as case specific or general. The results indicated that the outstanding supervisors made more didactic comments that were case specific about patients and techniques than did the good supervisors. The small number of supervisors included in this study and the limitations of the research design would seem to warrant a cautious interpretation of this data. Yet if future research confirms these findings, the cherished custom of avoiding direct didactic intervention in supervision would have to be reevaluated.

We can specify didactic material which is appropriate to use in supervisory work. DeRosis (1970-1973), in a fourteen-part series of articles, deals with specific interventions, approaches, and problems which she has identified as being of value to the beginning resident. Her approach to the use of material appears to be patient centered and specific rather than general.

Psychotherapy supervision that encompasses the didactic, interpersonal, and developmental needs of the supervisee is indeed an heroic undertaking for any one supervisor or any one supervisory process. Yet this is exactly what the supervisor is called upon to do. One solution to the problem is to divide the tasks among multiple supervisors; another is to use educational forms to achieve certain goals. The structure of the entire training program may help to meet other goals. Usually, this multifaceted approach is the one chosen. However, Volkan and Hawkins (1971) attempt to meet all of the beginning resident's needs through a broad patient-oriented learning group. The group meets often and is the setting for examination of psychotherapeutic techniques, didactic presentations (often with the aid of consultants), observation of group processes, and personal and professional growth experiences for the residents. The success of this approach seems to depend upon the unique qualifications of the leader, who must be broadly trained, a gifted teacher, a gifted therapist, optimistic, and possessed of a very high energy level. Obvious limitations of the process are the replicability of the individual instructor, the setting in which it would take place, and the extent to which the model is explicit enough to be reliably emulated.

If a comprehensive approach is not taken, then how detailed should the attempt be to meet each dimension of training? Sadock and Kaplan (1970) suggest meeting the trainees' interpersonal and developmental needs through a group psychotherapy experience in which the residents themselves are the patients. Another proposed supervisory method uses multiple therapy (more than one therapist) as a means of supervision. The recording of observations and post-therapy discussions are important dimensions of the process (see Rosenberg, Rubin, & Finzi, 1968).

The multiple therapy situation generally applies to work with one patient, a couple, or a family. Cotherapy in the group therapy setting is a widely used treatment modality and may also serve a supervisory function. The psychiatric resident working with a senior faculty member presents obvious advantages and poses some problems (see Anderson, Pine, & Mee-Lee, 1972).

Yet another approach is one in which the trainees supervise themselves as an adjunct to other supervision (see Winstead, Bonovitz, Gale, & Evans, 1974). Peer supervision fosters a sense of personal responsibility for professional development, but the conditions under which such a group can function successfully are not clear and may not be easily transplanted from one peer group to another.

STRATEGY AND TECHNOLOGY

The past several years have seen the introduction of structural and technological innovations that have been, in general, very well received. The role-playing exercises of the 1950s and 1960s have given way to the more easily controlled, more polished performances of actors in simulation exercises. In an elaborate and sophisticated use of simulated patients (Helfer, Black, & Teitelbaum, 1975), mothers are trained, for a minimum of twenty-two hours, to be interviewed by medical students. The students get feedback during a videotape replay of their interview with the mother of a sick child. Werner and Schneider (1974) describe the use of actors in a structured course on the doctor-patient relationship, while Froelich (1969) includes the use of "programmed" patients in a training model for teaching medical interviewing. Finally, Lamont and Hennen (1972) report on the use of live simulations as part of examination procedures. The advocates of simulation point out that the use of actors and actresses provides a measure of realism as well as a measure of safety for both student and patient. In addition, the instructor can control both the complexity of the problem and the diversity of patient types relative to the student's level of preparation.

Not surprisingly, the use of simulations has stimulated interest in controlled studies. One of the greatest obstacles to such studies in the past has been patient variability. The use of simulated patients minimizes the patient variable as a contaminating factor, but it raises other issues with which we will need to deal. When and where in a training program is it appropriate to use simulation? If simulations serve as a bridge between students' starting levels and their ultimate interactions with real patients, where in training and for how long should the simulations be used? Should the simulations become increasingly complex as a student progresses? Should actors be replaced by real patients who are paid a nominal fee for telling their stories and interacting with students? Should one finally graduate to "real" patients? It is also possible that in some aspects of patient interaction, simulations are actually counterproductive. Where simulation creates a sterile situation, reality may be distorted. A lack of practice in real situations may ultimately prove to be too reassuring and may lead to an unrealistic presentation and the diminution of appropriate anxiety.

Paper-and-pencil simulations also seem to have proliferated as a training device. Andrew (1972) describes one such technique, the patient management problem, which involves the use of a simulated patient's chief complaint and a description of that patient. The student is then required to do a diagnostic work-up and to make decisions regarding the management, therapy, and follow-up of the "patient." Following each request for diagnostic data, the student is given information just as he would receive it in an actual clinical setting. Every decision concerning management, therapy, or follow-up is accompanied by a description of that decision's effect on the patient's health status. As the student proceeds through subsequent stages in the clinical problem, he must deal with the consequences of the decisions he has previously made. A major limitation of such simulated problem-solving exercises is the "shaping" implicit in the structure of the model. However, little is known about the covert processes which expert diagnosticians actually use as they solve problems.

Computer-aided simulations in which the computer assumes the role of patient and the student that of practicing physician have also been introduced into psychiatric education (see Harless, Drennon, Marxer, Root, & Miller, 1971). The computer offers the obvious advantages of convenience, safety, and replicability; but it has at least two major disadvantages in psychiatric education. One is the amount of work required to create adequately realistic, sophisticated programs; and the second is that nonverbal data, which is so critical to psychiatric interactions, is entirely missing.

The Problem-Oriented Record, a systematic method of recording medical data, has received much attention as an improved form of documenting data in a manner that would permit better auditing (see Weed, 1969). Basically, the method consists of a four-part structure with a data base, a problem list, plans, and follow-up. Follow-up includes progress notes which are keyed to the original problem list. The system has been applied to psychiatric records (Grant, 1972). Further expansion on the idea proposes that it has potential in the evaluation of psychiatric learning (Grant, 1974). Implicit is the idea that such a record would aid in the supervision of trainees in diagnosis and management. As with any other method of recording data, the record is still only as good as the observations on which it is based. The data's organization in a particularly logical format may make it easier to audit than a traditional record, but this fact does not make it more accurate. We fear that the structure and logic of the format may create an appearance of accurate data observation even when that observation has been deficient. Thus, in terms of supervision, the Problem-Oriented Record would appear to have no advantages over other reporting techniques except in the area of data organization.

Structural innovations are being advocated, especially the incorporation of written behavioral objectives within systems approaches (see Stritter & Bowles, 1972). Criteria of a minimally acceptable performance usually follow from the stated behavioral objectives, and specific learning tasks are designed to insure the attainment of this performance level. One limitation of such systems is that the kinds of sensitivities necessary in psychotherapy and diagnosis are not so well understood that they can be carefully specified and programmed as minimal competence levels. Also, a great part of psychiatric education is directed toward attitudinal development. Another consideration is whether a professional person capable of a great deal of independent and self-regulated behavior can, in fact, be trained by the frequent use of extrinsically applied criteria and rewards when the ultimate goal is an intrinsically motivated professional.

A systems approach not based on behavioral objectives is advocated by Melges (1972). The use of a research design paradigm with individual patients ($N = 1$) is seen as a method of enhancing scientific thinking in psychiatric residents. The resident learns to measure change in individual subjects over a period of time and thus should be in a position to evaluate treatment against goals previously established for each patient.

One of the more obviously extrinsic approaches to supervision is the bug-in-the-ear method in which a resident hears instructions and suggestions from his supervisor through an audio receiver placed in his ear (see Boyleston & Tuma, 1972). The use of film and videotape to teach specific interviewing skills has also been developed and evaluated in controlled studies (Adler, Ware, & Enelow, 1970; Kagan, 1973; Werner & Schneider, 1974).

When one considers the complexity of the skills, attitudes, and behaviors which the psychiatric resident must learn in order to integrate into an efficient and practical interactive mode with patients, it is of little wonder that videotape recordings of the trainee in action have become widely accepted in psychiatric training programs. As with other educational devices, videotape can be used as a teaching tool to implement different learning and teaching forms.

Microteaching and microcounseling involve a process of instruction
in specific behaviors followed by an opportunity to practice the
specific behaviors on videotape (see Perlberg, Peri, Weinreb, Nitzan,
& Shimron, 1972; Ivey, Normington, Miller, Morrill, & Haase,
1968). A critique is made of the degree to which the desired behavior
was implemented, followed by repeated videotaping and instruction
until the behavior is mastered. Eye contact and verbal following are
among the skills which have been found to be quite easily taught
through the microcounseling model.

Other uses of videotape are advocated and practiced. Benschoter,
Eaton, and Smith (1965) describe the use of videotape playbacks as
a vehicle for discussion between the supervisor and trainee in which
they can observe "retrospective distortion" and the accuracy with
which nonverbal communication has been portrayed. They also cite
potential of the media for self-instruction through self-confrontation. Suess (1970) uses the term self-confrontation repeatedly but
seems to emphasize the advantage of videotape for providing "the
supervisor [with] a relatively unobtrusive entrée into the inherently
private setting of the interview process." He also notes that videotape permits a "more accurate, objective evaluation of the student's
strengths and weaknesses as a therapist [p. 282]."

Another use of the videotape playback is as a vehicle for stimulated
recall by one or both of the participants in the recorded session. In
Kagan's work with Interpersonal Process Recall or IPR (1973),
the system relies heavily on an individual's ability to learn through
a process of determining his covert affective states and cognitive
processes during a videotape playback of an interview. A series of
graded exercises begins with practice in specific response modes and
progresses to exposure to stressful interview stimuli through filmed
simulations. Next the student engages in interview activities which
are recorded on videotape; these activities are reviewed with an
instructor who attempts to help the student to describe and understand what he experienced and did rather than to justify or defend
his behavior. Finally, the student assumes the supervisory role and
engages in peer supervision. A reliable teaching technique is achieved
through the use of student and instructor manuals and standard film
stimuli. This model has been subjected to extensive research, and

its validity has been well established (Campbell, Kagan, & Krathwohl, 1971; Danish & Kagan, 1971).

Videotape playbacks and other technological innovations are tools which appear to be capable of aiding in the implementation of learning. All too often the advocates of various techniques present and describe their innovations as a curriculum rather than as a vehicle for implementing a curriculum. Many of the innovative methods do seem to have the *potential* for reliability. They are more clearly structured than traditional vehicles for teaching psychiatric skills, attitudes and behaviors, and so their outcomes are more reliably achieved.

EVALUATION

Having described varying supervisory practices for varying tasks, we will now examine the evaluation of supervision, which also varies with the task. Only a few studies have evaluated supervision in the areas of diagnostic skill acquisition, the recognition of behaviors and symptoms, the modification of specific therapist behaviors, and the production of specific patient responses. In our estimation, the greatest impediment to evaluating the supervision of clinical training has been the absence of instruments to measure these skills reliably. In recent years, scales and procedures have begun to emerge which may be prototypes for efficient methods of evaluation in the future.

We have previously referred to the Systems Analysis Index for Diagnosis and the research stimulated by the Psychiatry Learning System. These evaluative approaches stem from the work in the late 1950s of Geertsma and Stoller (1960) who assessed clinical judgment in psychiatry through the use of filmed interviews. Using a list of characteristics generated for each film, students indicated how characteristic each statement was of the film subject. Correlations between student ratings and expert ratings showed that students improved with training. In comparing students at varying levels to hospital volunteers, the authors found that in spite of all of the factors that go into becoming a first year medical student, the students possessed no more ability in judgment than did the volunteers. The reassuring conclusion is that the abilities eventually acquired are a result of medical education.

Using a similar procedure with an audio recording, Salzman and Goldstein (1961) found that progressive increments in ability accompanied training. Langsley and Aycrigg (1970) further modified the procedure to include a greater sampling of psychiatric types by using four 6-minute filmed excerpts of interviews. They similarly concluded that there was an increase in test scores with an increase in education. The procedures derived from the Geertsma and Stoller work clearly apply to audio or visual test stimuli but cannot automatically be transferred to evaluation in the clinical setting with live patients.

In another study using a somewhat different model, students were required to make more complex judgments about statements describing material presented on videotape (see Thurnblad, Muslin, & Loesch, 1973). The conclusions were different from those of the previously mentioned studies, for scores leveled off after the second year of medical school. The authors give a variety of explanations for this fact and conclude that the learning that obviously occurs during the clinical years is simply not measured by their examinations. These results highlight the fragility of the evaluation process, for small modifications in procedure can vastly alter results.

Evaluating the trainee's ability to recognize feelings has been accomplished through the use of a technique developed by Kagan (see Campbell et al., 1971; Danish & Kagan, 1971). The Affective Sensitivity Scale reflects personal growth in interpersonal sensitivity and uses a series of videotaped segments of interview sessions. The students respond in a multiple choice format by indicating what they would say to the patient at specific points, what they would want to say, and what the patient seems to be feeling about the interviewer. Significant differences have been found between the various levels of trainees, and the instrument reflects student gains resulting from a variety of training and supervisory experiences.

The application of evaluation procedures in supervision was demonstrated in the course described by Werner and Schneider (1974). In this instance precourse and postcourse testing used the Affective Sensitivity Scale and the evaluation of videotaped interviews by trained raters. Their highly specific supervisory model, derived from Interpersonal Process Recall, was successful in making students more aware of their responses to patients and their impact on the doctor-patient relationship. The students also learned new types of responses and behaviors.

The significance of such evaluation methods involves their potential to clarify the effects of supervision for specific skills. While the studies may at times be rudimentary and addressed to a very narrow area, they are a step in the right direction. Through the gradual definition of methods of effectively teaching specific skills, broadly based supervisory experiences should eventually emerge. These studies also indicate that methods for conducting studies of a comparative nature currently exist, but few of these methods have been used.

The obvious lack of evaluation of psychotherapy supervision is easy to explain and comes as no surprise to anyone who is engaged either in doing psychotherapy or in supervising trainees. Outcome studies involving patients in any kind of psychotherapy are still in their infancy. Well-validated criteria of patient improvement still do not exist, and agreement cannot be reached on the efficacy of treatment forms except in some isolated cases involving specific and limited symptomatology. Whether the absence of adequate outcome studies is a reflection of inadequate measures, inadequate treatment, or merely disagreement about treatment results based on different theoretical positions is not an issue in this review. Complete evaluation of the supervision of psychotherapists cannot exist until adequate outcome studies exist on the effects of psychotherapy. The ultimate measure of effectiveness will be when the supervisee has better treatment results when supervised by one method than by another.

Two of the methodologic problems inherent in the evaluation of psychotherapy supervision in psychiatry are the usually small number of trainees and the small number of supervisors. Controlled studies using such small numbers of subjects suffer from serious statistical limitations. The long training period raises another problem, for it is difficult to account for the possible effects of many other influences on the trainee during the training experience.

Psychiatry shares with other mental health professions the difficulties related to selecting patients for research programs that measure outcome criteria. A promising approach to patient variability in evaluating supervision is the goal attainment scaling method (see Cline, Rouzer, & Bransford, 1973). This technique makes use of goals formulated for each patient rather than universal characteristics of improvement.

CONCLUSIONS

The literature we examined for this review abounded with descriptive and unevaluated reports. We believe that papers describing programs have an obvious value, but when they dominate the literature and are not followed up with evaluations, they contribute little to the field. Many times authors fail to recognize the degree to which a particular program's effect is idiosyncratic to the institution in which it occurs. We do not mean to be critical of programs which are developed to serve specific functions, but we recognize that many such programs cannot be evaluated. However, journal editors must assume more responsibility than they have in publishing such programmatic descriptions.

Insufficient attempts have been made to define the various facets of supervision. Supervision must be multidimensional, as is the practice which it supervises. The tasks which must be supervised involve skills, knowledge, and attitudes. Thus specific educational forms must be designed to achieve supervision in these areas. Such supervision need not be accomplished by a single person or a single mode. A variety of supervisory techniques, instructional materials, and technical devices can now be employed. Certain traditional approaches continue to be highly regarded. The direct observation of the trainee by the supervisor, for example, consistently emerges as a chosen mode of supervision.

Supervisory processes need to be validated through studies on the impact of supervision on patient outcome; these same processes need to be defined so that they can be reliably implemented in other settings. Reliability may prove to be as difficult to achieve as has been the validation of effective practice.

In training undergraduates, the emphasis must continue to be directed toward those skills which are of importance to the generalist. Thus skills may need to be taught in the general medical setting which will most closely resemble the setting in which the future practitioner will work. While it is of the utmost importance that all physicians learn therapeutic skills, this goal will be reached more readily if we define those aspects of interpersonal relations which are important for the doctor-patient relationship and abandon the idea that this end can be accomplished only through psychotherapy training.

Reliability, validity, and outcome measures are issues that perplex all of medical education; and while the problems in psychiatry have unique aspects, they are mirrored in other specialties as well.*

REFERENCES

Ables, B. S., & Brandsma, J. The effectiveness of different learning experiences for teaching psychiatry. *Comprehensive Psychiatry,* 1973, **14,** 29-33.

Abroms, G. M. The new eclecticism. *Archives of General Psychiatry,* 1969, **20,** 514-523.

Adler, L. M., Ware, J. E., & Enelow, A. J. Changes in medical interviewing style after instruction with two closed-circuit television techniques. *Journal of Medical Education,* 1970, **45,** 21-28.

Anderson, B. N., Pine, I., & Mee-Lee, D. Resident training in cotherapy groups. *International Journal of Group Psychotherapy,* 1972, **22,** 192-198.

Andrew, B. J. An approach to the construction of simulated exercises in clinical problem-solving. *Journal of Medical Education,* 1972, **47,** 952-958.

Artiss, K. L., & Levine, A. S. Doctor-patient relation in severe illness. *New England Journal of Medicine,* 1973, **288,** 1210-1214.

Benschoter, R., Eaton, M., & Smith, P. Use of videotape to provide individual instruction in techniques of psychotherapy. *Journal of Medical Education,* 1965, **40,** 1159-1161.

---

*Like other fields in which applied training is the primary mode, psychiatry must continually confront the questions of what constitutes *improvement* and how improvement can be systematically measured. In the other training fields represented in this volume, the same questions must be asked about learning, the evidence of learning, and the measurement of learning. The overarching concern common to all these chapters is the degree to which supervisors and supervisory techniques affect training outcomes. All the authors contributing to this volume call for more research on the relationship between process and outcome.—ED.

Boyleston, W., & Tuma, J. Training of mental health professionals through the use of the "bug in the ear." *American Journal of Psychiatry,* 1972, **129,** 92-95.

Campbell, R. J., Kagan, N., & Krathwohl, D. R. The development and validation of a scale to measure affective sensitivity (empathy). *Journal of Counseling Psychology,* 1971, **18,** 407-412.

Cath, S. H. The student-teacher alliance and the formation of the professional ego. *International Journal of Group Psychotherapy,* 1965, **15,** 303-315.

Chien, C. P., & Appleton, W. S. The need for extensive reform in psychiatric teaching in T. Rothman (Ed.), *Changing patterns in psychiatric care.* New York: Crown Publishers, 1970.

Clare, A. W. Training of psychiatrists. *Lancet,* 1972, **2,** 753-756.

Cline, D. W., & Garrard, J. N. Evaluation of the SAID teaching program. *American Journal of Psychiatry,* 1973, **130,** 582-585.

Cline, D. W., Rouzer, D. L., & Bransford, D. Goal-attainment scaling as a method for evaluating mental health programs. *American Journal of Psychiatry,* 1973, **130,** 105-108.

Danish, S. J., & Kagan, N. Measurement of affective sensitivity: Toward a valid measure of interpersonal perception. *Journal of Counseling Psychology,* 1971, **18,** 51-54.

Dashef, S. S., Espey, W. M., & Lazarus, J. A. Time-limited sensitivity groups for medical students. *American Journal of Psychiatry,* 1974, **131,** 287-292.

DeRosis, H. A. Supervision of the first-year psychiatric resident. *Psychiatric Quarterly,* 1970, **44**(3) through 1973, **47**(4). (In fourteen parts)

Eckstein, R., & Wallerstein, R. S. *The teaching and learning of psychotherapy.* New York: Basic Books, 1958.

Elstein, A. S., Kagan, N., Shulman, L. S., Jason, H., & Loupe, M. J. Methods and theory in the study of medical inquiry. *Journal of Medical Education,* 1972, **47,** 85-92.

Engel, G. L. The deficiencies of the case presentation as a method of clinical teaching. *New England Journal of Medicine,* 1971, **284,** 20-24.

Engel, G. L. The education of the physician for clinical observation. *Journal of Nervous and Mental Disease,* 1972, **154,** 159-164.

Engel, G. L. Enduring attributes of medicine relevant for the education of the physician. *Annals of Internal Medicine,* 1973, **78,** 587-593.

Frazier, S. H., Campbell, R. J., Marshall, M., & Werner, A. *A psychiatric glossary.* (4th ed.) Washington, D.C.: American Psychiatric Association, 1975.

Froelich, R. E. A course in medical interviewing. *Journal of Medical Education,* 1969, **44,** 1165-1169.

Geertsma, R. H., & Stoller, R. J. The objective assessment of clinical judgment in psychiatry. *Archives of General Psychiatry,* 1960, **2**, 278-285.

Goin, M. K., & Kline, F. M. Supervision observed. *Journal of Nervous and Mental Disease,* 1974, **158**, 208-213.

Goldberg, D. A., & Goodman, B. The small-group system and training on an acute psychiatric ward. *Psychiatry in Medicine,* 1973, **4**, 173-181.

Grant, R. L. The problem-oriented record: A tool for teaching and evaluation of learning in the new psychiatric curriculum. In H. L. Muslin, R. J. Thurnblad, B. Templeton, & C. H. McGuire (Eds.), *Evaluative methods in psychiatric education.* Washington, D.C.: American Psychiatric Association, 1974.

Grant, R. L., & Maletzky, B. M. Application of the Weed system to psychiatric records. *Psychiatry in Medicine,* 1972, **3**, 119-129.

Grinker, R. R. Psychiatry rides madly in all directions. *Archives of General Psychiatry,* 1964, **10**, 228-237.

Halleck, S. L., & Woods, S. M. Emotional problems of psychiatric residents. *Psychiatry,* 1962, **25**, 339-346.

Harless, W. G., Drennon, G. G., Marxer, J. J., Root, J. A., & Miller, G. E. Case: A computer-aided simulation of the clinical encounter. *Journal of Medical Education,* 1971, **46**, 443-448.

Helfer, R. E., Black, M. A., & Teitelbaum, H. A comparison of pediatric interviewing skills using real and simulated mothers. *Pediatrics,* 1975, **55**, 397-400.

Ivey, A. E., Normington, C. J., Miller, C. D., Morrill, W. H., & Haase, R. F. Microcounseling and attending behavior: An approach to prepracticum counselor training. *Journal of Counseling Psychology,* 1968, **15**(5), 1-12. (Monograph supplement)

Kagan, N. Can technology help us toward reliability in influencing human interaction. *Educational Technology,* 1973, **13**, 44-51.

Kaufman, M. R. The teaching of psychiatry to the nonpsychiatrist physician. *American Journal of Psychiatry,* 1971, **128**, 610-616.

Kety, S. S. From rationalization to reason. *American Journal of Psychiatry,* 1974, **131**, 957-963.

Kilpatrick, D. G., & Randels, P. M. The use of psychological characteristics as performance predictors in medical students. Department of Psychiatry and Behavioral Sciences, Medical University of South Carolina, Charleston, S.C., 1974.

Kritzer, H., & Langsley, D. Training for emergency psychiatric services. *Journal of Medical Education,* 1967, **42**, 111-115.

Lamont, H. T., & Hennen, B. K. E. The use of simulated patients in a certification examination in family medicine. *Journal of Medical Education,* 1972, **47**, 789-795.

Langee, H., Glick, I. D., Hoffman, B., Silver, L. B., & Morrison, A. P. The requirements of a psychiatric residency program circa 1972. *American Journal of Psychiatry,* 1973, **130,** 1151-1152.

Langsley, D. G., & Aycrigg, J. B. Filmed interviews for testing clinical skills. *Journal of Medical Education,* 1970, **45,** 52-58.

Lazerson, A. M., Tufo, R. P., & Downey, L. The first experience in teaching psychiatry. *Psychiatry in Medicine,* 1973, **4,** 403-410.

Liske, R. E., Ort, R. S., & Ford, A. B. Clinical performance and related traits of medical students and faculty physicians. *Journal of Medical Education,* 1964, **39,** 69-80.

McKegney, F. P. Consultation-liaison teaching of psychosomatic medicine: Oportunities and obstacles. *Journal of Nervous and Mental Disease,* 1972, **154,** 198-205.

Melges, F. T. Integrating psychiatric research with clinical training: $N = 1$. *Journal of Nervous and Mental Disease,* 1972, **154,** 206-212.

Miller, P. R., & Tupin, J. P. Multimedia teaching of introductory psychiatry. *American Journal of Psychiatry,* 1972, **128,** 1219-1223.

Muslin, H. L., & Thurnblad, R. J. Supervision as an evaluative mechanism. In H. L. Muslin, R. J. Thurnblad, B. Templeton, & C. H. McGuire (Eds.), *Evaluative methods in psychiatric education.* Washington, D.C.: American Psychiatric Association, 1974.

Muslin, H. L., Burstein, A. G., Gredo, J. E., & Sadow, L. Research on the supervisory process. *Archives of General Psychiatry,* 1967, **16,** 427-431.

Ornstein, P. H. Sorcerer's apprentice: The initial phase of training and education in psychiatry. *Comprehensive Psychiatry,* 1968, **9,** 293-315.

Pattison, M. Residency training issues in community psychiatry. *American Journal of Psychiatry,* 1972, **128,** 1097-1102.

Perlberg, A., Peri, J. N., Weinreb, M., Nitgan, E., & Shimron, Jr. Microteaching and videotape recordings: New approach to improving teaching. *Journal of Medical Education,* 1972, **47,** 43-50.

Randels, P. M., McCurdy, L., Powell, W. S., Kilpatrick, D. G., & Keeler, M. H. The psychiatry learning system project: An educational research project. Department of Psychiatry and Behavioral Sciences, Medical University of South Carolina, Charleston, S.C., 1974.

Raskin, D. E. Psychiatric training in the 70s: Toward a shift in emphasis. *American Journal of Psychiatry,* 1972, **128,** 1129-1131.

Reiser, M. F. Training for what? *American Journal of Psychiatry,* 1972, **128,** 1128-1129.

Romano, J. The teaching of psychiatry to medical students: Past, present and future. *American Journal of Psychiatry,* 1970, **126,** 1115-1126.

Rosenberg, L. M., Rubin, S. C., & Finzi, H. Participant-supervision in the teaching of psychotherapy. *American Journal of Psychotherapy,* 1968, **22,** 280-295.

Rubinstein, B., & Levitt, M. An approach to humanism in a medical setting. *American Journal of Orthopsychiatry,* 1966, **36,** 153-159.

Sadock, B. J., & Kaplan, H. I. Long-term intensive group psychotherapy with psychiatric residents as part of residency training. *American Journal of Psychiatry,* 1970, **126,** 1138-1143.

Salzman, L. F., & Goldstein, R. H. Changes in clinical judgment as a function of psychiatric education. *Journal of Medical Education,* 1961, **36,** 914-923.

Schuster, D. B., Sandt, J. J., & Thaler, O. F. *Clinical supervision of the psychiatric resident.* New York: Brunner/Mazel, 1972.

Schwab, J., Clemmon, R. S., & Marder, L. Training psychiatric residents in consultation work. *Journal of Medical Education,* 1966, **41,** 1077-1082.

Shakow, D. The contribution of psychology in the teaching of psychiatry to medical students. *Journal of Nervous and Mental Disease,* 1972, **154,** 173-179.

Stritter, F. T., & Bowles, L. T. The teacher as manager: A strategy for medical education. *Journal of Medical Education,* 1972, **47,** 93-101.

Suess, J. F. Self-confrontation of videotaped psychotherapy as a teaching device for psychiatric students. *Journal of Medical Education,* 1970, **45,** 271-282.

Suess, J. F. Teaching psychodiagnosis and observation by self-instructional programmed videotapes. *Journal of Medical Education,* 1973, **48,** 676-683.

Thurnblad, R. J., Muslin, H., & Loesch, J. A test of clinical learning by medical students. *American Journal of Psychiatry,* 1973, **130,** 568-570.

Tischler, G. The transition into residency. *American Journal of Psychiatry,* 1972, **128,** 1103-1106.

Topham, M., & Smith, J. S. The use of experiential learning in undergraduate medical training. *The Medical Journal of Australia,* 1973, **1,** 1155-1157.

Volkan, V. D., & Hawkins, D. R. The "fieldwork" method of teaching and learning clinical psychiatry. *Comprehensive Psychiatry,* 1971, **12,** 103-115.

Weed, L. L. *Medical records, medical education, and patient care.* Cleveland: The Press of Case Western Reserve University, 1969.

Werkman, S. L., Landau, S., & Wakefield, H. Medical students view clinical psychiatry. *American Journal of Psychiatry,* 1973, **130,** 562-565.

Werner, A., & Schneider, J. M. Teaching medical students interactional skills. *New England Journal of Medicine,* 1974, **290,** 1232-1237.

West, L. J. The future of psychiatric education. *American Journal of Psychiatry,* 1973, **130,** 521-528.

Winstead, D. K., Bonovitz, J. S., Gale, M. S., & Evans, J. W. Resident peer supervision of psychotherapy. *American Journal of Psychiatry,* 1974, **131,** 318-321.

Worby, C. M. The first-year psychiatric resident and the professional identity crisis. *Mental Hygiene,* 1970, **54,** 374, 377.

Supervision in Counseling and Psychotherapy

LAWRENCE M. BRAMMER AND ARTHUR C. WASSMER

INTRODUCTION

"We have some contradictory ideas on the role expected of supervisors," note Hansen and Warner (1971), who also observe that "we know very little about how this role affects counseling trainees [p. 262]." While this statement is a severe indictment of supervision theory and practice, our review of the related literature on counselor education leaves us similarly convinced that an enormous gap exists between research and practice within that field. Instead of hard facts emerging from objective investigations of supervision functions, we found that 91 of the 110 articles and books reviewed were primarily informal thought pieces, speculations, or simple program evaluations. Only 19 made use of experimental or preexperimental designs. It is difficult to evaluate and subsequently improve the state of counseling supervision when we know so little about the variables involved and the ultimate effects of such variables. On the other hand, this review of counseling and psychotherapy supervision literature published since roughly 1960 suggests some basic styles, models, and goals for trainee supervision. Our main purpose is to present these ideas in the form of a systematic summary.

We will be concerned with the kinds of questions that must be asked in any evaluation of the supervision process:

What is supervision of counselors in training?
Who should be designated to perform supervisory functions?
Toward what goals is the process of supervision directed?
How do supervisors behave in order to achieve these goals?
What conditions in supervision facilitate or hamper the process of achieving these goals?
How do major theoretical approaches influence the supervisor?

Our second purpose is to present the answers to these questions as they appear in the available research and theoretical literature on counselor education. We will point out the limitations of these investigations, however, and will continue to remind the reader of the absence of scientific control when that absence renders conclusions highly tentative. When dealing with studies where the investigative methods are thorough and offer a useful model for future investigators, we will include detailed procedures and findings. Finally, we will issue an urgent call for future research in the areas where it is most needed.

Our initial section is organized around the conditions under which supervision is commonly performed—models, goals, and actual practice; that is, what supervisors want to do and what they actually do. The next section reviews the literature on theoretical approaches to supervision and the effectiveness of these respective behaviors and styles.

Definition of Supervision

We will begin by attempting to define supervision. As it appears to be practiced in most counselor and psychotherapist education programs, supervision is the assignment of an experienced person to help a beginning student learn counseling through the use of the student's own case material. Counselor educators agree that this is a critically important function; but beyond this basic generalization, agreement among supervisors and investigators of supervision is rare and tenuous, as our review will demonstrate.

While there are minor distinctions in usage between the terms counseling and psychotherapy, they will be considered synonymous for purposes of this review.

THE STYLE AND GOALS OF SUPERVISION

The term *supervisor* is applied somewhat loosely in the literature, depending on the style of supervision to which the author of the particular article is accustomed. Three structured styles of supervision are most evident. In the first style, students are enrolled in a counseling practicum; and during the course of treating several clients, they consult on an individual basis with a person who is called a practicum supervisor. In the second style, the student regularly attends group supervision sessions with his supervisor's other practicum trainees in addition to consulting individually with the supervisor. Thus the practicum supervisor is also the practicum group leader. In the third style, the student attends both group and individual supervisory sessions, but the practicum group leader and the individual supervisor may be different persons. We will focus primarily on individual case supervision.

Goals of Supervision

A difficulty which emerges quickly from inspection of literature on supervision is the failure of counselor educators to agree upon or even to state adequately operative goals for the supervision process. Paradoxically, the literature seems to contain many more statements about how supervision should be done than statements justifying those methods. There is general agreement on the goal of increasing the beginning counselor's level of skills and knowledge, but there is little agreement on the definitions of such skills and knowledge.

Supervision as Interpersonal Learning

The literature contains a number of deductive, philosophically derived statements made by respected counselor educators concerning the goals of supervision and the nature of the supervisory process. Arbuckle (1963), for example, in a bold article stating the covert sentiments of many counselor educators, suggests that the goal of supervision is to draw the beginning counselor into an interpersonal learning process. While most occupations, he reasons, involve the mastery of specific tasks, the task of the counselor is to engage his client in an interpersonal process. Arbuckle maintains that the only appropriate way for counseling students to learn this task is to themselves engage in this same interpersonal process. In this process the relationship of counselor educators to their students is identical to the relationship of counselors to their clients. For Arbuckle, the goals of supervision are self-awareness and engagement in both interpersonal and intrapersonal processes. Altucher (1967) supports Arbuckle's conceptualization of the goals and aims of supervision and observes that "learning to be a counselor is both an emotional and an intellectual experience, and of the two, the emotional part is the most crucial [p. 165]."

Supervision as Cognitive Learning

Other counselor educators see the goals of supervision as being primarily cognitive and didactic in nature. Walz and Roeber (1962) attempted to define the counselor supervisor's role by surveying the attitudes of supervisors toward their own activities. The typescript of a counseling interview was sent to twenty-nine counselor educators in the north central region of the United States with directions to respond to the typescript as if it had been generated by one of their own trainees. These supervisors demonstrated a strong tendency to focus on the counselor's behavior rather than on the client's. Upon further analysis, 73 percent of the supervisors' responses were found to be questioning or instructive in nature. The authors concluded that supervisors are primarily teaching oriented and do not seem to have an underlying rationale for their supervisor behaviors. Minimally, however, we may conclude that whether or not a practicing supervisor has a conscious image of the goals of supervision, he behaves as if his goal is to teach. If this finding is accurate, it would seem that most supervisors in the Walz and Roeber sample did not functionally subscribe to the Arbuckle conceptualization of the supervisor as counselor.

Supervision as Personal Growth

Patterson (1964) takes the findings of Walz and Reober as documentation of the "woefully inadequate" state of supervision, and hypothesizes that if supervisors are "more concerned with techniques than with attitudes, with content than with feelings, with specific responses than with the relationship," then supervision may be "more harmful than helpful to the student [p. 47]." On the other hand, Patterson takes exception to Arbuckle's conceptualization of the supervisor as counselor, arguing that "making the supervisory session a counseling or therapy session is to impose counseling on a captive client [p. 48]." The supervisory session, suggests Patterson,

> falls between teaching and counseling. . . . Supervision, while not therapy, should be, like all good human relationships, therapeutic. Supervision is a relationship which is therapeutic, and in which the student learns. This learning is more like the kind of learning which takes place in counseling and psychotherapy. It is concerned with the development of sensitivity in the student, of understanding and the ability to communicate that understanding, of therapeutic attitudes, rather than techniques, specific responses, diagnostic labeling, or even identifying or naming presumed personality dynamics in the client [p. 48].

Patterson concludes that supervision is an "influencing situation" directed toward certain changes in the student's behavior which are presumed to be therapeutic for clients.

As we have previously stated, a major weakness in these expressions of supervision goals is their failure to communicate operationalized meanings. Of Arbuckle we may ask, "How do we know when our students are engaged in the process of which you speak?" If Walz and Roeber's inferences are correct, we may ask of practicing counselor educators, "Since you behave like teachers, what is it you are trying to teach, and how will you know if and when you have taught it?" Of Patterson, we ask "Can you be more explicit about how supervision may influence students in becoming effective counselors?"

Perhaps, as Gross (1968) suggests, such efforts to operationalize and evaluate are premature. No clear-cut set of principles elaborates what constitutes an effective counselor and how to distinguish him from an ineffective counselor. "It is," Gross feels, "somewhat incongruent to base evaluation of these goals on such undefined principles [pp. 78-79]." Stemming from this fundamental incongruity, we may see the remaining supervision literature in terms of two distinct strains. The first represents an attempt to isolate and elaborate the characteristics of effective counseling in the hope that these characteristics may be adopted as goals for supervision. The second represents an attempt to define and understand supervision phenomena as they actually exist.

Supervision as a Combination Didactic-Experiential Style

Attempts to isolate and define the behaviors of the ideal counselor have been carried on primarily by researchers of the client-centered orientation. Rogers' work on supervision in the 1950s heavily influenced Arbuckle and Patterson. Rogers rejected the style of most earlier supervision, which emphasized learning counseling and therapy techniques, in favor of stressing the affective and relational aspects of the therapist's behavior. Rogers (1957) suggested that if certain "necessary and sufficient" conditions were present in the therapist's behavior, the client would move in the direction of therapeutic change regardless of what techniques the therapist employed. Conversely, if these conditions were not present, therapeutic change would be unlikely to occur. The necessary and sufficient conditions described by Rogers are empathic understanding, unconditional positive regard, and personal congruence or genuineness. Carkhuff (1969) operationalized these concepts in the following manner:

> facilitators communicate an accurately empathic understanding of deeper as well as the surface feelings of the second persons(s); they are freely and deeply themselves in a nonexploitative relationship; they communicate a very deep respect . . . they are helpful in guiding the discussion of personally relevant feelings and experiences in specific and concrete terms [p. 171].

The effective provision of these necessary and sufficient conditions in producing therapeutic change in clients is adequately documented elsewhere (see Carkhuff, 1969b; Carkhuff & Berenson, 1967). The application of these conditions to the process of supervision is based on the following assumptions: (1) that by offering to supervise the necessary and sufficient conditions, supervisors model for their trainees the ways in which a facilitative person may offer these conditions; and (2) that in offering students a relationship containing the necessary and sufficient conditions, supervisors provide an atmosphere in which students can freely explore their own feelings, special difficulties, and questions which they encounter in the process of learning to be counselors and psychotherapists.

Training programs which have emerged from the necessary and sufficient conditions concept were described by Truax, Carkhuff, and Douds (1964) as the didactic-experiential approach. With some refinements and modifications, this approach stems from Rogers' recommendations in 1957 on the training of psychotherapists. At that time he stressed the importance of learning counseling by first doing it. While incorporating appropriate didactic material in such areas as personality and learning theory, the experiential base of the training program constituted the essential starting point.

Research on the Didactic-Experiential Approach

A number of research efforts have been directed toward assessing the effectiveness of the didactic-experiential approach in producing counselors who can provide such conditions as empathy, warmth, and genuineness. Carkhuff and Truax (1965) compared graduate and lay training programs on these growth-facilitating dimensions. At the end of training, taped excerpts from each trainee's interviews were rated by trained raters on the dimensions of empathy, unconditional positive regard, the therapist's self-congruence, and the depth of the client's self-exploration. These ratings were compared to ratings of commercially available interviews by experienced therapists. On each dimension, experienced therapists ranked first, graduate students next, and lay personnel last. Since these differences were not significant, however, the authors concluded that a program of training specifically directed toward the necessary and sufficient conditions could, in a relatively short time, raise graduate and lay persons to a level of functioning similar to that of experienced therapists.

Berenson, Carkhuff, and Myrus (1966) attempted to demonstrate the effectiveness of the didactic-experiential training approach in developing these interpersonal skills in counseling trainees. Eighteen male and eighteen female undergraduates were randomly assigned to one of three groups: (1) the treatment group, which specifically employed scales that operationally defined various levels of functioning on the relevant interpersonal dimensions and which, in addition, received a quasi-group therapy experience; (2) a training control group, which met regularly and was presented with the same counseling theory but which did not employ either the research scales or the group experience; and (3) a control group, which received no training. Measures were taken before and after the experience on a number of dimensions—empathy, positive regard, genuineness, client self-exploration (taken from objective tape ratings), client ratings, "significant other" ratings, and self-report ratings—and the findings supported the authors' hypotheses concerning the effectiveness of the didactic-experiential approach in training on these interpersonal dimensions. With variations in each case on one or more indices, group 1 demonstrated the greatest gains in interpersonal functioning, and group 2 demonstrated greater gains than did group 3.

Granted that existing research supports the efficacy of the didactic-experiential approach in producing counselors who function at comparatively higher levels of interpersonal facilitation, what implications do these findings hold for the process of supervision? Hansen and Barker (1964) correlated the quality of the relationship between students and their supervisors with the students' relative levels of experiencing, as measured by the Experiencing Scale developed by Gendlin (1961, p. 161). Twenty-eight graduate students enrolled in an NDEA guidance institute during the 1962-63 academic year were asked, following their last supervision session, to rate their supervisors on the Barrett-Lennard Relationship Inventory (Barrett-Lennard, 1959). Supervisors were also asked to rate their trainees using the same instrument. At the conclusion of the practicum experience, each trainee recorded an interview with his supervisor in which the trainee was asked to cite what was particularly significant to him. Randomly selected segments of these tapes were rated by judges according to the Gendlin Experiencing Scale. Analysis of this data indicated that trainees in group 1, together with the supervisor of this group, rated their relationships significantly higher than did the trainees and supervisor of group 3. Correspondingly, trainees of trainer 1 scored consistently higher than trainees of trainer 3 when judges rated their level of experiencing ($p < .01$). Hansen and Barker's interpretation of these findings is

> that trainees in Group 3 were more remote from their experience and from their feelings and more likely to be cautious and defensive in their relationship. Experiencing had to be safely in the past before meanings could be drawn from it, while trainees in Group 1 were more sensitive to the changingness of their experiencing and feelings [p. 110].

Hansen further hypothesizes that "because the trainees in Group 1 perceived the supervisor as being congruent, as having a high level of regard, empathic understanding and unconditional regard for them, they felt the atmosphere safe enough to examine their feelings and experiences (p. 110)."

Pierce, Carkhuff, and Berenson (1967) examined the effects of the supervisor's level of functioning, as measured on research scales of empathy, positive regard, genuineness, concreteness, and self-disclosure upon trainee gains along the same dimensions. Of seventeen volunteers in a mental health counselor training program, eight were assigned to a supervisor rated as functioning at a high level, while nine were assigned to a supervisor rated as functioning at a low level. All trainees were given training from the didactic-experiential model. Of the nine trainees of the supervisor rated as low, only four finished the program, while all eight trainees of the supervisor rated as high completed the program. On posttraining measures the trainees of the highly rated supervisor showed significant gains ($p < .05$), while the trainees of the other supervisor showed no gains.

In perhaps the most powerful demonstration of the relationship between the supervisor's level of functioning and gains in the trainee's level of functioning, Carkhuff (1969b) assembled supporting data from sixteen studies of training programs from various status levels in the helping professions. Three variables emerged as critical to the explanation of trainee changes along relevant interpersonal dimensions—(1) trainee level of functioning, (2) trainer level of functioning, and (3) type of program. In all cases, trainees were found to move on the research scales of interpersonal functioning in the direction of their trainers. Significantly, this tendency held even in cases of downward movement; that is, in those cases (including two Ph.D. training programs in clinical psychology) where the trainers were functioning at lower levels of interpersonal skills than their trainees at entry, the interpersonal functioning of the trainees tended to deteriorate over the course of the training program. A second finding suggests that as a general rule, trainees tend to move on these scales in the direction of their trainers and to the degree of approximately half the difference in ratings between themselves and their trainers.

These findings, then, tend to support Rogers' contention that the differentiating factors between effective and ineffective therapists lie less in the techniques they utilize than in the facilitative conditions they provide within the context of the therapy relationship. Insofar as these criteria have been applied in research on supervision, the findings tend to support Arbuckle's belief that supervision bears certain similarities to counseling. The facilitative characteristics which, when found in therapists, produce the greatest gains in clients seem identical or closely related to those characteristics which, when found in supervisors, produce the greatest gains in trainees.

WHAT SUPERVISORS DO

There are some descriptions of the world of supervision as it exists, with little or no editorializing about the characteristics of ideal counselors or supervisors. As a group, these studies seem to suffer from two major weaknesses: (1) a fundamental lack of continuity or relatedness, a lack of agreement on the effect of relevant criterion variables on those of experimental design, and (2) a general weakness of research design. Nevertheless, we regard these studies as valuable contributions to the field in that they provide systematic information about supervision as it is currently practiced in counselor education. As such, they constitute necessary preexperimental data gathering which subsequently can help to generate hypotheses that deserve true experimental investigation.

These studies seem to describe the actual practice of supervision as being very different from the ideals presented by the client-centered writers. A cogent example is the Walz and Roeber (1962) study cited earlier which showed that supervisors' responses are primarily didactic, with little supporting rationale.

Delaney and Moore (1966) surveyed beginning students' expectations of their supervisors. The Supervisor Role Analysis Form, constructed by Gysbers and Johnston (1965), was administered to 123 prepracticum graduate students, none of whom had had previous practicum experience. The Supervisor Role Analysis Form contains forty-six Likert-type items based on supervisory functions drawn from the literature on supervision. The subjects were instructed to rate each item on a five point scale ranging from "absolutely must" to "absolutely must not" in terms of the perceived importance of that supervisory role. Analysis of the data yielded fifteen significant factors related to trainee expectations of supervisors, and these expectations could be grouped under four major headings—didactic-instructive, instructive-consultative, counseling, and critique of counseling performance.

Nine factors are related to the didactic-instructive function and indicate, by item content analysis, that trainees expect the supervisor to direct the work of the trainee, to provide information about the trainee, to instruct the trainee, to demonstrate counseling techniques, and to provide for the support and security of the counselor in practicum. They further expect the supervisor to instruct and demonstrate clerical procedures, to act as an instructor in administration, and to direct counselors, while supporting them or providing for their support and demonstrating counseling techniques and procedures by carrying a regular case load of counselees.

The three factors grouped under the instructive-consultative heading indicate that trainees expect the supervisor to be a nondirective person who charges the trainee with the responsibility for his own professional growth while consistently making himself available for consultation with the student. Only one factor indicated expectations that the supervisor would function as a counselor for counselors, and it comprised only 5 percent of the total factor loadings. It would appear that trainees concur with the supervisors' orientation toward their teaching roles, as reported by Walz and Roeber.

Two studies indicate, however, that student expectations may undergo modifications as a result of actually experiencing a supervisory relationship. Gysbers and Johnston (1965) administered the Supervisor Role Analysis Form (cited in the Delaney and Moore study) to fifty-one enrollees and ten supervisors during a six-week practicum at the University of Michigan. The instrument was administered on the first day of the practicum, again in the middle of the third week, and again on the final day. Analysis of the responses to the first administration indicated that these students with no previous practicum experience had definite expectations of their supervisors. Specifically, Gysbers and Johnston note that

> they wanted demonstrations of counseling techniques, tapes of good interviews, help with test selection, direct assistance in handling students and parents, writing interview notes, and even counseling for themselves (a role they expected their supervisor would assume). They also felt the supervisor should serve as an evaluator of their performance, both assessing their counseling behavior and assigning or recommending a grade in practicum [p. 69].

Although some changes in these expectations were evident upon analysis of the responses to the second administration, the pattern of these changes became more clear in the analysis of data gleaned from the final administration.

Responses to twenty-seven of the items show significant changes at the p .01 level or better, results that support the authors' conclusion that during the course of supervision students came to see their supervisors less as teachers and more as consultants. Concomitantly, they seemed to place a significantly higher value on the freedom to learn and explore counseling in their own day and at their own pace. The authors made several other observations on the basis of their data. First, a number of basic role functions are agreed upon by almost all supervisors, while some functions (such as counselor to trainee) were controversial. Second, while there was diversity of opinion among supervisors about roles, there was also diversity of opinion among trainees. Finally,

> The data also indicated differing perceptions of the supervisor's role existing between enrollees and their supervisors. There was no evidence, however, to suggest this interfered with or detracted from the supervisor's effectiveness. . . . In fact, it may produce a minimal tension that aids the enrollee's growth in practicum [p. 73].

At the same time that Gysbers and Johnston were exploring trainees' expectations of the supervisor's role, Hansen (1965) was using the Barrett-Lennard Relationship Inventory to examine trainees' expectations of the kind of relationship they would have with their supervisors. This instrument (Barrett-Lennard, 1959), which is based on the measurement of Rogers' necessary and sufficient conditions of personality change, contains four subscales indicating levels of regard, congruence, empathic understanding, and unconditional regard. Since Hansen first administered the inventory before the trainees had contact with their supervisors, items were modified to the future tense. At the conclusion of the ten-week practicum, the instrument was administered a second time in order to determine how the trainees actually perceived the relationship with their supervisors. The variance of the group scores was analyzed and yielded significant differences on three or four subscales in what the trainees expected and actually received from their supervisors and from the total relationship. The level on the regard scale, which narrowly missed significance at p .05, indicated that while the trainees held very high expectations concerning the supervisors' regard for them, their perceptions of their supervisors' regard in fact somewhat exceeded their expectations. While they expected the supervisors to be only moderately congruent with them, they in fact perceived the supervisors to be far more congruent than they had expected ($p < .05$).

Trainees in this study also anticipated a low level of empathic understanding, but at the end of the practicum they perceived their supervisors to be a great deal more empathic than they had expected ($p < .05$). The trainees' greatest surprise in the supervisory relationship was the level of unconditional regard which they received from their supervisors. The unconditional regard scale differs from the level of regard scale in that it measures the degree of nonjudgmentalness associated with the regard. The first administration scores showed a tremendous difference between the trainees' expectations of the level of regard (33.73) and unconditional regard (6.90). Therefore, the data seem to indicate that students expected to be valued by their supervisors as good students but not particularly as persons. Second administration scores on the unconditional regard scales indicated that the trainees perceived that they had in fact been valued as persons far more than they had ever expected ($p < .01$).

These studies support the views advanced by Rogers and Arbuckle about the nature of the supervisory process and how learning of counseling takes place within it. Anticipating the practicum, students feel somewhat insecure about their level of ability. They see the supervisor as a teaching person (Delaney & Moore, 1966; Gysbers & Johnston, 1965), but they do not expect much from him by way of helpful interpersonal relationships (Hansen, 1965). Gysbers and Johnston point out that supervisors, in turn, seem to hold an image of their functions consistent with the trainees' expectations; and according to Walz and Roeber (1962), they see themselves primarily as teachers with didactic and instructive functions. The supervisors, however, seem to function as counselors; and when they actually participate in a supervisory relationship, they are perceived as providing far greater facilitative conditions than their trainees had expected (Hansen).

As a result of these facilitative conditions, trainees become more open to their own experiencing (Hansen & Barker, 1964) and to their expectations and desire for more freedom to explore and develop their own style (Gysbers & Johnston, 1965). According to the degree to which these facilitative conditions are present in the relationship, their own abilities to provide these conditions to clients are increased (Pierce et al., 1967).

The studies we have cited fit into a composite picture of counselor supervision. A number of additional studies, which are more delimited or have less clearly defined criterion variables, speak to specific aspects of this broad supervisory picture.

Research on the Impact of Supervision
Behavior on Trainees

The reader will recall that Delaney and Moore's study (1966) was among the first pieces of research we cited in exploring the changes in trainees' expectations of the supervisor and perceptions of the supervisor's role. Delaney and his team (Delaney, Long, Masucci, & Moses, 1969) later probed the extent to which these changing attitudes and expectations are related to positive changes in the behavior of counselor trainees. The hypothesis of this study was that as a result of experiencing the supervised practicum, counselor trainees would demonstrate behavioral increases on the dimensions of empathy, warmth, and genuineness and would at the same time demonstrate positive attitudinal changes on certain semantic differential concepts. Subjects for this study were ten post-master's degree students enrolled in a counseling practicum at the University of Illinois. Research scales developed by Truax and Carkhuff (1967) to measure the behavioral dimensions of empathy, warmth, and genuineness were applied to three-minute tape excerpts drawn from the counseling sessions of each student at the beginning, middle, and end of the practicum experience. As measures of attitudinal changes, nine sets of bipolar semantic differential scales that called for responses to activity-loaded words, potency-loaded words, and evaluation-loaded words were administered at the same points at which tape excerpts were taken. Analysis of the data showed statistically significant increases ($p < .01$) along all three dimensions of counselor behavior from the beginning of the practicum to the end. Unfortunately, the study was not designed to elaborate on the factors in the practicum experience which produced these changes. No significant changes were found in responses to the word-concept items of the semantic differential, except for "professional."

Four other studies examined the effects of particular aspects of supervisor behavior on trainee behavior. Davidson and Emmer (1966) explored "the position of a counselor's attitude along a continuum ranging from concerned with client to concerned with self [p. 27]" in relation to its effect on the counseling trainees' focus of concern. The aspect of supervisory behavior under examination was the extent to which the supervisor's techniques were supportive or nonsupportive. We note in passing that their definitions of supportive and nonsupportive techniques sound very much like descriptions of the characteristics which client-centered researchers have termed facilitative and nonfacilitative (Rogers, 1957) or high functioning and low functioning (Pierce et al., 1967). The term *supportive techniques* refers to supervisor behaviors which emphasize the positive aspects of the counselor-client relationship and are calculated to promote the student's self-confidence, while nonsupportive techniques are largely evaluative or didactic in nature and emphasize the negative aspects of beginning counselors' performances in their dealings with clients (Davidson & Emmer, 1966, p. 27). The authors hypothesized that the counselor's focus of concern would become more self-centered when the techniques of the supervisor were mainly nonsupportive.

Twenty-eight beginning counselors attending an NDEA institute at the University of Michigan were asked to select a five-minute taped section of one of their counseling interviews to serve as the basis for an experimental supervision interview. The subjects next completed an instrument containing twenty-two items designed to measure the focus of concern (Davidson and Emmer do not give the name or source of this instrument). Two supervisors then conducted twenty-minute sessions with each trainee. Each supervisor did seven supportive and seven nonsupportive interviews. In order to determine whether different treatments had taken place, trainees responded to a semantic differential instrument on the word *supervisor*. Analysis of the mean scores of the two groups did indeed yield a significant difference ($p < .01$). Following the supervision interviews, trainees completed the focus of concern measure for a second time. A two-way analysis of variance was performed on the pre- and postinterview measures of focus of concern, and the results supported the authors' hypothesis; a significant difference ($p < .05$) was observed in a direction which indicated that after the interview, those trainees who had received nonsupportive supervision were more concerned about themselves than they were about their clients.

Blane (1968) studied the effects of positive supervision, negative supervision, and no supervision upon trainees' gains on the behavioral dimension of empathy. Thirty enrollees of an NDEA guidance institute at the University of Florida were divided by age and sex into three equal groups which were then randomly assigned to treatments of positive supervision, negative supervision, or no supervision. Each counselor conducted a thirty-minute interview with one of two paid volunteer clients, and this interview was rated for empathy using Carkhuff's Empathic Understanding in Interpersonal Processes II Scale. Each counselor was next given a fifteen-minute supervision interview which was either positive or negative, depending on the treatment group to which he was assigned. The ten-subject control group received no supervision. Twenty positive and twenty negative statements (compiled from a pilot study in which three expert judges rated fifty comments as strongly, mildly, or weakly positive or negative) were used by the supervisor in these sessions. Immediately following the supervision session, each subject conducted another thirty-minute interview with a second client, and this interview also was rated for empathy using Carkhuff's Empathic Understanding in Interpersonal Processes II Scale. Analysis of the data yielded the following results. First, no significant differences in empathy were observed prior to the supervisory session. Second, subsequent to the supervisory session, the group receiving positive supervision demonstrated significant ($p < .01$) gains in empathic behavior, while neither the control group nor the group receiving negative supervision demonstrated such changes. Blane concludes:

A positive supervisory experience significantly increases the level of empathic understanding a counselor is able to offer his client. The level of empathic understanding does not change without supervision during the time period investigated here. Receiving a negative supervisory experience does not significantly increase a counselor's level of empathic understanding [pp. 42-43].

As the author points out, a major question stemming from this study concerns the effects of time and repeated exposure to these styles of supervision upon relevant counselor learning.

The Supervisor-Trainee Relationship

The findings of the previous two studies support data suggesting that a critical variable in the supervision process, indeed perhaps the most critical variable, is the relationship between the supervisor and trainee. The Davidson and Emmer (1966) study indicates that the supervisor who behaves in an unsupportive manner, that is, in a didactic and evaluative manner, causes the counseling trainee to shift the focus of his concern away from the client and toward himself (presumably because he feels inadequate and fears evaluation). We can then account for Blane's (1968) findings in terms of trainee anxiety which blocks the learning of empathic behavior and, perhaps more importantly, in terms of trainee self-concern which, by definition, is the antithesis of empathy.

An apparent contradiction to these conclusions arises in a study (Payne & Gralinski, 1968) of the effects of both counseling and technique-oriented supervision on trainees' learning of empathy. The authors constructed a counseling supervision analogue using forty-two male undergraduate students in introductory psychology as student counselors and fourteen graduate students as supervisors. The subjects were divided into two treatment groups and a control group and were to receive counseling-oriented supervision, technique-oriented supervision, or no supervision. All subjects were exposed to a thirty-minute recorded orientation to the meaning of empathy. Subjects in the experimental groups then responded as counselors to seven client statements played to them on a tape recording. Each experimental subject was then given a twenty-minute supervision session, with the analogue supervisor making use of either the technique-oriented or counseling-oriented style of supervision. Counseling-oriented supervisors were instructed to model their supervision interviews after a nondirective counseling relationship, setting as the primary goal the establishment of an empathic relationship with the student counselor. Technique-oriented supervisors also were instructed to work toward a positive interpersonal relationship, but they were to focus on discussing the student counselors' success in providing empathy and their general counseling techniques. Following the analogue supervision interviews, all subjects responded to seven more recorded client statements. The responses of all subjects were then rated on a seven-point empathy scale based on research scales developed by Truax (1971) and Barrett-Lennard (1959). Analysis of the presupervision and postsupervision empathy scores revealed (1) that supervision does provide an effect ($p < .01$), and (2) that students receiving technique-oriented supervision obtained significantly higher ($p < .05$) scores in empathy than did those receiving counseling-oriented supervision.

Upon initial inspection, these findings seem to contradict many of the studies we have reviewed thus far. Indeed, Payne and Gralinski (1968) comment that

> within the limits of this exploratory use of a supervisory analog, some questions are raised concerning widely stated views on counselor training. Although a technique orientation is frequently disparaged as mechanistic and artificial, it produced greater gains than the more commonly advocated counseling approach. It would appear that the theorized threat and disruption of the technique orientation did not prevent counselor learning [p. 520].

The authors go on to furnish some possible reasons for these somewhat surprising results. For instance,

> It may be that the counselors in the counseling group expected criticism and evaluation . . . and their absence proved to be disruptive. In particular, the initial orientation of recorded examples may have created expectancies for supervision which

were congruent with the technique-type but conflicted with the counseling-type supervision. And, of course, it may be that the effects of a counseling-type supervision are slower in taking effect [p. 520].

Several other possible explanations occur to us for this apparent contradiction. First, the experimental subjects were not counselor trainees but rather undergraduates taking introductory psychology. It could be that their level of investment in becoming good counselors was so low as a group that the technique-oriented supervision failed to draw from them the defensive responses which might shift their focus of concern from the client to themselves (Davidson & Emmer, 1966), and this failure would block their effective learning of empathy. Second, all of the studies cited thus far were conducted with real (albeit experimental) clients, but this study was conducted within a constructed analogue using recorded client statements instead of real clients. Thus we may be encountering the results of that difference. Third, in telling the counseling-oriented analogue supervisors to "model their supervision after a nondirective counseling relationship," the authors may have been guilty of creating a caricature rather than an analogue of a supervision relationship characterized by empathy, warmth, and genuineness. Finally, by directing the technique-oriented supervisors to offer the same high level of empathy as the counseling-oriented supervisors, it seems to us that the researchers in fact created an additive treatment rather than a differential treatment. Nevertheless, these findings present a contradiction to other findings we have cited.

A final study on the effects of supervisor style upon counselor performance was conducted by Demos and Zuwaylif (1962) in an attempt to measure how changes in trainee orientation over a practicum experience were related to the theoretical orientations of the supervisors. Prior to the first meeting of the practicum, enrollees completed the Porter Attitude Test, which classifies reponses according to five categories—evaluative, interpretive, supportive, probing, and understanding. Trainees were then randomly assigned to three supervisors who represented client-centered, eclectic, and more directive clinical orientations. At the end of the training period, the trainees again completed the Porter Attitude Test. Analysis of the two sets of results revealed that the entire group demonstrated significant changes in the direction of becoming less evaluative, less supportive, less probing, more understanding, and more interpretive. When analyzed according to type of supervision, trainees of the client-centered supervisor showed significantly more understanding and fewer probing responses ($p < .05$) than did the trainees of the other two supervisors. The authors make little attempt to explain this difference other than to suggest that the client-centered supervisor probably would tend to reinforce the understanding responses and would not tend to reinforce the probing responses.

Summary of Supervisor Role Perceptions

It would appear from the existing literature that supervisors conceive, although perhaps not consciously, of their role primarily as that of a teacher (Walz and Roeber, 1962). This conception conforms to the expectations of beginning counseling students (Delaney & Moore, 1966; Gysbers & Johnston, 1965), but somehow these expectations change over the course of the supervision process in the direction of the student's greater desire for freedom to explore and develop his own style of counseling (Hansen, 1965). It has been theorized that this change is related to the degree to which the supervisor provides relational conditions in the supervisory relationship that are similar to those conditions which we know are helpful to clients in a counseling or therapy relationship (Rogers, 1957). Indeed, it has been demonstrated that those trainees who receive the conditions of empathy, warmth, genuineness, and unconditional regard from their supervisors become significantly more open to their own experiences (Hansen & Barker, 1964) and are more successful in developing these helpful behaviors for themselves (Blane, 1968; Pierce et al., 1967). One possible explanation of the latter phenomenon, which has been supported by research, is that while didactic and evaluative supervision focuses a trainee's concern on his own fears and anxieties about becoming a good counselor, supervision which is supportive (that is, provides Rogers' necessary and sufficient conditions of personal change) frees the student counselor to focus his concern upon his client (Davidson & Emmer, 1966). This focus of concern is the underlying affective stance from which empathic behavior proceeds. Evidence suggests that trainees receive significantly more than they had hoped from the supervisory relationship (Hansen). It may be that just as a client who enters therapy for the first time expects advice and instead receives helpful conditions under which to resolve his own problems (Rogers, 1957), the trainee who enters supervision for the first time expects instruction and instead receives helpful conditions under which to develop his own understanding and counseling skills (Arbuckle, 1963). It would appear, however, that within the framework of a truly supportive supervisory relationship, counseling technique can be successfully taught (Payne and Gralinski, 1968); but the research evidence indicates that a highly developed interpersonal relationship is the sine qua non of counselor learning.

SUPERVISOR BEHAVIORS AND STYLES

Thus far we have been speaking of supervision with little reference to the nature of supervision activities, which is a bit like talking about dinner without referring to the menu. What actually goes on in supervision? How is it conducted? The supervision literature is filled with descriptions of supervision techniques, but few studies include research findings which support their usefulness as training devices. The appropriateness of specific techniques, of course, rests on the supervisor's primary goals. Hosford (1969), in an unpublished review of supervision literature, suggests that the primary trainee outcomes may be grouped under five major categories:

1) gaining greater awareness and understanding of one's own personality; 2) building and maintaining a counseling relationship; 3) refining past learning, incorporating theoretical constructs into counseling practice; 4) understanding the dynamics of one's own behavior and their effect on the client; and 5) integrating research findings with counseling practice [p. 7].

We feel that these goals can be further generalized under the following groupings: personal-emotional development (Hosford's categories 1 and 4), practical skills (Hosford's category 2), and cognitive structuring (Hosford's categories 3 and 5).

Personal-Emotional Development

Rogers (1956) and Arbuckle (1963) advocate personal-emotional goals for supervision, as do Ekstein and Wallerstein (1958), who represent the psychoanalytic psychotherapy orientation. A major assumption underlying all techniques which spring from this goal orientation is, according to Altucher (1967), that "learning to be a counselor is both an emotional and an intellectual experience, and of the two, the emotional is the most crucial [p. 165]." Altucher goes on to state that students' difficulties in learning counseling stem largely from their characteristic patterns or styles of behavior. When they are confronted by demands for change in these characteristic patterns, they feel anxiety, and this anxiety blocks their ability to learn things that would otherwise (Altucher seems to imply), be relatively simple. The supervisor's task, then, is to manage the trainee's level of discomfort and anxiety at a level high enough to produce the motivation for learning and yet low enough so that the student is not overwhelmed by the anxiety. Altucher feels this balance is achieved "by careful attention to specific instances, going over the counselor-client interactions with the counselor one by one, over and over, in the most painstaking way [p. 167]."

It seems clear from other articles that supervisors who hold practical or skill acquisition goals also make extensive use of the technique of examining client interactions. For Altucher and other supervision theorists of the personal-emotional orientation, however, the primary tool is the student counselors' confrontations of themselves and their characteristic patterns of behavior rather than their learning specific kinds of skill-related responses.

The most frequently cited technique for accomplishing this task of examining counselor-client interactions is the use of recordings, both audio and video, although most references to the use of recordings come from a practical skills orientation. Walz and Roeber (1962) give an account of trainees' confrontations of their interview behavior through the use of videotape playbacks. Patterson (1964) tells of his use of tape recordings in the service of the students' own learning processes rather than in the service of a practical skills orientation to training.

Anderson and Brown (1955) provide a very concrete anecdotal

account of how recorded material can be used in a personal-emotional, non-technique-oriented supervision session. Other techniques associated with the personal-emotional orientation to supervision are role playing, psychodrama, and adjunctive group counseling (Betz, 1968).

Practical Skills

Let us first consider microskills methods. Few systematic training programs have been developed for the training of specific practical skills. Of those techniques which have been reported, few provide evaluative findings as documentation of their effectiveness. A striking exception is a system of behavioral training developed by Ivey, Normington, Miller, and Haase (1968) which has become known as microcounseling. This approach consists of a series of scaled-down counseling interactions or analogue counseling interactions in which a trainee's attention is focused upon specific counselor behaviors. The basic microcounseling model includes the following steps: (1) the student counselors conduct an interview or analogue interview with no specific directions regarding the behavior to be learned; (2) they read a short section of a manual which describes the behavior to be learned; (3) they view effective and ineffective videotaped examples of the skill to be learned, comparing themselves to the interviewer in the taped example; (4) they talk with the trainer/supervisor about their interviews in light of the new information they have received; and (5) they go back to the session or analogue session and consciously try to implement the new behavior.

Bellucci (1972) elaborates on the supervisor's role in this behavioral system of counselor training. While actual instructional content is provided in the materials (most notably, the training manual used in the microcounseling process), the supervisor functions to reinforce correct behaviors by utilizing positive verbal reinforcement, positive nonverbal reinforcement, qualified reinforcement (for example, "That's great, but . . ."), or positive post hoc reinforcement (the supervisor remembers a previous response and then reinforces). The supervisor attempts to shape the student counselor's behavior according to the microcounseling models developed by Ivey and his team.

Skills fall into three major categories, according to Ivey's (1971) presentation of the microcounseling model. These categories are (1) facilitative interview skills, (2) conceptual strategy skills, and (3) skills dealing with feelings. Ivey contends that the psychoanalytic, client-centered, and didactic-experiential training models are inadequate in terms of comprehensiveness and specificity. He feels, however, that the microcounseling model fulfills the requirements of a training model by discriminating, describing, and modeling, as well as by providing practice and feedback for each skill to be learned.

Three studies reported by Ivey, Normington, Miller, Morrill, and Haase (1968) demonstrate both the technique and the effectiveness of the microcounseling approach. The first study focused on attending behavior, that is, on teaching counselors how to reinforce their clients by paying attention to them. An additional training goal in this study was to practice verbal following behavior, which consists of a counselor response that attends to the client's last comment without introducing new data. Subjects for this study were thirty-eight dormitory counselors who were randomly divided into experimental and control groups. The experimental group was trained by the microcounseling technique, while the control group performed only two interview sessions and did not have the intervening training. Evaluation of this study was accomplished in three ways: (1) videotapes were rated for attending behavior using a scale developed by microcounseling researchers, with an interrater reliability of .843; (2) transcripts of all interviews were rated for verbal attending behavior by two trained raters; and (3) all clients completed a semantic differential on counselor effectiveness. Analysis of the data only revealed a significant difference ($p < .05$) in the eye contact behavior on the direct tape ratings. Clients also rated the experimental group higher ($p < .05$) on the Counselor Effectiveness Scale.

A second study included in this report (Ivey et al., 1968) focused on the training of student counselors to reflect feelings. This skill is operationally defined as behavior by the counselor which communicates to the client, "I am with you. I can accurately sense the world as you are feeling and perceiving it." Ivey and his associates state that "this communication is a communication of empathic understanding, a key aspect of an effective interpersonal relationship [p. 5]." Eleven beginning counselors, three of whom had had no counseling experience whatever, were used as subjects in this study. Clients were eleven paid volunteers drawn from a university population. The microcounseling training model used for this study proceeded as follows: (1) each student counselor conducted a five-minute videotaped interview with the experimental client, and this session was to be conducted as the student wanted; (2) trainees next read the "Reflection of Feeling Manual" and discussed the nature of the skill with a supervisor; (3) videotaped models of the effective and ineffective reflection of feelings were presented to the trainees, coupled with discussion of the skill involved; and (4) trainees then were shown the videotapes of their initial sessions and were asked to identify instances where feelings were reflected or instances where the skill might have been utilized. The skill was reinforced by the supervisor through positive verbal reinforcers. A videotape was made of a three-minute role-playing practice session in which an experienced counselor played the client and expressed feelings very freely, thus giving the trainee ample opportunity to utilize the feeling skill. The supervisor and the two role players then viewed the videotape and noted instances of the effective reflection of feelings. The trainee conducted a second interview with the same client, with instructions to practice reflecting client feelings. The trainee and supervisor reviewed the tape of the second interview and analyzed the trainee's use of the skill. The supervisor rewarded accurate reflections of feeling with positive verbal reinforcements. The trainee conducted a third interview with the original client, again with instructions to practice the reflection of feelings. Then the final interview was viewed and discussed by the trainee and supervisor. This entire training process took approximately two hours.

Evaluation of this study was accomplished by: (1) client ratings of the student counselor on the semantic differential Counselor Effectiveness Scale (Ivey et al., 1968) and on a relationship questionnaire adapted from Truax and Carkhuff (1967); (2) counselor self-ratings on a semantic differential self-concept scale and on a rating scale for the accurate reflection of feelings administered at the end of each interview session; and (3) judges' ratings of the videotapes for the accurate reflection of feelings. Analysis of the data emanating from each contact with the original client was accomplished by use of a linear trend design.

Results of the judges' ratings revealed highly significant ($p < .001$) increases in the trainees' abilities to reflect client feelings accurately. Clients confirmed this judgment by noting highly significant increases ($p < .001$) in their counselors' abilities to establish and maintain relationships and in their general counseling effectiveness. Counselors-in-training concurred with these judgments by rating themselves as significantly more able ($p < .001$) to accurately reflect feelings. Concomitant with this rise in their estimates of their abilities, trainees reported significant ($p < .001$) changes in their self-concepts. It would appear from this study that significant changes in trainees' mastery of this skill can produce positive changes in their self-concept.

The third and final study reported by Ivey and his associates involved training in the skill of summarizing feelings. This skill, while an extension of the skills of attending and reflecting feelings, is seen by the authors as "attending to a broader class of client response," and it demands "the skill to bring together seemingly diverse elements into a meaningful Gestalt [Ivey et al., 1968, p. 13]." Ten beginning counselors who had had no previous counseling experience participated as trainees in this study, while ten paid students, randomly assigned to the counselors, served as clients. The microcounseling technique utilized was identical to that used in the reflection of feelings study, except that a "Summarization of Feeling Manual" was substituted for the "Reflection of Feeling Manual" and videotaped examples emphasized the skill of summarizing feelings. Evaluation was also identical to the reflection of feelings study, except that the criterion variable became accurate summarization of feelings. Finally, the trend analysis design for treating the data also was identical to that used in the earlier study. Results showed highly significant increases ($p < .001$) on all four dimensions measured—judges' ratings of accurately summarized feelings, clients' ratings of counselor ability to establish and maintain an effective relationship, counselors' self-ratings on the ability to summarize feelings, and counselors' reports of their own levels of self-development. The authors concluded that "summarization of feeling is a discrete, identifiable skill, which can be taught to beginning counselors quickly and effectively *via* the microcounseling paradigm [p. 15]."

It is difficult to know whether to class the microcounseling approach as client-centered or behavioral. Ivey describes attending behavior, reflection of feelings, and summarization of feelings as reinforcers; but he sees training in these skills as a more complex process than simply rewarding desired client behavior. Training involved cue discrimination through the presentation of models, training materials, and supervisory comments. It involved positive reinforcement of operants by the supervisor through rewarding appropriate attending behavior. In short, the training process was designed to model the behavior and then reinforce the behavior once it had occurred.

The social learning model of Bandura and Walters (1963) provides an essentially relevant discussion of some of the techniques employed in this study. Specifically:

> Attending behavior . . . can be taught as a technique, but unlike pure technique ("Say the client's name at least three times"), attending implies real interaction. In order to engage in the attending behavior of following content by relevant statements, the person must listen to content. To follow communication of feeling by appropriate changes in voice timbre and quality and by appropriate statements, one must attend to the feeling that is being communicated [p. 10].

In microcounseling, then, we seem to have criteria which are based essentially on client-centered counseling theory. Attending behaviors, for example, are analogous to the characteristics of warmth, genuineness, positive regard, and recognition of feelings. Ivey and Gluckstern (1974) have developed a videotape series that includes instructor and student manuals and is designed to teach basic helping skills by way of the microcounseling method. A similar instructional approach, with accompanying video materials, has been developed by Carkhuff (1973). His supporting research is reported in his earlier two-volume work (Carkhuff, 1969).

A second major approach to practical skills involves Interpersonal Process Recall, a method of supervision which defies strict classification within one of our theoretical orientations. Originally developed by Kagan and Krathwohl (1967), the IPR approach to supervision grew out of the authors' initial dissatisfaction with supervision conducted in the absence of both objective data from the counseling session and information relating to the client's thoughts and feelings during the interview. Kagan's formulation of the problem is a cogent critique of supervision as it often is conducted in counselor education:

> Our initial concern was that the education of counselors and therapists is currently based on a very small portion of the available client responses, namely those which could be recorded on an ordinary tape recorder. Although techniques of supervision vary, training typically consists of having the trainee counselor audiotape record his interviews, listen to the recording with a counselor educator and discuss the recording in terms of how he handled the session. With one-way mirror systems the supervisors may watch an occasional interview or a part of an interview with a client, and only by these time-consuming means can he make suggestions about the face-to-face behavior. Even where videotaping is used there is very little understanding of the various mannerisms, facial expressions, and other nonverbal cues which accompany the client's verbalizations [1967, p. 4].

Kagan goes on to raise questions about missed information and to suggest solutions to the problem:

> Did the trainee miss opportunities to influence the client because he didn't perceive or understand some of the more subtle client cues? Was he so preoccupied with projecting a "proper" counselor image that he was not really focused on the client's communication? Had he accurately understood the communication of the client but was frightened that the client might "fall apart" or get angry with the trainee, or, even worse, cry, if the trainee responded to the client's cues? Was he simply not well enough informed about counseling theory? . . . In the absence of knowledge of the nature of specific develop-

mental counselor tasks, supervisors frequently adopt a supervisory "posture" with the trainee. The supervisor tends to
maintain this posture as *his approach* throughout the trainees'
supervised experience.

We concluded that if we could give a subject enough clues
and cues to help him relive the experience, we could explore in
depth at a later time various points in the interaction, the
thoughts, feelings, changes in thoughts and feelings, and the
meaning of various gestures and expressions. This formulation of the problem suggested that if we could capture the
relevant stimuli in the situation in such a way that we could
recreate it at a later time, we could help the person relive the
original situation [Kagan & Krathwohl, 1967, pp. 4-5].

In addition to the counselor and client, the IPR procedure involves
a third person, an "inquirer." The potential inquirer watches the
counseling interview from behind a one-way mirror, and the interview is also videotaped. When the counseling session is concluded,
the inquirer enters the counseling room and takes the counselor's
place. Inquirer and client watch the videotape of the interview together, stopping the tape frequently to allow the client to comment
or the inquirer to ask about what the client was feeling and experiencing at that point in the interview. The inquirer avoids interacting directly with the client. The sole purpose of this interview is
to help the client relive the original interview and to elaborate on
his or her internal experience during that session. The counselor
trainee observes this process. Later, the counselor is interviewed
about his thoughts and feelings during the counseling interview.

In IPR supervision, the inquiry session is also videotaped. This
tape is viewed by the supervisor and trainee together. The supervisor in effect becomes the inquirer, pushing the counselor trainee
to examine thoughts and feelings experienced during the session.
An additional supervisory technique is to conduct the inquiry of
both client and counselor simultaneously.

Kagan and his associates hypothesized that the education of a
counselor involves a series of developmental tasks, four of which
are identified as: (1) becoming aware of the elements of good coun-

seling; (2) becoming sensitive to client communication (a goal served by the counselor's exposure to the client's recall under the inquiry process); (3) becoming aware of and sensitive to one's own feelings during the counseling session (a goal served by direct inquiry by the counselor); and (4) becoming sensitive to the bilateral nature of the counseling interaction (a goal facilitated by a mutual recall process with the client).

The first study performed to measure the effectiveness of IPR as a supervision technique yielded unexpected results. The authors suspected that their initial failure to demonstrate the effectiveness of IPR over traditional methods of supervision was due to defects in the research design and to the enormous complexity of the counseling situation. Indeed, a second, more rigorously constructed experiment comparing IPR to traditional supervision methods yielded more positive results. Two groups of beginning counseling students (*N* not provided) were selected for treatment and control groups. An initial state, consisting of a thirty-minute counseling session with a high school student, was identical for all subjects. For the remainder of the practicum, the treatment group was given intensive supervision under the IPR method for one hour following each session, including both exposure to client recall and exposure to counselor recall under the supervisor. The control group was given one hour of supervision following each session, using only tape recordings and stressing that the student understand himself and his own psychodynamic processes and that he understand his relationship with the client. At the end of the practicum experience, the IPR Counselor Verbal Response Scale and the Wisconsin Relationship Orientation Scale (Steph, 1963) were readministered to each subject. Data items were analyzed by means of a *T* test for paired observations, and the results supported the idea that the IPR approach was the more effective treatment within the parameters of this study. The authors note that similar results were obtained in three separate replications of this experiment.

On the basis of these promising initial findings, our intuitive response to Kagan's conceptualization of the process, and our awareness of the inadequacies of traditional methods of supervision, we feel the IPR techniques are a productive technical development in counseling supervision. The major difficulties with the method seem to be the need for a relatively sophisticated videotape apparatus and the need for a skilled inquirer/supervisor. These difficulties would seem to put a fully implemented IPR supervision program out of the reach of most current counselor education programs. Nevertheless, further research into several applications of the IPR technique appear to be most promising.

Kagan concluded from his years of research on the IPR process that counseling was too complex a behavior to learn through one type of supervisory experience. He therefore designed a teaching strategy and supporting materials which incorporated the basic elements of IPR method. The sequence moves from concepts to simulation exercises, affective stress experiences, video feedback from clients, and video feedback of oneself in action. The methods have been packaged in a program lasting thirty to fifty hours and including six hours of stimulus films (Kagan, 1972).

Our investigation of the literature pertaining to supervision techniques uncovered no meaningful research either supporting or refuting the effectiveness of cognitively oriented supervision. Two articles, however, were often cited as offering a strong rationale for supervision which proceeds from a cognitive orientation. The first of these (Krumboltz, 1967) describes supervision as a process of changing the behavior of behavior changers. Though Krumboltz never actually describes the process by which these changes are effected, he does state four goals and a theory of counselor education. Specifically,

> 1) The counselor should learn, for each individual client, to specify the objectives of counseling in terms of changes in the client's behavior mutually desired by client and counselor. . . .
> 2) The counselor should learn to apply facts about the learning process to the modification of client behavior. . . . 3) The counselor should learn that the responses of his client, not the judgment of his practicum supervisor, provide the criterion for the success of his counseling. . . . 4) The counselor should learn to examine the research literature and to participate in research studies in order to find improved ways of helping clients [p. 223].

Unfortunately, the supervisory techniques by which these goals are implemented have to be inferred from the Krumboltz article.

Cognitive Structuring

Dreikurs and Sonstegaard (1966) provide us with an example of a group supervision method approached from a cognitive orientation. The authors trace the roots of group supervision to Adler, who commonly interviewed children and their families before groups of counselors and teachers for training purposes. Adler's practice grew into "multiple psychotherapy," that is, the use of two counselors, one experienced and the other inexperienced, to treat one client. In line with this historical development, Dreikurs and Sonstegaard practiced both counseling and supervision within the context of the entire training group. An advantage of this approach is that the trainee,

acquiring knowledge and skill in counseling in a group setting of his peers, experiences inestimably valuable feedback from the observations and questions of his colleagues during and after each counseling session. As students observe and participate in the counseling and discussion of all cases, they are confronted with a wide range of problem situations, thereby increasing their understanding and insight and further developing their skills. Each student counselor, as he counsels before the group and the instructor, thus contributes to the learning experiences of each member of the group, as he, in turn, learns from them [p. 19].

The Dreikurs and Sonstegaard study (1966) also suggests that the above form of supervision, while perhaps not consistent with other systems of counseling theory, is entirely consistent within the framework of Adlerian psychology. If one believes that clients' problems spring from their own psychopathology and intrapsychic conflict, then it follows that being interviewed in a group setting would not only be futile but would be potentially damaging. If one believes that the sources of a client's help spring from the quality of the interpersonal relationship between the client and therapist, then it seems incongruous to subject the client to an interview situation before a group in which he or she might be interviewed by several different therapists. But if, as the authors point out, one views "the deficiencies and maladjustment of the child not as a consequence of pathological processes, but as an expression of wrong ideas and mistaken goals, as we do, then one can explore and discuss them in front of others [p. 19]."

Dreikurs and Sonstegaard go on to describe the process of group supervision. Practicum groups, comprised of ten to twelve counseling students, meet as a group for counseling sessions with parents and children. Students are instructed in interview technique and format, apparently aimed at uncovering the clients' "wrong ideas and mistaken goals." The client is counseled by one student as far and as fast as the student can profitably go (one assumes that the practicum instructor makes this judgment). At this point, another student takes over, and so on, until the interview time is exhausted. At some point during the interview, the supervisor takes over the counseling for demonstration purposes. Following the interview, the students and instructor evaluate the session.

A similar approach was utilized by Brammer and Springer (1971) in training staff development specialists during a school counselor training program. When Washington State adopted a competency basis for counselor education and certification, practicing counselors as well as new candidates were required to meet specified performance standards. A training model was utilized in which peer assessment was a dominant feature. The program incorporated microskills methods, Interpersonal Process Recall techniques, and development groups.

The common thread which seems to bind the cognitive approaches (the behavioral orientation of Krumboltz, the Adlerian group approach of Dreikurs, and a variety of supervision styles grouped under the heading "clinical orientations") is the emphasis placed upon the conceptual-theoretical evaluation of the client. We might say in retrospect that the personal-emotional orientation emphasizes the personal development of the trainee, whereas the practical skills orientation emphasizes the conceptualization and treatment of the person and problem. However, we need not be limited to such a simplistic generalization. One can imagine the client-centered therapist undergoing a practical skills supervision process (as in the microcounseling model), just as one can imagine the behavioral therapist undergoing a personal-emotional supervision process with the aim of changing his behaviors in order to become a more effective counselor or therapist.

SUMMARY AND IMPLICATIONS

We have given an account of the experimental literature of the nature and conditions of the supervision process in counseling and psychotherapy. We also have presented several techniques associated with these approaches. Figure 1 shows a schematic summary of the information contained in this chapter. Classifications such as this are arbitrary; and the reader should be aware that in any one supervisor, there is considerable overlap in basic styles of supervision. While some have done research in one style, their supervisory methods tend to be broader.

From the experimental literature, certain conditions appear to be "givens" in the supervisory process. It appears that when supervisors are asked to account for their roles, they emphasize the instructional nature of their work. Students, at least in anticipation of supervision, see their supervisors as teachers; but these expectations change during the course of the training period in the direction of the students' greater desire to explore the learning of counseling in their own way and at their own pace. Client-centered theorists have hypothesized that growth changes are related to the degree to which the supervisor provides relational conditions in the supervisory process that are similar to the growth conditions which we know are helpful to clients in counseling. Some research suggests that when supervisors provide Rogers' necessary and sufficient conditions for therapeutic personality change, the students become more open to their own experience and less defensive. They also have more success in developing their abilities to offer these same conditions to their clients.

Trainees receive a great deal more than they expect by way of the relational conditions in supervision; and within the context of these facilitative conditions, they grow and develop into effective counselors. This is not to suggest, however, that specific techniques cannot

FIGURE 1

A Schematic Summary of the Supervision Literature

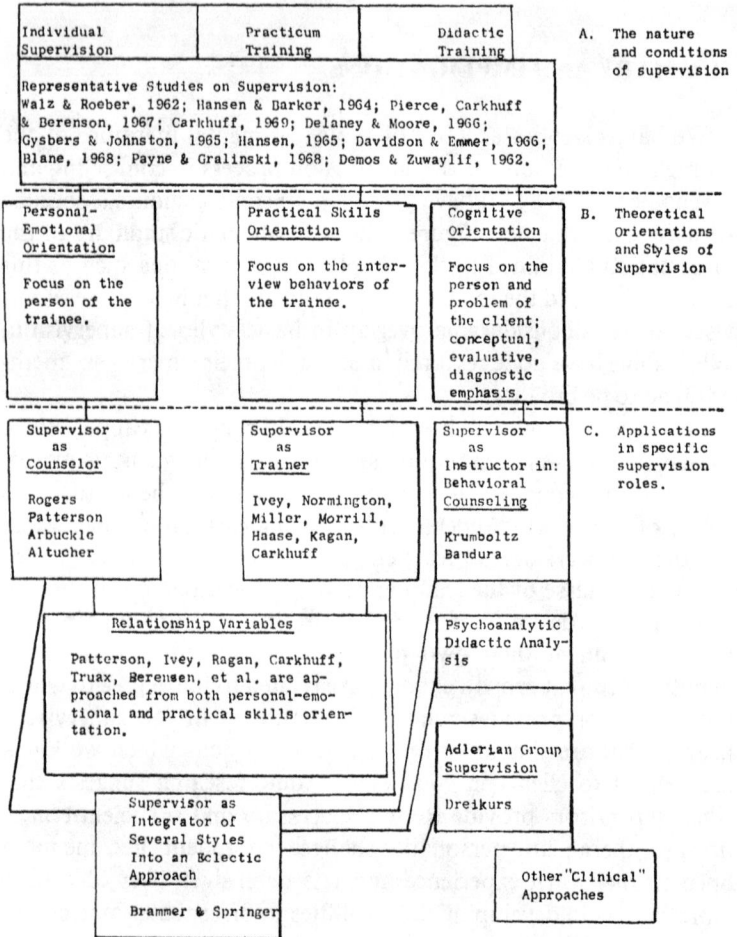

Individual Supervision	Practicum Training	Didactic Training	A. The nature and conditions of supervision

Representative Studies on Supervision:
Walz & Roeber, 1962; Hansen & Barker, 1964; Pierce, Carkhuff & Berenson, 1967; Carkhuff, 1969; Delaney & Moore, 1966; Gysbers & Johnston, 1965; Hansen, 1965; Davidson & Emner, 1966; Blane, 1968; Payne & Gralinski, 1968; Demos & Zuwaylif, 1962.

Personal-Emotional Orientation Focus on the person of the trainee.	Practical Skills Orientation Focus on the interview behaviors of the trainee.	Cognitive Orientation Focus on the person and problem of the client; conceptual, evaluative, diagnostic emphasis.	B. Theoretical Orientations and Styles of Supervision

Supervisor as Counselor Rogers Patterson Arbuckle Altucher	Supervisor as Trainer Ivey, Normington, Miller, Morrill, Haase, Kagan, Carkhuff	Supervisor as Instructor in: Behavioral Counseling Krumboltz Bandura	C. Applications in specific supervision roles.

Relationship Variables

Patterson, Ivey, Ragan, Carkhuff, Truax, Berensen, et al. are approached from both personal-emotional and practical skills orientation.

Psychoanalytic Didactic Analysis

Adlerian Group Supervision

Dreikurs

Supervisor as Integrator of Several Styles Into an Eclectic Approach

Brammer & Springer

Other "Clinical" Approaches

be taught successfully within a good interpersonal relationship; but the overwhelming weight of research evidence indicates that a highly developed relationship between the trainee and supervisor is a necessary condition for learning counseling or psychotherapy.

Systems of supervision are susceptible to differentiation under three distinct orientations—personal-emotional, practical skills, and cognitive-theoretical. Supervisors of the personal-emotional orientation hold that the learning of counseling is most importantly an emotional experience, and as such it demands the trainee's personal confrontation and exploration of feelings, behaviors, and experiences in counseling. Since these confrontations and explorations often prove too difficult for the trainee to handle alone, the primary role of the supervisors of this orientation is to counsel students, to facilitate their efforts to cope with their feelings, behaviors, and experiences. The supervisors also help them to derive important personal learning from their experiences. Advocates of this orientation in the supervision literature are Rogers (1957), Arbuckle (1963), Patterson (1964), and Altucher (1967).

Supervisors of the practical skills orientation, while not explicitly stating so at the philosophical level, seem to believe that the differences between effective counseling and ineffective counseling lie in the performance of certain key behaviors by the counselor. Furthermore, they feel that these behaviors can be taught effectively to counseling students or indeed to lay persons without either excessive attention to personal feelings or lengthy didactic instruction. In this approach, the role of the supervisor becomes that of a trainer or behavioral consultant whose aim is to assist the trainee in developing a system of behaviors which will contribute to effective counseling practice. Prominent positions which we see as falling under this grouping are the relational approach of Truax, Carkhuff, and Berenson and the microcounseling approach of Ivey, Normington, Miller, Morrill, and Haase.

Cognitive orientations stress the trainee's mastery of a certain body of knowledge as a prerequisite to the effective practice of counseling. This body of knowledge may be learning theory applied to behavioral counseling, Adlerian theory as advanced by Dreikurs, psychoanalytic theory for doing analysis, or the diagnostic skills demanded by the various clinical approaches. The role of the super-

visor in the various cognitive orientations is primarily that of instructor and professional role model.

Needless to say, we suspect that supervision of a pure type from
any one of these orientations occurs very rarely in the real world of
counselor education. When it does, we feel that the supervisor in
question is probably more devoted to the system of supervision than
to the real educational needs of his trainees. Nevertheless, we believe
that examination of these admittedly caricatured orientations to
supervision may help practicing supervisors to formulate and tighten
the rationale for their supervisory operations.

THE NEED FOR FURTHER RESEARCH: WHERE
DO WE GO FROM HERE?

Our exploration of the literature on counselor supervision leaves
us convinced of the need for further research on supervision in
general and specifically of the need for: (1) further exploration of
given conditions in supervision as it is practiced with beginning as
well as with advanced trainees; (2) definitive elaboration and operationalization of the qualities and behaviors viewed as desirable
outcomes of the supervision process by various schools of counseling and counseling supervision; (3) assessment techniques by which
to measure the effectiveness of supervision in attaining the preceding outcomes; and (4) development and evaluation of training
for potential supervisors.

We see the descriptive studies on the existing nature and conditions of supervision as highly valuable preexperimental work. But
in the end, we concur with Hansen and Warner's (1971) concluding
comment on the status of research in supervision:

> The obvious question at this point is: What have we learned
> from these studies? The answer is almost as obvious as the
> question: very little. In short, not much of a definitive nature
> has been added to the useful knowledge of counselor educators.
> This is not to say that the research reviewed here has been a
> waste, for the reports raise many interesting questions for
> further research. It would seem highly appropriate at this

time to subject these questions to more refined study. What is needed is an end to description and a move toward solid experimental investigation [p. 271].

Counselor educators of the practical skills orientation have been the most active in the explication and operationalization of ideal terminal behaviors for the supervision process. Carkhuff's (1969b) scales for the measurement of empathic understanding and his training system, for example, along with scales developed by Ivey and his associates (1971) for measuring the learning of verbal attending behavior constitute a specificity of concepts and a willingness to subject ideal outcomes to actual measurement. One has the impression that these measures appear frequently in the experimental literature not so much because they represent ideal supervision outcomes as because they are among the very few outcome statements sufficiently operationalized for research. Would it not be possible, for instance, for supervisors of the personal-emotional orientation to specify the directions of personal growth which they hope their trainees will experience, to develop means of measuring this growth, and to subject their work to evaluative research? Is it not possible for cognitively oriented counselor educators to specify their goals for supervision and to develop measurement instruments by which to gauge the success of their training programs in terms of their own training goals? If it were possible to say in what ways and at what levels counselors of various orientations were functioning in terms of behaviors deemed desirable within those orientations, it would be much easier to approach the question of which counselor behaviors result in help for clients.

Finally, we view as critically important the many unanswered questions concerning the qualifications and preparation of counseling supervisors. The American Personnel and Guidance Association committee on training, licensing, and certification recommended in 1958 that counselor supervisors have the doctoral degree in counseling or a related area, or its equivalent. In 1963, an American Psychological Association committee added the recommendation that supervisors have several years of counseling experience. Clearly, these recommendations are not followed in many counselor education programs. Roeber (1962) proposes a graduated system of supervisor status based upon education, experience, and job responsi-bilities. Smith (1962) argues that status definitions alone are not tenable and that education and experience do not constitute compe-tence. Hansen and Stevic (1967) recognize the need to prepare super-visors and propose a special practicum on supervision to be offered as part of the doctoral program in counseling. Brammer and Springer (1971) have reported on the only such practicum or supervisor train-ing program. Until such training is available, the counselor renewal program involving fourteen-hundred school counselors in Wash-ington State has been handled by eighty "staff development spe-cialists" who were specially trained in supervision technology and methodology. These practicing counselors were interested in train-ing and were invited to help implement the new competency-based program.

We suspect that supervision will continue to be a highly individual, sometimes rigorous, sometimes haphazard, always unregulated, "sometime" thing, which no amount of descriptive research will substantially improve. The task before us is at least twofold. First, our lack of knowledge of the nature and conditions of supervision, our lack of outcome criteria, and our lack of knowledge of the comparative effectiveness of various supervisory strategies all de-mand a moratorium on further speculation and a redoubled effort toward descriptive, evaluative, and experimental research. Second, the current theory and practice of supervision needs to be rebuilt and should be based solidly upon research findings and validated experience rather than upon speculations.

REFERENCES

Altucher, N. Constructive use of the supervisory relationship. *Journal of Counseling Psychology,* 1967, **14,** 165-170.

American Personnel and Guidance Association; Professional Training, Licensing, and Certification Committee. Counselor preparation: Recom-mendations for minimum standards. *Personnel and Guidance Journal,* 1958, **37,** 162-166.

American Psychological Association, Division of Counseling Psychology. The role of psychology in the preparation of rehabilitation counselors. Unpublished manuscript, American Psychological Association, 1963.

Anderson, R. P., & Brown, O. H. Tape recordings and counselor trainee understandings. *Journal of Counseling Psychology,* 1955, **2,** 189-194.

Arbuckle, D. S. The learning of counseling: Process, not product. *Journal of Counseling Psychology,* 1963, **10,** 163-168.

Aubrey, R. F. Elementary school counseling practicum: Suggestions for experiences and expectations. *Counselor Education and Supervision,* 1967, **7,** 13-19.

Austin, B., & Altekruese, M. K. The effects of group supervisor roles on practicum students' interview behavior. *Counselor Education and Supervision,* 1972, **12,** 63-68.

Bandura, A., & Walters, R. *Social learning and personality development.* New York: Holt, Rinehart, and Winston, 1963.

Barrett-Lennard, G. T. Dimensions of perceived therapist response related to therapeutic change. Unpublished doctoral dissertation, University of Chicago, 1959.

Bellucci, J. E. Microcounseling and imitation learning: A behavioral approach to counselor education. *Counselor Education and Supervision,* 1972, **12,** 88-97.

Berenson, B., Carkhuff, R., & Myrus, P. The interpersonal functioning and training of college students. *Journal of Counseling Psychology,* 1966, **13,** 441-446.

Bergland, B. W., & Quatrano, L. Systems evaluation in counselor education. *Counselor Education and Supervision,* 1973, **13,** 190-198.

Betz, R. L. Effects of group counseling as an adjunctive practicum experience. *Journal of Counseling Psychology,* 1968, **16,** 528-533.

Blane, S. M. Immediate effect of supervisory experiences on counselor candidates. *Counselor Education and Supervision,* 1968, **8,** 39-44.

Bocknek, G. Supervision of counseling: An overview. *Journal of Education,* 1971, **3,** 3-6.

Brammer, L. M., & Springer, H. A radical change in counselor education and certification. *Personnel and Guidance Journal,* 1971, **49,** 803-808.

Brown, D., & Sibalus, D. J. The effect of supervisory style upon trainee self-conception and their specific self-perception of counseling ability. Symposium presented at the meeting of the American Personnel and Guidance Association, New Orleans, 1970.

Carkhuff, R. R. Training in the counseling and therapeutic practices: Requiem or reveille? *Journal of Counseling Psychology,* 1966, **13,** 360-367.

Carkhuff, R. R. Critical variables in effective counselor training. *Journal of Counseling Psychology,* 1969, **16,** 238-245. (a)

Carkhuff, R. R. *Helping and human relations.* New York: Holt, Rinehart, and Winston, 1969. 2 vols. (b)

Carkhuff, R. R. *The art of helping.* Amherst, Mass.: Carkhuff Associates, 1973.

Carkhuff, R. R., & Berenson, B. G. *Beyond counseling and therapy.* New York: Holt, Rinehart, and Winston, 1967.

Carkhuff, R. R., & Truax, C. B. Training in counseling and psychotherapy: An evaluation of an integrated didactic and experiential approach. *Journal of Consulting Psychology,* 1965, **29,** 333-336.

Clark, C. M. On the process of counseling supervision. *Counselor Education and Supervision,* 1965, **4,** 64-67.

Colten, S. I. Supervision: Joint encounter in learning. *Journal of Education,* 1971, **3,** 7-18.

Davidson, T. N., & Emmer, E. T. Immediate effect of supportive and nonsupportive supervisor behavior on counselor candidates' focus of concern. *Counselor Education and Supervision,* 1966, **11,** 27-31.

Delaney, D. J. A behavioral model for the practicum supervision of counselor candidates. *Counselor Education and Supervision,* 1972, **12,** 46-50.

Delaney, D., Long, T., Masucci, M., & Moses, H. Skill acquisition and perception change of counselor candidates during practicum. *Counselor Education and Supervision,* 1969, **8,** 273-283.

Delaney, D. J., & Moore, J. C. Students' expectations of the role of practicum supervisor. *Counselor Education and Supervision,* 1966, **6,** 11-17.

Demos, G. D. Suggested uses of tape recordings in counseling supervision. *Personnel and Guidance Journal,* 1964, **45,** 704-705.

Demos, G. D., & Zuwaylif, F. Counselor attitudes in relation to the theoretical positions of their supervisors. *Counselor Education and Supervison,* 1962, **11,** 8-11.

Dilley, J. S. Rating scale statements: A useful approach to counselor evaluation. *Counselor Education and Supervision,* 1965, **11,** 40-43.

Dreikurs, R., & Sonstegaard, M. A specific approach to practicum supervision. *Counselor Education and Supervision,* 1966, **6,** 18-25.

Eisenberg, S., & Delaney, D. J. Using video simulation of counseling for training counselors. *Journal of Counseling Psychology,* 1970, **17,** 15-19.

Ekstein, R., & Wallenstein, R. *The teaching and learning of psychotherapy.* New York: Basic Books, 1958.

Foreman, M. E. T-Groups: Their implications for counselor supervision and preparation. *Counselor Education and Supervision,* 1967, **7,** 48-53.

Frankel, M. Effects of videotape modeling and self-confrontation technique on microcounseling behavior. *Journal of Counseling Psychology,* 1971, **18,** 465-471.

Friesen, D. D., & Dunning, G. B. Peer evaluation and practicum supervision. *Counselor Education and Supervision,* 1973, **12,** 228-235.

Gazda, G., & Ohlsen, M. The effects of short-term group counseling on prospective counselors. *Personnel and Guidance Journal,* 1961, **41,** 634-638.

Gendlin, E. Experiencing: A variable in the process of therapeutic change. *American Journal of Psychotherapy,* 1961, **15,** 171-176.

Gladstein, G. A. In-service education of counseling supervisors. *Counselor Education and Supervision,* 1970, **9,** 183-188.

Gross, D. R. A theoretical rationale for the practicum aspects of counselor preparation. Unpublished doctoral dissertation, University of Wisconsin, 1968.

Gust, T. Extending counselor supervision. *Counselor Education and Supervision,* 1970, **9,** 157-161.

Gysbers, N. C. Strategies for practicum supervision. *Counselor Education and Supervision,* 1964, **3,** 149-152.

Gysbers, N. C., & Johnston, J. A. Expectations of a practicum supervisor's role. *Counselor Education and Supervision,* 1965, **4,** 68-74.

Gysbers, N. C., & Moore, E. J. Using simulation techniques in the counseling practicum. *Counselor Education and Supervision,* 1970, **9,** 277-285.

Hansen, J. C. Trainees' expectations of supervision in the counseling practicum. *Counselor Education and Supervision,* 1965. **2,** 75-80.

Hansen, J. C., & Barker, E. N. Experiencing and the supervisory relationship. *Journal of Counseling Psychology,* 1964, **11,** 107-111.

Hansen, J. C. & Stevic, R. Practicum in supervision: A proposal. *Counselor Education and Supervision,* 1967, **6,** 205-206.

Hansen, J. C., & Warner, R. W. Review of research on practicum supervision. *Counselor Education and Supervision,* 1971, **10,** 262-272.

Horan, J. J. Behavioral goals in systematic counselor education. *Counselor Education and Supervision,* 1972, **11,** 162-171.

Hosford, R. Counselor supervision: Related research. Unpublished manuscript, University of Wisconsin, 1969.

Ivey, A. E. *Microcounseling.* Springfield, Ill.: Thomas, 1971.

Ivey, A. E., & Gluckstern, N. *Basic attending skills.* 72 Blackberry Lane, Amherst, Mass.: Authors, 1974. (Student manual, instructional manual, and half-inch videotapes)

Ivey, A. E., Normington, C., Miller, C. D., Morrill, W. H., & Haase, R. F. Microcounseling and attending behavior: An approach to prepracticum training. *Journal of Counseling Psychology,* 1968, **15** (5), 1-12. (Monograph supplement)

Johnson, J. A., & Gysbers, N. C. Practicum supervisory relationships: A majority report. *Counselor Education and Supervision,* 1966, **1,** 3-10.

Johnston, J. A., & Gysbers, N. C. Essential characteristics of a supervisory relationship in counseling practicum. *Counselor Education and Supervision,* 1967, **6,** 335-340.

Kadushin, A. Observing the interview in counselor training and supervision. *Personnel and Guidance Journal,* 1956, **35,** 405-408.

Kagan, N. *Influencing human interaction.* Instructional Media Center, Michigan State University, East Lansing, Mich.: 1972. (Manual and film series)

Kagan, N., Krathwohl, D., & Miller, R. Stimulated recall in therapy using videotape: A case study. *Journal of Counseling Psychology, 1963,* **10,** 237-243.

Kagan, N., & Krathwohl, D. R. *Studies in human interaction.* East Lansing, Mich.: Educational Publishing Service, 1967.

Kell, B., & Meuller, W. J. *Impact and change: A study of counseling relationships.* New York: Appleton, Century, and Crofts, 1966.

Krumboltz, J. E. Changing the behavior of behavior changers. *Counselor Education and Supervision,* 1967, **6,** 222-229.

Lanning, W. L. A study of the relation between group and individual counseling supervision and three relationship measures. *Journal of Counseling Psychology,* 1971, **18,** 401-406.

Lister, J. L. Supervised counseling experience: Some comments. *Counselor Education and Supervision,* 1966, **5,** 55-60.

Matarazzo, R. G., Wiens, A. N., & Saslow, G. Experimentation in the teaching and learning of psychotherapy skills. In L. Gottschalk & A. Auerbach (Eds.), *Methods of research in psychotherapy.* New York: Appleton, Century, and Crofts, 1966.

Mazer, R. C., & Segrist, A. E. Implementing the on-site supervision model. *Counselor Education and Supervision,* 1973, **12,** 206-212.

Orton, J. W. Areas of focus in supervising counseling practicum students in groups. *Personnel and Guidance Journal,* 1965, **44,** 167-170.

Patterson, C. H. Supervising students in the counseling practicum. *Journal of Counseling Psychology,* 1964, **11,** 47-53.

Payne, P., & Gralinski, D. Effects of supervisor style and empathy upon counselor learning. *Journal of Counseling Psychology,* 1968, **15,** 517-521.

Payne, P. A., Winter, D. E., & Bell, G. O. Effects of supervision style on the learning of empathy in a supervisory analogue. *Counselor Education and Supervision,* 1972, **11,** 262-269.

Peters, H. J., & Hansen, J. C. Counseling practicum: Bases for supervision. *Counselor Education and Supervision,* 1963, **2,** 82-85.

Pierce, R., Carkhuff, R. R., & Berenson, B. G. The differential effects of high and low functioning counselors upon counselors in training. *Journal of Clinical Psychology,* 1967, **23,** 212-215.

Roeber, E. C. Position paper: Practicum and internship. In *Counselor education: A progress report on standards: Discussion, reaction, and related papers.* Washington, D.C.: American Personnel and Guidance Association, 1962.

Rogers, C. R. Training individuals to engage in the therapeutic process. In C. R. Strother (Ed.), *Psychology and mental health.* Washington, D.C.: American Psychological Association, 1956.

Rogers, C. R. The necessary and sufficient conditions of therapeutic personality change. *Journal of Consulting Psychology,* 1957, **21,** 95-103.

Ruble, R. A., & Gray, H. D. Student centered approaches to practicum supervision. *Counselor Education and Supervision,* 1968, **7,** 143-144.

Smith, G. E. Reaction-state supervisor. *Counselor education: A progress report on standards: Discussion, reaction, and related papers.* Washington, D.C.: American Personnel and Guidance Association, 1962.

Steph, J. A. Responses to hypothetical counseling situations as a prediction of relationship orientation among school counselors. Unpublished doctoral dissertation, University of Wisconsin, 1963.

Sundblad, L., & Feinberg, L. The relationship of inter-personal attraction, experience, and supervisors' level of functioning in dyadic counseling supervision. *Counselor Education and Supervision,* 1972, **11,** 187-193.

Truax, C. B. An approach to counselor education: Counseling training. *Journal of Education,* 1971, **3,** 46-54.

Truax, C. B., & Carkhuff, R. R. *Toward effective counseling and psychotherapy: Training and practice.* Chicago: Aldine, 1967.

Truax, C. B., Carkhuff, R. R., & Douds, J. Toward an integration of the didactic and experiential approaches to training in counseling and psychotherapy. *Journal of Counseling Psychology,* 1964, **11,** 240-247.

Walz, G. R., & Roeber, E. C. Supervisors' reactions to a counseling interview. *Counselor Education and Supervision,* 1962, **1,** 2-7.

Yenawine, G., & Arbuckle, D. S. Study of the use of audiotape and videotape as techniques in counselor education. *Journal of Counseling Psychology,* 1971, **18,** 1-6.

Supervisory Thought and Practice in Teacher Education

GERALD R. SMITH

INTRODUCTION

This chapter examines supervision in teacher education, a subject that has been practiced steadily and analyzed periodically for the past seventy years or more. The chapter's purposes are: (1) to review supervisory practices that have been and are being implemented; (2) to examine the theories, models, and formal structures that are used to explain such practices or that provide an orienting framework for them; and (3) to analyze the evaluation designs, instruments, and techniques by which the adequacy of the practices has been judged. The main intent of the task is description, but analysis, integration, and even speculation enter into the discussion as well.

There are two ways to examine current practices in any field, and both have their strengths and weaknesses. One way is to go out and look. Although such an approach provides firsthand knowledge, it also requires a considerable period of time. The other way is to look at the literature and presume that it accurately reflects what is going on in the field. Although this method is less direct, making use of secondary sources, it can be managed in a reasonable time frame. Moreover, if care is taken to include the results of empirical studies, it should provide a fairly accurate picture. Then, too, some aspects of the field theories and models, for example, are probably better acquired through this approach. For better or worse, this is a report of practice as provided in the literature, and the reader will do well to keep this fact in mind. The only exceptions are those instances where the author himself has firsthand knowledge, and comments accordingly.

Before proceeding, it does seem essential to stake the boundaries of the supervision territory. For our purposes, supervision in teacher education means primarily the supervision of student teachers by cooperating public school teachers and by college or university supervisors. (For variety, "college" and "university" will be used interchangeably in referring to such supervisors.) However, the practice of supervision in teaching internships and other forms of field experience will not be ignored.

For the most part, the discussion does not attempt to distinguish between the supervision of student teachers in elementary education and those in secondary education. While there are some differences in the typical periods of student teaching and in other aspects of the arrangements, the relationships and variables involved are quite similar, if not the same. Moreover, when differences do occur, they are seldom clearly attributable to the persons or programs of elementary or secondary teacher education. In the rare instances where such differences are clear, they are discussed when the results are reported.

Probably more material has been written about school supervision than about supervision in teacher education. School supervision includes the responsibility of the principals, department heads, and other supervisory personnel in the school system for maintaining and improving the instructional program of the schools. One aspect of this responsibility is teacher evaluation, particularly in relation to tenure, where both the procedures used and the relationships established often parallel those between the student teacher and supervising teacher on the one hand or the student teacher and the college supervisor on the other. Some of this material is included in the review.

Finally, a vast body of management literature exists on supervisory practice in business, government, industry, hospitals, and other organizations. While some reference is made to the concepts, principles, and practices found in this literature, it was not examined in any systematic way.

SUPERVISORY PRACTICE

Organizational Patterns

Student teaching was known to have been a part of teacher training in the United States from a very early date. Newell (1900) notes, for example, that prospective teachers worked under supervision in Philadelphia as early as 1818. Since teacher education was not much of an enterprise in those days, the process more nearly resembled an apprenticeship than the culminating stage of professional training. By 1909, according to Learned (1920), almost all normal schools, the teacher training institutions of the period, required student teaching—approximately half for a full year and another third for two quarters. Learned also notes that a large percentage of the normal schools (80 percent) made use of their own laboratory schools (called "model" schools) for this purpose. Although the public cooperating schools had made their appearance much earlier—Newell reported one as early as 1844—they were still not used very widely by the early 1900s. Presumably the model schools provided a more controlled environment for training purposes, especially since many public school teachers had little training themselves. Most normal schools were at the level of high schools and accepted grade school graduates as students. Thus the model schools enabled the teacher educators to administer a program of supervision they probably felt was more adequate than what students would have received in public schools under the tutelage of untrained persons.

By 1900, most programs continued to place students in model (that is, laboratory) schools, but public school placements gradually became the more accepted mode. This development probably resulted from (1) increased student enrollments in teacher education, (2) an increasingly better-prepared group of public school teachers to serve as supervisors, and (3) pressures from the states to make public school placements mandatory for certification purposes.

The pattern for such placements, which remains the standard to this day, may best be described as "dispersed," for small numbers of student teachers are placed in a great many schools and systems across a given state. The dispersed pattern probably continues to be the standard for a number of reasons. For one thing, schools are still organized around the self-contained classroom where the individual teacher continues to operate in relative isolation. For another, such an arrangement lends itself to a low budget and is convenient for the college or university to administer. Finally, one of the prevailing myths in teacher education is the widespread belief that a prospective teacher can best learn to teach by doing an apprenticeship with *one* other teacher.

Under the dispersed pattern of providing for student teaching, supervision is carried out by a uniquely American institution known in the vernacular of education as the "roadrunner," more officially known as the college supervisor. This person serves as liaison between the school, the teacher, and the student teacher on the one hand and the college or university on the other.

While no national norms are available, common practice presents the following picture. The college supervisors direct anywhere from ten to thirty student teachers. They visit each student teacher from three to six times each semester, spend an average of thirty minutes in the classroom, and frequently do not have time for a conference afterward. The problem of inadequate time is faced by most college supervisors. In large university settings, the supervisor is usually a graduate student pursuing his or her own studies as well. Where the supervisor is a faculty member, he generally teaches, and his courses may bear no relevance to his supervisory functions, a psychic split at best. (Although a mixture of pronouns is used as referents, it is sometimes awkward, as in the preceding sentence, to use more than one. In such cases, *he* is employed as a matter of convention.)

While the dispersed pattern of placement for student teachers continues to flourish, it has been widely criticized for the following reasons: (1) the weak relationship between the schools and the university (Barnes, 1967); (2) the large number of student teachers who proceed through it without any organized orientation (E. Smith, 1969); (3) the high turnover rate among supervising teachers (Taylor & Fields, 1964); (4) the failure to focus on individual student needs (Richardson, 1968); (5) the lack of trained supervisors (Association for Student Teaching, 1963); (6) the greater possibility of a personality clash with only two persons involved (Cole, 1963); and (7) the student's exposure to a single philosophy of education and teaching (Cole, 1963).

These and similar criticisms have led to the development of a "concentration" pattern of placement in which students are concentrated in a smaller number of locations often called "teacher centers." These centers were created to reduce the gap between the largely theory-oriented world of the university classroom and the real world of the public schools. The student usually carries out a program of observation during his junior year and spends his senior year as an intern with the same teacher.

Supervision in a Multi-Institutional Teacher Education Center (Maddox, Holt, Stebbins, & Young, 1972), for example, is carried out by several persons. The role of the college supervisor is generally construed as a resource person to the teacher rather than as a supervisor to the student teacher. The school-based coordinator, also called a clinical professor, has a dual appointment from the school and the college or university. His or her responsibilities are in harmony with the way the role has been visualized by Conant (1963) and others. Finally, the clinical supervising teacher has responsibilities similar to those of any supervising teacher, but an attempt has been made to stimulate greater involvement and communication among the persons participating in the supervision process.

The creation of such centers suggests many of the advantages that have been claimed for their operation. First, they broaden the base of responsibility and decision making in teacher education, particularly during the critical student-teaching period. In some cases, the school district and the university have participated in the joint appointment of a coordinator for the center. Closer cooperation between school and university personnel has been achieved in the supervision of student teachers and in the development of the program. Often, but not always, the establishment of centers has led to a longer period of student exposure to the school program, the allocation of specific times for teachers to work with student teachers, and an improved program of supervision from both college and school personnel.

Most readers understand, of course, that teacher centers engage in many more functions than preservice training. Yarger and Leonard (1974) offer the following list of functions: "1) the enhancement of skills for teaching children, 2) skill development for making materials, 3) skill development in professional areas, and 4) recreational or social functions [p. 35]." While their discussion emphasizes the professional development or inservice role of such agencies, it acknowledges the fact that some centers "deal exclusively or almost exclusively with *preservice* teacher education [p. 10]."

While the center programs concentrate student teachers in a smaller number of locations, the numbers placed in each building may still be quite small. The next logical step, then, was to move toward the placement of greater numbers in a single building. (It is not suggested that the logical sequence is the actual sequence that occurred.) Since the principle calls for the saturation of a building with large numbers of student teachers, this pattern of placement has been designated a "saturation" pattern. In such models, where as many as fifteen to twenty students may be placed in a single building, it is feasible to offer methods classes, training in supervisory skills, and other forms of inservice development for teachers at these locations. Moreover, the larger numbers make it economically feasible and convenient to do so. In general, all of the features of the concentration pattern are inherent in the saturation pattern, only more so. Because methods classes may be offered at the site, the methods professors can add their own subject matter focus to the program of supervision. Also, teachers can be conveniently brought into methods classes, thus enhancing the possibilities for cooperative activity. While the saturation pattern might be expected to occur as a logical extension of the concentration pattern, descriptions of such a pattern are not found in abundant numbers in the literature.

The Indiana TTT Project made use of a saturation pattern in its Professional-Year Program (Smith, Harste, Mahan, Clark, Mc-

Ginty, & Shimer, 1974). It placed from sixty to ninety prospective elementary teachers in four, and in some years, five elementary schools of Monroe County, Indiana, for a full academic year. Four major methods and student teaching were offered through an integrated program of experience and instruction. In addition, the student teachers were supervised by teachers, methods instructors, and doctoral student interns. A program of supervisory skill training was offered to teachers; curriculum development and inservice training were carried out in each school; and teachers were involved in the development and operation of the program, including participation in methods instruction.

The saturation pattern apparently does have some distinct advantages, at least as represented in the TTT model. It provided a greater base of supervision, achieved a reasonable degree of coordination between methods and student teaching, and was quite highly regarded as a total program. However, there are some disadvantages or problem areas that are likely to arise if a saturation pattern is employed. For one thing, it requires that all or nearly all of the teachers participate in the supervision program, and all may not be interested in or capable of such participation. Also, it poses some logistical problems for the schools. For example, the school must be sufficiently underenrolled to make unused classroom space available to university faculty and students. The additional numbers also place a heavier burden on the cafeteria, lounge, and parking facilities, on the use of supplies and equipment and on other aspects of the school's operation. Until very recent years, schools have tended to be overcrowded, and this single factor may account for the limited use of the saturation pattern.

The movement from a dispersed pattern of placement to a more concentrated pattern of placement and then to a pattern of saturation such as that described in the Indiana TTT leads logically to a pattern of wholly shared responsibility which, to the author's knowledge, has never been tried. Such a pattern would be similar to that of a teaching hospital in the medical field. The staff, comprised of both school and college personnel, would have dual responsibility for carrying out a program of school instruction for elementary or secondary students and a program of teacher education for students in training. Some would argue that such a pattern has already been tried in the laboratory school; but the laboratory school, with rare exceptions, was never a public school and never offered an opportunity for shared responsibility. Even when university-appointed persons taught in the school, they did not have dual responsibility for instruction of children and teacher education.

Although a variety of arrangements have been employed for the placement of student teachers, most institutions make use of one pattern or another and offer little if any choice to students. In a national survey of 478 institutions of higher education approved by NCATE (National Council for Accreditation of Teacher Education), Yoder (1971) confirmed the lack of alternatives in secondary student teaching, noting that "of the institutions which responded to this survey, 63.1% did not offer any alternative programs [p. 129]." In other words, "all student teachers had approximately the same experience and little choice in what their experience would be [p. 129]."

The Supervisor-Supervisee Relationship

Having just examined the patterns for organizing student teaching and supervision, it may be useful to take another look at these arrangements not so much by way of reviewing ground already covered as to view them psychologically from the perspectives of the key participants. What is it that the participants know about student teaching from a psychological perspective? Whether they have thought about it or not, they are aware of the following things:

1. Student teaching lasts for a specified period of time, which all of the participants are aware of in advance.

2. It represents the last significant hurdle in the training program.

3. It takes place in a location that is likely to be quite foreign to the student teacher and the college supervisor.

4. It requires the student teacher to behave in ways that are completely different from similar situations in the past. He was a student in schools before, and now he is a teacher.

5. The relationship between the student teacher and supervising teacher is embedded in the physical and psychological setting of an immediate classroom. Moreover, the fact that it is the supervising teacher's classroom is scarcely lost on the student teacher. Whatever

the student teacher does or thinks about doing, he is reminded that he does so by the leave of the supervising teacher. The student teacher is clearly a guest in the teacher's territory.

6. For reasons already alluded to, the teacher who serves as the student teacher's supervisor holds enormous power over him in the present and over the course of his life for years to come. This power and the other elements of the situation place considerable stress on the student teacher to "get along with" his or her supervising teacher.

7. The link between the student teacher's present professional experience and his past training, the college supervisor, is a tenuous one at best. In most cases, the supervisor knows the student teacher only superficially and sees him relatively infrequently.

There are two closely related implications in these statements. One is that the supervising teacher has more influence on the student teacher, for better or worse, than the college supervisor. The other is that a power relationship exists between the student teacher and the supervising teacher. Both of these implications are documented in the material which follows.

A power relationship has been reported by Edgar, Warren, and Brod (1970) in a longitudinal study of beginning teachers and their supervisors. In a related article, Edgar (1972) sees the central issue as a balance "between control and autonomy (who is to set tasks and goals, how these are to be performed, and how such performance is to be evaluated) [p. 169]." According to this theory of occupational socialization, the new teacher's experience and status are relative to the significant evaluator. The degree of positive feeling between him and his evaluator modifies the influence of the evaluator on the trainee's attitudes toward autonomy and on the behavioral autonomy he can achieve in practice.

Edgar reports that where high affect existed between a teacher and his supervisor, "autonomy attitudes changed significantly more from pretest to posttest toward those held by the evaluator than did those [attitudes] of low affect teachers [p. 170]." It also appears that the movement occurred in both directions (from high autonomy on pretest to low autonomy on posttest and vice versa). The data on behavioral autonomy reinforces the importance of affective relationships. "Satisfaction with the way teaching methods were allocated and evaluated" and "the way in which disciplining students as a task area was evaluated" were both rated higher by high affect teachers (p. 170).

The importance of the relationship between the supervising teacher and the student teacher has also been documented in studies of openness. Using a Q-sort technique, Freeze (1970) measured the openness of 145 secondary teachers, 131 supervising teachers, and 16 college supervisors before and after student teachings. One hypothesis, that student teachers would become more open when placed with supervising teachers and college supervisors who were above average in openness scores, was not confirmed. Although changes were in the predicted direction, they were not significant. However, student teachers placed with less open supervisors showed a significant decrease in openness. In a follow-up study, Elliott (1970) found that significant negative changes occurred in the openness scores of both elementary and secondary student teachers and that these changes were significantly related to the openness scores of their *supervisory teachers* but *not* to the scores of their *college supervisors*. A study by Hart (1964) relating openness to interaction analysis categories yielded similar results. It appears, then, that the openness characteristics of supervising teachers, but not of college supervisors, do influence the openness characteristics of student teachers and that the greatest impact lies in a negative direction.

Others have addressed themselves to the critical nature of the relationship between the student teacher and the supervising teacher. For example, Sorenson and Halpert (1968), in a study of student teacher discomfort, concluded that "whether the apprehension which most prospective teachers experience in the early stages of student teaching is quickly overcome, or whether it persists, will be determined in part by the relationship between the candidate and supervising teacher [p. 32]." Price (1961) noted that the attitudes of student teachers change considerably during student teaching and that their attitudes tend to shift in the direction of the attitudes held by their supervising teachers. In some instances, even their teaching practices reflect those of the cooperating teacher.

As a result of the attention given to the student teacher-supervising teacher relationship and the various attitudinal and personality factors that enter into it, several researchers have explored the potential for matching student teachers with their public school supervisors. Hayes (1969) reported data indicating that such matches may improve student teacher attitudes, although he also reported that the predisposition of student teachers was more important than "external influences" during student teaching. Lindsey and Monahan (1968) examined the congruence of student teachers' educational attitudes. Correlations were found to be significant between four predictor variables and final evaluations.

One fairly large and comprehensive study by Leslie (1971) revealed little support for matching on the basis of such variables as sex, socioeconomic status, religious preferences, age, physical proximity, or four personality variables—sense of security, autonomy, innovativeness, and progressivism. In offering an explanation, the author notes that "the effect of a single individual upon the student teacher appears to be too mild to compete with the overall trauma of the student-teaching experience [p. 308]." Another feasible explanation, according to Leslie, is

that the student teacher who is mismatched reacts positively by attempting to compensate [his] students for an ineffectual cooperating teacher. This would appear to be an illustration of cognitive dissonance (learning by reaction against the cooperating teacher behavior), suggesting matching different rather than similar typologies [p. 308].

Like Freeze and Elliott, Leslie suggests that a negative relationship, a mismatched pair, may have the greatest impact. Fortunately, Leslie also concludes that the outcome may be positive, at least as far as the classroom pupils are concerned.

Another point that is reinforced is the minimal impact of the college supervisor upon the student teacher. While the findings cited thus far have been limited to the concept of openness, studies on other concepts hold similar implications. Stoller and Lesser (1963) reported, for example, that neither the method of supervision nor the particular college supervisor had any great impact on student teachers. Zahn (1965) observed that the effect of the supervising teacher upon the student teacher's attitude appeared to be greater when students were supervised with conventional techniques than when the college supervisor used interaction analysis.

Role Expectations of Supervisors

A number of studies speak to the questions of how student teachers view the role of the supervisor and how the supervisors view their own roles in the supervision process. In his investigation of student teachers' expectations of very effective and very ineffective supervisory behaviors, Scholl (1966) analyzed 311 reports and concluded that effective college supervisors were expected to make specific suggestions to student teachers on how to improve teaching skills. Also, effective supervisors were seen as helping with problems related to self-evaluation, interpersonal relationships, and student teaching requirements.

In another study, Kaplan (1967) compared the perceptions of student teachers, cooperating teachers, and university supervisors and found little agreement, especially concerning the role of the supervisor as evaluator and resource consultant. He also noted that the lack of agreement was further complicated by the lack of communication among the three groups.

Delaney and Moore (1966) administered the Gysber and Johnston Supervisor Role Analysis Form (SRAF) to prepracticum counselor trainees to determine their expectations of their supervisors. They found the primary role expectation was that of teacher followed, respectively, by the roles of counselor and critic. Students first wanted to be taught, then counseled, and then evaluated by their counselor supervisors.

Johnson and Knaupp (1970) replicated the Delaney and Moore study using students enrolled in an introduction to education course. The student reactions were based on a microteaching supervisor. The first factor—"teach me," "tell me," and "show me"—appeared quite similar to Delaney and Moore's didactive-instructive factor. The second factor, unlike Delaney and Moore's second factor, suggested "a desire for unhampered practice, for experimentation [p. 339]."

McConnell (1960) put together two lists of suggestions made over a five-year period from student teachers to supervising teachers.

The first list contained thirty-one specific ideas on how supervising teachers had been helpful. The second list contained suggestions that student teachers wished the supervising teachers had put into practice. Both lists are more reflective of human concern and common courtesy than they are of any specialized professional knowledge or skill.

Student teachers appear to differentiate very little in their expectations of the two types of supervisors. When asked to list how college supervisors helped them, student teachers tend to mention the same kinds of items as they do for supervising teachers. In a study of student teacher expectations of college supervisors, Edmund and Hemink (1958) reported that from 49 to 65 percent of the students mentioned one of the following items:

Encouraged the students, showed personal interest in them and were understanding and sympathetic.

Gave constructive criticism. Were frank and honest in their criticism.

Set good examples of how to be friendly and professional [p. 57].

In the same study, when student teachers were asked how the college supervisors could be more helpful, from 12 to 20 percent listed the following items:

Observe the student's teaching performance more often and observe for longer periods.

Participate in three-way conferences. Be more frank and honest in criticizing the student's performance.

Give more time to conferences with student teachers.

Keep appointments promptly [p. 58].

These results do not vary greatly from those reported by Garner (1971) and Trimmer (1961) on the expectations that student teachers have of cooperating teachers. In other words, instead of considering the differences in the roles, responsibilities, physical proximity, and other factors between the two groups, the student teacher perceives the role of each in relation to his own needs. Since there is little likelihood that the college supervisor can hope to meet these expectations without a drastic restructuring of his assignment, there is every possibility that high dissonance will remain between the expectations of the student teacher and the actions of the college supervisors.

Supervisory Style

When one thinks about supervisory style, several frames of reference come to mind. One has to do with the extent to which the supervisor is seen as being very direct in his efforts to change the behavior of the student teacher or beginning teacher. Where carried to an extreme, it results in what Wilson (1963) has labeled "super supervision," a process which overemphasizes planning and staying with the plans no matter what. Another approach to direct and indirect supervision was employed by Blumberg (n.d.), who made use of Flanders' (1960) concepts of direct and indirect influence to identify four supervisory styles—high direct, high indirect; high direct, low indirect; low direct, high indirect; and low direct, low indirect. The first style (high direct, high indirect) simply means that supervisors in that group were perceived by teachers as having exhibited a high frequency of both direct behaviors (giving information, expressing opinions, and making critical comments, for example) and indirect behaviors (accepting feelings, praising and encouraging, accepting and using ideas of the other person and so forth). Using the Barrett-Lennard Relationship Inventory as a measure of interpersonal relations, Blumberg found that "those behavioral styles that are seen as having a relatively heavy loading on indirect behavior seem to result in a set of interpersonal relations that are more positive than those where such a loading is not present [p. 11]." He also found that "the greater the perceived directness the more chance there is that the unconditionality score [one of the subscores of the Barrett-Lennard Inventory] will be lowered [p. 11]." This result leads Blumberg to speculate that the more indirect the behavior displayed by the supervisor, the more likely he will be to operationalize Likert's (1961) "Principle of Supportive Relationships [p. 103]" in his supervisory style.

Selection and Training of Supervisors

The Association for Student Teaching (1963) reported a survey of 282 institutional representatives who were asked to identify the problems encountered in student-teaching programs. The three most frequently checked problems were related to the identification and preparation of cooperating teachers. Some of the "matching" studies already cited speak to the selection issues. One component of the Indiana TTT Project (McIntosh and Jackson, 1973) actually employed a mutual selection process, allowing student teachers and supervisors to choose each other. Although this factor was judged to have been one of the reasons for the program's success, the numbers were small, and placements were made within a single school system. With large numbers and a more widespread system of placements, such an approach would encounter serious logistical difficulties.

As far as this author could see, the question of how to select supervising teachers has never been examined very extensively. Most states have some criteria that are used, but these are largely formal and minimal and in many cases are not rigidly followed. Indiana requires a master's degree and five years of teaching experience, and most states have similar requirements.

In one unusual study, Roth (1961) employed Flanagan's (1954) critical incident technique to identify the behaviors of supervising teachers which were judged to be outstandingly effective or ineffective. From these behaviors, Roth developed nineteen behavioral criteria which could be used in the selection of elementary school supervising teachers.

Roth's list of criteria leads to two interesting observations. First, many of the items appear to be easy to learn to implement. Surely anyone can learn to arrange for conferences, interrupt appropriately, study children, and so on. Thus if there is any validity to these criteria, they could be taught to teachers to improve their supervisory capabilities. Second, there is by implication a thread of good human relations or interpersonal skills running through many of these criteria. To the extent to which supervising teachers can be selected because they exhibit such skills or can be taught to exhibit such skills even more effectively, a more informed basis for selection will become possible. The studies cited earlier on openness in supervisors certainly support this statement. By way of specific illustration, Emmerling (1963) found that more open teachers were seen by their students as congruent, empathic, positive, and unconditional in their regard. Although this study is based on a teacher-pupil relationship, there is every reason to believe from similar studies of supervising teachers that such factors are operative there as well.

The State of Georgia has had a training program for supervising teachers since 1949. Three studies were carried out in the early 1960s to analyze and evaluate the effectiveness of this program. Prince (1961) found that "provisionals" (supervising teachers participating in the professional sequence) were more effective than "professionals" (those who had completed the three-course sequence). Two years later, Perrodin (1963) said the evidence seemed to favor the professionals, but the results were not statistically significant. He also found no relationship between supervising teacher groups and their resulting influence on student teacher attitudes.

The literature on the selection and training of supervising teachers scarcely gives one confidence that all that needs to be done is to establish selection and training programs in every state, and improvement in supervisory practice will follow. The one bright spot seems to lie in the possibility of reinforcing selection criteria with training procedures. By developing procedures for selecting more open supervisors and training programs to expand their awareness and use of such characteristics as empathy and unconditional regard, state educational agencies and institutions of higher education may have their best opportunity for making an impact upon future student teachers. At any rate, it seems to be one of the few avenues offering a reasonable chance of success. Edgar's (1972) research on affect certainly bears out this assessment.

Objectives of Supervision

In recent years, one can hardly turn to a piece of educational literature without encountering some discussion of goals, purposes, or objectives. In Illinois, the Office of the Superintendent of Public Instruction (Bakalis, 1972) published a set of educational goals for the 1970s that were derived through a process involving three thousand Illinois citizens. This emphasis on educational objectives has certainly been noted in teacher education with discussions of competency-based programs, accountability, and similar concepts.

With such developments taking place in education as a whole and in teacher education in particular, it would scarcely be surprising to find a similar trend in the literature of educational supervision; and in one respect, this expectation is fulfilled. There are a number of references to the objectives to be achieved by student teachers. Dussault (1970), who has performed the most thorough review in this area, reports two major categories of objectives in the non-research literature, the professional and the personal. He divides professional objectives into six major themes:

the student teacher as an inquirer into the educational process; the competency and effectiveness of the prospective teacher; his autonomy; his creativity; his understanding of the school, of the school system, and of the community; his membership in the teaching profession [p. 61].

Under personal objectives, Dussault includes: "the development of a valid self-concept, openness to experience, personal and psychological adjustment, breadth of interests, and development and clarification of values [p. 88]." For each objective listed under the two major categories, Dussault cites a number of references which I will not attempt to duplicate here. Most of the research references, according to Dussault, dealt with teacher competence, membership in the profession, and changes in student teacher attitudes.

Although Dussault cites more than fifty references dealing with objectives and outcomes, they are, almost without exception, statements of educational goals expressed in terms of the actions and responsibilities of student teachers rather than supervisors. Presumably, if student teachers achieve their goals, the supervisor has done his work well; but if student teachers fail in their efforts, so has the supervisor. The last statement should not be interpreted as an objection to linking the work of the supervisor to the success of the student teacher. However, we need intermediate objectives that are tied to the behavior of the supervisor and are linked empirically to student teacher outcomes.

Iannaccone and Button (1964) make an interesting point that is relevant to this discussion. They assert that the manifest functions of student teaching are not clearly defined and that it may be more useful to look at its latent functions for an explanation of why people continue to see it as important without agreeing about why. Perhaps the latent functions of supervision, particularly supervision by the college supervisor, are more important to the process than its manifest functions are. To this author's knowledge, no analysis of these functions has ever been performed. What would these latent functions be? The following points are purely speculative but do at least suggest some possibilities.

1. University supervisors are an overt symbol of the university's control over what is generally acknowledged to be the most important part of the training process. Without their presence, the schools would be granted what in fact they already have, an almost complete monopoly over this most important part of teacher education.

2. Supervision is an easily justified form of employment for graduate students, who are used as supervisors.

3. "Double" supervision creates the appearance, for certification and public relations purposes, of a carefully supervised student-teaching program.

It should be stressed again that these potential latent functions of the college supervisor role are not documented in the literature. They are offered to stimulate thought and research in this area. Such research appears to be what is needed more than anything else in the whole area of supervisory objectives.

Methods, Strategies, and Techniques

The specific tools employed by supervisors emerge from the process of supervision as it is understood and practiced in teacher education. Although there are many variations in the basic format, the key elements are invariably the same whether the supervising teacher or the college supervisor is involved. These elements are: (1) the visit, and the observation of the student teacher that accompanies it; (2) the conference, and the content, procedures, and participants involved; (3) the transition, a collection of procedures designed to continue the cycle of supervision; and (4) the implications of technology, a new element.

The "visit" takes place in a slightly different context depending upon which supervisor is involved. For the supervising teacher, who is in regular if not daily contact with the student teacher, the visit may represent an agreement that on a particular day or at a particular time, the teacher will be making a formal observation of the student teacher conducting the class. Not every supervising teacher arranges for such visits; some prefer to use the more informal day-to-day contact as a basis for their supervisory discussions.

For the college supervisor, the visit is, of necessity, a more formal event. In the first place, it invariably involves some travel on the part of the supervisor, even if it is only across town, and takes place infrequently enough so that some advance notice of its occurrence is called for. Otherwise, as the rationale goes, the college supervisor could easily drop by on a day when tests were being administered, a field trip was in process, or any one of a number of other things was happening to prevent his observation of the student teacher. In this context, the visit means a trip to the school at the very least, and in many cases it may mean the actual observation of the student teacher in action. Although many of the following observations probably could be applied to the supervisory visit under either circumstance, it is important to recognize that two different contexts exist and to take them into account when it is useful to do so.

Regardless of the supervisor, one purpose of the visit that is generally agreed upon is observation; and the purpose of observation is to be of assistance to the teacher or student teacher. Within the context of school supervision, Goldhammer (1969) feels that the supervisory encounter provides an opportunity for one person (and under the best of circumstances, for each person) to test his own observations and perceptions against those of another. In the case of teacher education, at least, it is a more mature "other." Perhaps this is one explanation of why affect is so important in the relationship. According to findings reported by Edgar (1972), affect apparently provides the basis for changes in attitudes toward autonomy and in behavioral autonomy on the part of beginning teachers. The higher the affect, the more likely a student teacher's scores are to move in the direction of the supervisor's values, regardless of whether that movement is toward autonomy or dependency. When these results are added to those already cited on openness, we see the significance of the visit and the spirit in which observation is conducted.

When Schueler and Gold (1964) compared supervision based upon personal visitation, supervision performed through the use of kinescopes, and a third method combining the first two, they found no significant difference in objective scores. They did find, however, that both student teachers and supervisors were "strongly in favor of the use of the new medium as a tool in teacher education [p. 362]."

Barbour (1968) trained supervising teachers in the use of an observation schedule and conference guide which he developed in order to bring about changes in their orientation toward supervisory behavior. He reported significant pretest and posttest shifts in the direction of greater objectivity.

Another purpose for supervisory visits is demonstration. In the Sandberg study (1963), the supervisors' demonstrations of new materials and methods were seen as effective by beginning teachers. Supervisors appeared somewhat cautious about using demonstrations and felt they might reduce the teachers' potential for using their own capabilities. Although the data do not reveal it, there may have been some rationalization in the supervisors' views.

According to a study of school supervision by Fisher (1959), teachers rejected the idea of the supervisor as an agent of change. They saw the supervisor's job as "an inspirational, thought-provoking role in which the supervisor takes responsibility to stimulate a broad look at the curriculum [p. 504]." With one exception, "the teachers rejected the idea that a supervisor's main job is to make suggestions for changes in teaching [p. 504]." What is not clear from the study is whether the teachers were rejecting a direct style of supervision, a focus on changing teaching behavior, or both. A similar theme is sounded by Cogan (1973), who reports that teachers have "a need to exert powerful controls over the kinds of supervision practiced in the schools, expressing itself sometimes as a demand for self-supervision or for supervision mainly by invitation [p. 16]."

Although lacking complete documentation, these points suggest an excellent psychological explanation for why teachers, as supervisors of student teachers, frequently do not engage in careful observation and feedback designed to bring about changes in teaching behavior. Their distaste for having supervision carried out in this way with their own teaching could lead to their failure to make use of it more extensively with student teachers.

Those who view the purpose of supervision and observation as bringing about changes in teaching are not likely to recommend that the supervisor take sole responsibility for pinpointing the behaviors that need to be changed. A more likely position is taken by Redfern (1963), Hill (1968), and Unruh and Turner (1970). These individuals all view the process as a cooperative one in which heavy responsibility is given to the teacher himself. Still others, including Combs (1965), attest to the importance of having the teacher or student teacher select his own targets for improvement. According to this view, the individual is always motivated from within, for behavior is a function of the person's perceptions. By permitting the teacher or student teacher to select his own targets of change, the supervisor makes use of this self-motivation. The supervisor is more of a resource person within this framework.

Observation Instruments

Instrumentation provides the means for transforming observation from a casual, subjective process into a specifically focused, objective one. The Barbour (1968) study cited earlier demonstrated shifts in supervisory behavior in the direction of objectivity through the use of specialized instruments. Unfortunately, the use of any form of instrumentation is neither commonplace nor evenly distributed throughout the profession. As Cogan (1973) points out, "Systematic observation of classroom interaction has arrived late in the history of education. What little there is of it has been done by researchers rather than supervisors [p. 134]." The norm of practice is still one of casual observation.

Interaction analysis is one of the most frequently used techniques for observing the student teacher's behavior, and Flanders' system is among those most widely employed for this purpose. Flanders (1960) developed a system for classifying verbal interactions between teachers and pupils into ten categories. Seven are related to teacher-initiated talk, and three are related to student-initiated talk. Amidon Kies, and Palisi (1970) summarized the findings from several studies that employed the Flanders system as follows:

After training, teachers were observed as: 1) more encouraging and accepting, 2) less critical, 3) more indirect, 4) more positive in their attitudes toward teaching, 5) more successful (by supervisors' ratings) in student teaching, 6) talking less, 7) giving fewer directions, and 8) permitting more student-initiated talk [p. 220]).

Moskowitz (1970) tried to determine whether training in the use of interaction analysis techniques (using the Flanders system) made a difference in the attitudes of cooperating teachers and student teachers toward one another. Four treatment conditions were employed—(1) both groups received the training, (2) only student teachers received the training, (3) only cooperating teachers received the training, and (4) neither received the training. Scores on attitude questionnaires were not significantly different but did appear to support the following generalizations:

1. Training cooperating teachers in interaction analysis appeared to have a positive effect upon the interpersonal relationship between them and student teachers.

2. Training both groups appeared to produce more positive attitudes.

3. Training only student teachers had a negative effect on their attitudes toward teachers.

In what appeared to be a carefully devised study, Zahn (1965) compared the use of conventional supervisory techniques to the use of interaction analysis and found that student teachers exposed to interaction analysis had more positive teaching attitudes than those exposed to conventional supervision. He also found that the influence of the cooperating teacher upon the attitude of the student teacher appears to be greater when students are supervised using conventional techniques than when they experience supervision through interaction analysis. For those concerned about the perils of socializing student teachers into the status quo of the profession, interaction analysis appears to counter this process.

Studies by Gellman (1968) and Lohman (1966) support Zahn's contention that student teachers trained in interaction analysis have more positive attitudes toward teaching and encourage more student-initiated talk in their own teaching. In one of the few articles that is critical of interaction analysis, Mitchell (1969) examines some of the methodological problems that arise from its use. While his criticisms are directed at the Flanders system, they probably apply to the Amidon-Hunter system as well as others derived from Flanders. Flanders' instrument is not the only one dealing with classroom interaction. Simon and Boyer (1970) describe seventy-six separate observation instruments or systems for analyzing behavior in a wide variety of interactive settings. Their bibliography also lists approximately seven hundred references dealing with such systems. Most of these instruments—the Flanders System of Interaction Analysis (FSIA), the Amidon-Hunter Verbal Interaction Category System, Bales' Interaction Process Analysis, Bellack's System, and Medley's Observation Schedule and Record (OSCAR)—examine verbal behavior in the classroom. A few—the IPI Student Observational Form, the Spaulding Teacher Activity Rating Schedule (STARS), and the Galloway System—focus on nonverbal behavior.

Given the rather comprehensive resource already available in Simon and Boyer's work and the space limitations of this review, it seems fruitless to try to summarize these instruments. It is undoubtedly true that not all of the instruments have been used in supervisory settings; but it is also true that most, if not all, would be appropriate for use in such settings.

Audio- and videotape recorders and monitors have been employed primarily for recording classroom activities and, in a few instances, the supervisory conference. Although these devices have received wide application as research and training tools, they have been used mainly in teaching and microteaching situations, which have not been considered here except as a framework for examining supervisory concepts and practice.

Generally, the use of technical equipment has produced positive results. Acheson (1964) established that its use in supervisory conferences reduced teacher monologue. Lange (1971) reported the use of the videotape model to demonstrate a specific set of behaviors. He found that the use of such a model "produced a significant amount of the same behavior in student teachers who observed it [p. 153]." These results have been supported by Bandura (1965) and Krumboltz (1967). It also appears that the use of videotape equipment is generally well received. Raby (1968) and Schueler and

Gold (1964) observed favorable reactions to the use of kinescope recordings.

The potential for using microteaching techniques to train supervisors is explored by Allen (1968), one of the pioneers in the use of microteaching methods. Among the items he feels can be examined are "testing and looking at alternatives for supervision, varying the time and length of visits, and letting teachers select the time for supervision [p. 237]."

Brigham Young University (Edelfelt, 1969) permitted students to use microteaching on an experimental basis as a partial fulfillment of the student-teaching requirement. During microteaching, students were expected to demonstrate seven teaching skills. A university supervisor analyzed the videotapes to determine whether each student's performance was satisfactory. If not, the student practiced the skills until his performance improved.

Although Allen and Young (1967) discuss the values of using videotape in the context of microteaching, much of what they say is also applicable to standard supervisory situations. They point out that the videotape provides a common frame of reference, that it permits the display of positive teacher behaviors for reinforcement by the supervisor, that it can be stopped to pinpoint problems or points for discussion, that it can be reversed to permit second or third viewings of a particular segment, and that it provides a relatively permanent record of the student's performance for use throughout the student-teaching period.

With all these advantages, with the positive attitudes and the positive results that generally have been reported, one wonders why the impact of technology upon supervision has not been even greater.

The Conference

Perhaps more has been written about the conference in supervision than about any other single element. Taken together with the visit, it represents the heart of the supervisory process. Just as the visit and observation provide the data for analysis, the conference provides the occasion and opportunity for it. Everything else either leads up to or proceeds from the visit and the conference. For an excellent review of the supervisory conference, the reader is directed to Dussault's work (1970) citing 159 references, most of which deal directly with the supervisory conference.

In most instances, the conference is a meeting of two individuals; and in student teaching, the two individuals most frequently involved are the student teacher and the supervising teacher. On a few occasions during the semester, the college supervisor may replace the supervising teacher as the second party in the conference. In school supervision, which has many parallels to supervision in student teaching, the teacher is one party to the conference; and the principal, department head, or some other supervisor is the second person involved. In some contexts, to be discussed in a moment, more than two persons are involved, but this arrangement does not appear to be the norm.

Since practice varies considerably from institution to institution and from supervisor to supervisor, it is all but impossible to specify a median or mean for the number of conferences held during the student-teaching period. The situation is complicated by the fact that one supervisor, the public school teacher, has daily access to the student teacher and can, at least theoretically, conduct a daily conference. In contrast, the college supervisor is not likely to make more than three to five visits during the student-teaching period. Therefore, even if a conference is held during each visit, the total number is likely to be relatively small. The difficulty is further compounded by lack of agreement about what constitutes a conference. How does one equate a ten-minute chat in the teachers' lounge amid several interruptions with a half-hour session using a specific instrument and focus. Both of these extremes are operational definitions for some supervising teachers and college supervisors. In sum, there appears to be a real lack of empirical data on which to base any normative statements about supervisory practice with regard to the conference. For this reason, normative statements are more likely to be made on the basis of general knowledge of supervisory practice derived from experience.

The best rationale for supervisory conferences, without benefit of data or theory, is found in the literature on school supervision. Young (1971) recommends a systems approach to achieve "an *orderly* analytic study of the supervisory process to enable the supervisor to identify a preferred course of action from among possible alternatives. [p. 1].'' He defines the subfunctions of the supervisory conference as follows:

1. Plan teaching strategies.
2. Provide encouragement to teachers.
3. Provide training for the acquisition of specific teaching behavior.
4. Provide for the improvement of a teacher's self concept.
5. Provide teachers objective feedback on performance—to improve the accuracy of perception about their behavior.
6. Develop the teacher's ability to analyze his own performance without the aid of a supervisor.
7. Modify a teacher's behavior.
8. Evaluate a teacher's performance [p. 6].

While Young admits this list is not exhaustive, it does provide a good overview of the important sub-functions. Goldhammer (1969) has divided conferences into at least two categories, the preobservation conference and the supervision conference. He also makes use of a third, the postmortem conference, in those instances where group supervision is used. The first conference prepares the teacher and supervisor for the observation, and the second presents data collected during the observation. Where the third is employed, its purpose is to examine the process of supervision in order to decide how it is working and what modifications need to be made. When the term ''conference'' is used without a modifer, it almost invariably refers to the analytical conference, the one in which the data is examined.

McGeoch and Lindsey (1967) feel the conference should focus on the teaching performance of the student teacher. Reed (1964) believes the purpose of the conference is to help the student teacher evaluate his own teaching style. Wilhelms (1967) and Segar (1968) express concern that a student teacher is likely to become dependent on the supervisor during student teaching. For reasons already discussed, a dependent relationship is more likely to develop between the student teacher and the public school supervisor. Some approaches to supervision and a positive affective relationship between the two may increase the likelihood that this will happen. To counteract this tendency, both Wilhelms and Segar recommend that the supervisor assist the student teacher to become more independent. While this suggestion is easy to make, it is probably much more difficult to carry out in practice, particularly in the context of student teaching, where the student teacher is making use of the supervising teacher's classroom and must remain in his good graces in order to continue to do so with any effectiveness. Success in this attempt probably requires an unusual supervising teacher, an unusual student teacher, or both.

An interesting research study could be carried out using content analysis and similar techniques to determine how closely changes in the conceptions of the supervisor as teacher follow changes in the view of teaching itself and what the typical time lag is between these changes. Similarly, comparative studies could be carried out on the nature of supervision in English and American primary schools. Does the model of supervision in each case proceed from the model of teaching practiced in the schools?

Providing feedback is one of the primary reasons given for the conference. Festinger (1954) has hypothesized a basic human need for feedback on one's behavior. He believes that decisions are a function of perceptions of how one is doing in relation to what one hopes to do. Both objective and subjective data are used for feedback. According to Amidon and his associates (1970), the first step in setting up a successful program of group supervision is deciding on the ground rules for giving feedback. Among the rules established by a faculty group working with the Amidon team were: (1) describe, don't evaluate; (2) provide feedback in areas where change is most likely to occur; (3) give feedback only upon request; (4) base feedback on current material; (5) do not require rebuttal; and (6) focus on specific teaching arts (see p. 222).

In a study comparing three methods of providing feedback, Acheson (1964) found the use of videotape recordings with conferences to be more effective in reducing teacher monologue than either the conference without videotapes or no conference at all.

Ishler (1967) concluded that feedback could be effective in producing more learner-centered verbal behavior on the part of student teachers.

In another study, Kyte (1962) examined the sequence in which feedback was given and the emphasis placed on each item of feedback. He concluded that the conference should include no more than four or five items and that these items should be presented as follows. The first item should be used to establish rapport; the second and third items should be given major stress; the fourth item could be given either major or minor stress depending upon how much it was to be considered in subsequent teaching; and the fifth item should be given passing attention and probably should be related to one of the earlier items. The last item should have a pleasing effect on the teacher regardless of its value for subsequent teaching.

Studies by Bryan (1963) and Tuckman and Oliver (1970) found that teachers receiving feedback from students changed their behavior more than teachers who received no feedback. However, Tuckman and Oliver found that "supervisory feedback added nothing to the student feedback effect when they were combined [p. 428]." In fact, "feedback from supervisors alone produced a significantly greater negative shift (i.e., a change in the opposite direction of that recommended by the feedback) than no feedback at all [p. 432]." Tuckman and Oliver conclude that teachers probably react in this way because they are defensive or hostile toward administrators.

From this author's casual knowledge, there is a wealth of information and research results available on feedback and other aspects of the supervisory conference. Although much of it lies in such fields as counseling, psychotherapy, organizational development, and industrial management, at least one article (Fuller & Manning, 1973) is within teacher education. In their review of the self-confrontation literature, Fuller and Manning sift through a variety of sources and examine such topics as feedback, focus, confrontation processes, and outcomes. Although the review discusses self-confrontation in several settings, much of the material is applicable to supervision. This article and Dussault's review should be examined carefully by those who wish further information on the conference.

THEORIES, MODELS, AND APPROACHES

We have just spent some time examining supervisory practices in teacher education with particular reference to student teaching. Now it is time to examine the ways in which such practices are represented by explanatory systems. As the terms in the title of this section imply, some of these systems are little more than logical structures. Others are more elaborate systems that are tied explicitly to philosophical, psychological, or sociological concepts. Usually these more elaborate systems are considered to be formalized theories or models.

Theories

In education and indeed in many academic circles, the words "model" and "theory" are overworked to the point where they no longer have much meaning. If we look at the extremes, the word "theory" has been employed on the one hand to glorify someone's loosely structured speculations about reality and on the other to represent a highly formalized set of metaphysical statements untraceable to reality through any known empirical methods. Most people recognized as theorists would employ a definition similar to the one given by Werkmeister (1959), who states that a "theory, reduced to its bare essentials, consists of a set of definitions and postulates from which certain theorems and laws descriptive of observed facts can be logically derived [p. 48]." Similar definitions are advanced by Feigl (1951), Brodbeck (1959), and Campbell (1920).

Theories are designed to be tested by empirical data. Brodbeck (1959) points out this fact very clearly in the following statement:

A theory is a deductively connected set of laws. Some of these laws, the axioms or postulates of the theory, logically imply others, the theorems. The axioms are such only by virtue of their place in the theory. Neither self-evident nor otherwise privileged, they are empirical laws whose truth is temporarily, at least, taken for granted in order to see what other empirical assertions, the theorems, are true, if they are. Since empirical laws are inductive generalizations, they are also called hypotheses [p. 378].

According to such a definition, very few theories exist in education and only one exists in the supervision of teacher education. Dussault (1970) has developed what he terms a "middle-range theory of supervision in teacher education programs [p. 154]." He makes explicit use of Rogers' (1959) theory of therapy and personality change as a model from which he has retroduced his own theory. In deriving this theory, he uses comparisons

between the process of therapy and the variables within the supervisory conference, between the outcomes of therapy and the inputs into the supervisory conference, and finally between the conditions of therapy and the variables within the supervisory conference [p. 158].

By his own acknowledgment, Dussault's theory is limited to the teaching function of supervision as carried out within the context of the supervisory conference. This fact is not so much a criticism of Dussault's theory as a statement about its applicability. To my knowledge, the theory has not been tested by the collection of empirical data, although, as Dussault himself points out, some research has been done with some of the variables. While other uses of the word "theory" have undoubtedly occurred in the literature on educational supervision, particularly if one includes school supervision, no other references in the literature on supervision in teacher education fit the more formal definition of theory.

Models

At the speculation end of the theory continuum lie several conceptions of what supervision is and what supervisors do. These conceptions or "models" represent a consistent view of how the supervisor functions with a student teacher or some other person in training. Table 1 compares three of the most common models in teacher education along several dimensions. The reader may wish to spend some time examining the similarities and differences in these models before reaching the fuller description of each which follows. In practice, the teaching model appears to dominate the scene, with perhaps one exception. A fourth model, really a non-

TABLE 1

Three Models of Supervision in Teacher Education

Points of Comparison	Model 1: Teaching	Model 2: Criticism	Model 3: Counseling
View of Teacher	Teacher is a technician	Teacher is a performer	Teacher is a person
View of Supervisor	Supervisor is an expert	Supervisor is a critic	Supervisor is a counselor
Philosophy of Supervisor	I can show you how to improve, or we can deter-mine it together	I can pinpoint what you are doing wrong	I can help you clarify who you are as a person and a teacher
Supervisor/ Supervisee Relationship	Superordinate/ Subordinate	Superordinate/ Subordinate	Colleagueship
Purpose of Supervision	Professional development	Organizational performance	Personal fulfillment
Focus of Supervisory Process	Improvement in technical knowledge and skills	Remediation of weaknesses	Examination of personal feelings and beliefs
Approach to Supervision	Direct, rational	Direct, rational	Indirect, psychological
Tone of Supervision	Positive to neutral	Negative to positive	Positive

model, probably is used more than any other. I have termed it "laissez-faire," and as practiced by many supervisors, it involves "letting things slide" on the assumption that they will take care of themselves. Gauging the extent to which the non-model is employed is a difficult and indirect process. It is difficult because not many supervisors want to admit they use it. It is indirect in that most of the references to it are negative ones. Nevertheless, judging by the frequency of such references, it is a well-tried approach. Dussault's (1970) use of "the teaching function of supervision [p. 37]" fits the first model. Not surprisingly, the literature on school supervision frequently makes use of the supervisor-as-teacher theme. Enns (1968) and Goldstein (1972) both view the supervisor as a teacher and, by implication, the teacher as a student. Cogan (1973) acknowledges that this view is widespread, although he rejects it in favor of his own model, "clinical supervision." Unruh and Turner (1970) see a direct relationship between the program of supervision and the continuing education of teachers. In other words, the supervisor becomes an extension of the college professor and provides a continuous program of inservice education.

In teacher education, a similar view is common. Olsen (1968) and Stratemeyer and Lindsey (1958) see the supervisory conference as a teaching and learning situation, while Smith (1964) and Curtis (1964) view the supervisor as a tutor. In Johnson and Knaupp's (1970) study of student expectations in a microteaching situation, the single most important element, which accounted for 31 percent of the variance, was a "teach me" factor. Moffett (1966) made explicit use of an instructional model in working with student teachers and found that the pupils of student teachers who used this model "better achieved the goals of instruction [p. 2430]."

A major historical theme in the literature of supervision, whether in education or in industry, is the supervisor-as-critic. As McKean and Mills (1964) point out in tracing the development of educational supervision in this country, "Initial attempts at supervision were marked by an emphasis on autocratic inspection. Laymen set standards and through examinations and visitations sought to weed out teachers who were judged to be deficient [pp. 1-2]." This early emphasis on deficiencies, weaknesses, and critical examination continue to be the hallmarks of the supervisor-as-critic model of supervision.

Another term that is used to convey this model is "evaluator." According to Dussault (1970), the function of the supervisory conference most often mentioned in the nonresearch literature is evaluation. Those who use the term evaluation often express quite different views of what it means. To Stradley (1968), "Supervising a student teacher is just like teaching a class [p. 18]." Evaluation is seen in the context of teaching, and its purpose is "to strengthen his [the student teacher's] weaknesses and help eliminate his frustrations [p. 21]." In this sense, its intent is the constructive improvement in the student teacher's performance, a function very consonant with, if not part of, the teaching process.

A second view of evaluation requires the act of critical examination or the rendering of a judgment about the effectiveness, value, or appropriateness of various teaching behaviors. According to Seif (1970):

> Supervisors who use this "criticism" approach to supervision will, when watching a teacher, look for things that the teacher does wrong. A teacher may teach "erroneous" content; he may "not be able to control the class"; his strategy may not get the students "involved." The supervisor looks primarily to the teacher during supervision and looks for things that "go wrong" during the course of a lesson [p. 1].

While it is likely that some teachers and college supervisors rely on criticism, no one seriously advocates it as a systematic model to be employed. Indeed, Curtis (1964) and Smith (1964) advocate that it *not* be employed. No data exists on how extensive the practice of offering criticism is, and there is no operational definition at present to distinguish between the constructive use of evaluation in a teaching model and its more threatening use through a critical approach.

There is some evidence to indicate that student teachers do not feel they get enough critical feedback from their supervisors. Trimmer (1960) reports that student teachers want "to know their deficiencies [p. 538]" and want supervision. Harven (1964) did what she termed "a comprehensive study of the research findings and the thought pertaining to the supervising teacher" and concluded that "most of the criticism of the supervising teacher's work was focused on *the lack of guidance given to student teachers* [italics added] in planning for the learning activities of pupils [p. 2601]." Indeed, one of the single most dominant themes in the literature of supervision is not that supervisors are overly critical but that they are not critical enough. In Edmund and Hemink's study (1958), two of the four most frequently mentioned ways in which student teachers said supervisors helped them were "gave constructive criticism" and "were frank and honest in their criticism [p. 57]." In the same study, when student teachers were given a chance to offer suggestions to their supervisors, three of the four most frequently mentioned were: (1) participate in three-way conferences, (2) be more frank and honest in criticizing the student's performance, and (3) give more time to conferences with student teachers.

Cogan (1973) suggests that a critical focus is only necessary when a single weakness "threatens possible irreparable consequences" or when a pattern of weakness "is so defective as to bar his [the teacher's] students from even minimally adequate learning [p. 202]." In all but these two instances, he concludes that "the weakness strategy is not likely to be very productive [p. 202]."

Although the supervisor-as-critic model may have had some utility during an earlier period in this country when teachers had little or no professional training, one wonders why it has continued to persist in practice despite the widespread criticism it has received in the literature.

Another frequently used supervision model is the supervisor-as-counselor, helper, or therapist. This model is probably in more widespread use in counseling and the other helping fields than it is in teacher education. We can speculate that the most dominant model of supervision in any field is the model most consonant with the primary practice of the field. If this observation is accurate, teaching would be the dominant supervisory model in teacher education as would counseling in counselor education and psychotherapy, criticism in the performing arts, and so on.

The preceding observation notwithstanding, the supervisor-as-counselor is a current model of supervision in teacher education. Perhaps this fact reflects a shifting conception of the role of the teacher to one that is less didactic and more facilitative. Whatever the reason, the model is well established, at least in the literature. Dussault's theory (1970), which we have already discussed in some detail, is established upon a therapeutic model and makes use of such variables as congruence, openness to experience, self-esteem, acceptance of others, and similar concepts. Bridges (1970) believes the supervisor-as-counselor "acts as a helper rather than a judge [p. 190]." Symonds (1955) carries the idea of helper one step further by identifying effective supervision with psychotherapy. Mosher and Purpel (1972) recommend use of the ego-counseling approach which is primarily concerned with the teacher-as-person. All of these variations rely heavily on Rogers' (1958) conception of a helping relationship. According to Fiedler (1950), everyone from experienced psychotherapists to laymen can recognize a good helping relationship. In keeping with a self-as-instrument concept of good teaching, Combs (1965) favors a personal approach to supervision. To carry out such an approach, he calls for the following shift in the basic orientation of supervisors: "Instead of focusing attention on what students do, they [supervisors] must learn to concentrate on how student teachers feel, think, believe about themselves, their students, their purposes, and the subject matter they are charged with teaching [p. 107]."

The view of supervisor-as-helper is one that emphasizes a concern for teachers as people and focuses on their development. Unlike the supervisor-as-evaluator role, the helper avoids making formal value judgments and encourages the teacher to select information and suggestions that will be of personal use.

Although the previous models have received most of the attention in the literature, others are at least mentioned. Bridges (1970) suggests that supervisors may also serve as integrators, designers, and experimenters, while Unruh and Turner (1970) imply that the supervisor's primary role is as an agent of change. These models are mentioned not so much because they are considered viable ones in the context of teacher education as because they help to give the reader a sense of the full range of models being discussed. The fact that they are being discussed in the school supervision literature means they may have some impact on teacher education. In this author's opinion, their impact is likely to be negligible in the near future.

Summary on Models

The literature on school supervision and supervision in teacher education does make reference to a number of models of how supervisors do or should behave in their interactions with teachers and student teachers. The three most frequently mentioned models have already been summarized, and the following conclusions appear to be appropriate:

1. The teaching model represents the most dominant model in the literature and in practice as well. With some exceptions, the views of teaching expounded in such models are fairly traditional.

2. Although it is found in the literature, the counseling model probably is not practiced very extensively in teacher education. Since some aspects of this model fit changing views of the teacher (as facilitator rather than dispenser of knowledge), it may be combined with the teacher model in some instances.

3. While the role of the critic is probably a viable one in some fields (the performing arts, for example), the critical model as a complete model is not advocated in the literature of teacher education. Criticism is practiced as a technique in conjunction with other models (teaching, for example), but there is little agreement about its value. Some authors advocate that it *not* be used, while students seem to want more critical input. However, students often react negatively to supervisors who are too critical. The attitude and manner of the person providing the criticism may be important.

4. Perhaps the most general conclusions that can be made are that no model is employed with any great consistency and that the non-model appears to be employed at least as frequently as any other, including an eclectic one.

Systematic Approaches

This section would not be complete without an examination of some formal approaches to supervision not associated with specific theories or models. One such approach makes use of the term "clinical supervision." The term probably emerged from the field of medicine where "clinic" and "clinical" were given their initial meanings and later from Conant's (1963) concept of the "clinical professor." Both Goldhammer (1969) and Cogan (1973), who have constructed very similar approaches to school supervision under the clinical banner, allude to the term's earlier tradition in the medical field.

While these researchers acknowledge the term's medical heritage, they also feel the need to make it appropriate for educational use. Cogan (1973) cites *Webster's Third International Dictionary* to justify his use of clinical to mean "involving or depending upon direct observation," which he notes as a distinguishing character-istic of clinical supervision. Apparently, the dictionary also supports the use of clinical in the sense of "the presentation, analysis, and the treatment of actual cases." Goldhammer (1969) gives a very similar explication and notes that when we have "close observa-tion, detailed observational data, face to face interaction between the supervisor and teacher, and an intensity of focus that binds the two together in an intimate professional relationship, the meaning of 'clinical' is pretty well filled out [p. 54]."

Similar definitions lead to similar approaches. Goldhammer's approach has five stages and Cogan's has eight, but both cover essentially the same ground—planning for observation, observing, analyzing the data from the observation, planning for the confer-ence, holding the conference, and completing the cycle by initiating another round of planning for observation. Both approaches are logical and systematic. They would fit quite comfortably with the didactic and critical models of supervision.

Yet another similar approach is employed by Seif (1970), although he does not call it clinical supervision. He emphasizes the collection of accurate descriptions in order to identify significant events and their determinants and consequences. Seif also stresses the need to achieve objectivity in the collection and analysis of data.

Team or group supervision is another approach that appears in the literature. The teaching clinic provides an example of this ap-proach in action. Its process stages are almost identical, though the terms differ slightly, to the five stages outlined by Goldhammer. The real difference is in the number of participants and the way they function. As Olsen, Barbour, and Michalak (1971) point out, "the teaming of professional peers to observe, analyze, and refine their teaching skills gives special significance to the teaching clinic [p. 1]." Furthermore, when supervisors are included, "their function is to facilitate the work of the group [p. 1]." Each participating teacher takes his turn at planning a lesson, being observed, and being ana-lyzed while the other teachers in the clinic assist him by serving as observers. The roles of clinic leader, resource person, and coordi-nator are filled by the supervisory group. Procedurally, a great deal of emphasis is placed on nonjudgmental description as the coin of the realm for clinic sessions. The teaching clinic also provides (or is supposed to provide) a supportive climate in which the process of change—its goals, directions, and strategies—is under the control of each individual.

In teacher education, O'Hanlon (1967) and Readling & Blom (1970) all mention the use of team supervision. O'Hanlon views team teaching and team evaluation as two phases of the same process. A teacher and student teacher teach together and evaluate their teaching together. Readling and Blom view team teaching as a humanistic approach to accountability. Lindman and her colleagues found they were able to serve student teachers better when they functioned as a team.

Team supervision in teacher education makes the most sense in the context of teaching centers, which were discussed earlier under patterns of supervision. These centers usually encourage a variety of university personnel (methods instructors, clinical professors, and others) to team with members of a school faculty in order to provide an enriched program of supervision. Several different roles may be defined and carried out by the persons involved. In some of these situations, experimentation is going on in an attempt to implement a form of peer supervision among the undergraduate students. The advocates of this approach argue that student teachers acquire evaluation skills in the process.

EVALUATION

The intent of this section is to examine the extent to which systematic evaluation procedures are employed to provide data on supervisory practice. Since evaluation is a commonly used term in educational circles and since it often has a different meaning from the one intended here (particularly in supervision), an initial discussion of its meanings may be useful. Evaluation in supervision frequently means the procedures used by supervisors to describe or judge the performance of the person being supervised. In school supervision, the supervisee is most frequently the teacher and the supervisor is a principal, department head, or subject matter specialist. In teacher education, the supervisee is the student teacher, intern, or some other person in training; and the supervisor is the cooperating teacher or the college supervisor. References to evaluation in these contexts are common in the literature of school supervision and supervision in teacher education, but such procedures are not the focus of this section. They are treated under the practice of supervision through such topics as the conference, feedback, and observation devices. This section is concerned solely and exclusively with the extent to which evaluation procedures are used to examine the effectiveness of a given *program* of supervision.

As it is used here, evaluation has several closely associated meanings. First, it refers to a set of procedures by which programs or practices are examined to determine their effectiveness in achieving stated goals. Thus if one of the goals of a particular program of supervision is to produce self-renewing teachers, evaluation provides the procedures for measuring its accomplishment, using whatever operational definition of self-renewal seems appropriate for the task. By extension, this definition of evaluation is also concerned with differentiating the influence of key program elements on the results. For example, it tries to isolate the effects of supervisory type (teacher versus college supervisor) from those of method in the determination of a specific outcome.

Another goal of evaluation is to isolate the influence of key program or activity variables, such as those just mentioned, from variables that are external to the program—for example, the school environment, student teacher characteristics, and selection factors. Some writers include a judgment of worth in evaluation activity. Scriven (1967) and Glass (1971) agree that it is not enough for an evaluator to determine that a particular program has achieved its goals; he must also arrive at some judgment of how worthwhile those goals are.

Since this review has already examined a number of research studies from the supervision literature, it may be useful to distinguish between research and evaluation. This task is not easy for two reasons. First, research and evaluation make use of similar methodological techniques to accomplish their aims. Among the areas that overlap are: the identification or development of instruments and techniques for data collection, the administration of these instruments in particular settings, the application of statistical methodology for the interpretation of the data, and the reporting of results in appropriate forms. Second, both are well grounded in the values of scientific inquiry with its regard for systematic, objective, and conclusive evidence.

But there are differences as well. One of the most important distinctions between research and evaluation has to do with the extent to which the activity is focused on decision making. The researcher is not particularly interested in decision making. He has identified some hypotheses to test, and he collects his data accordingly. If the data can be used by decision makers, that is fine; but he does not conceptualize his study with such use in mind. The evaluator, on the other hand, must be concerned with providing useful data to decision makers, for that is the purpose of his being involved. His designs must be practical. They must employ the most effective and efficient techniques for collecting data for a given investment of resources, a concern shared by the researcher. They must also be capable of providing guidance for the short-term modification of practice, a feature which is uniquely the concern of the evaluator and the decision makers with whom he works.

A research project is concerned with building on refining knowledge in some generalizable sense. The researcher wants to be able to understand the variables in a situation well enough to predict their influence in similar situations at different times and in different places. In order to do so, he structures the situation in ways that enable him to control the interaction of the variables through the use of such techniques as random sampling, random assignment to treatments, and the use of control groups. Because of this orientation, the researcher is often criticized for not intervening in the situation with techniques and activities he feels will bring about desirable results. His need to produce generalizable results prohibits him from intervening prematurely, particularly with the so-called control group.

By contrast, evaluators usually work with larger units of activity and within the constraints of intact groups, existing structures, and typical operating procedures. They are not able to change the situation to fit their needs; they must adapt their techniques to fit the demands of the situation. Moreover, their techniques are governed to a great extent by objectives that have been established by other persons. Under the best of circumstances, evaluators may participate in the identification and clarification of goals; but even then, they are one group among many. More often than not, they are brought in after goals have been established and are asked to adapt their techniques to goals and programmatic activities as they exist.

In some cases, of course, the programs are new or recently revised, but innovation is not required to make productive use of an evaluator's skills. What is required is an ongoing set of activities that represent a coherent program; that is, a set of objectives, however vaguely established, and a set of structures, procedures, and personnel with particular responsibilities for achieving those objectives. Thus while researchers *may* work within the context of an organizational framework, evaluators invariably do. Moreover, evaluators tend to focus on the entire set of activities that are represented by the program whereas researchers select some important variables over which they can exert more control.

It is important to remember that these differences do not describe completely independent processes and functionaries. As processes, research and evaluation have much in common; and the background and training of researchers and evaluators are often quite similar. The differences are more a matter of emphasis and orientation arising out of the contexts in which these individuals function rather than any inherent differences in the techniques or the persons involved.

The similarities and differences do provide a useful starting point for a discussion of the supervision literature. For one thing, they lead to the tentative observation that, as an activity, research is much more prevalent than evaluation. The observation is tentative because it is not grounded in empirical studies. Rather, it is based upon impressionistic data and as such is open to subjective judgment and distortion. Nevertheless, the statement can be tested somewhat by an examination of that portion of the supervision literature that is data oriented, for this literature can be classified as research or evaluation.

Several major types of research are represented in this literature. Three of the more commonly accepted types are survey research, correlational and factor analytic studies, and experimental studies. Each of these will be described briefly, and illustrations will be provided from the literature to document their presence.

Surveys

Surveys are descriptive studies of the status of a particular supervisory practice. Yoder's study (1971) of alternatives in secondary student teaching, Prince's study (1961) of the Georgia program for training supervising teachers, and Snyder's study (1961) of effective techniques in the supervision of student teachers in music are examples of surveys.

Correlational and Factor Analytic Studies

These studies are static in the sense that no treatment is applied. Data is collected and analyzed for correlational trends or to identify underlying factors. Predictive studies are also included in this group. Kracht's study (1967) of the relationship between student teachers' attitudes and anxiety scores and the supervising teacher's evaluation of their performance is an example in this category. Other illustrations of factor analytic techniques are Johnson's study (1954) of the ability of supervisors to predict their subordinates' responses and Johnson and Knaupp's study (1970) of trainee role expectations.

Experimental Studies

These research studies require the manipulation of treatment or independent variables in order to examine effects upon dependent variables. They invariably employ the random assignment of individuals to experimental and control groups. Ishler's study (1967) of the effectiveness of feedback in changing the student teacher's verbal behavior fits this category. In a similar study, Hinckley (1969) trained supervising teachers in interview techniques by using videotaped feedback and modeling techniques. Finally, Acheson's study (1964) of the effects of feedback from television recordings and three types of supervisory treatment on selected teacher behaviors fits into the experimental category.

Other widely acknowledged forms of research—instrument development and validation, case studies, analytical studies involving content analysis, historical studies, and literature reviews—were also identified in this review; but enough references have been cited to make the point that there is a body of research literature in supervision. Incidentally, I have said nothing so far about the quality of the research literature; and while much of it leaves something to be desired, it is present in sufficient quantity to be noteworthy.

Now we face the question of whether the same point can be made about evaluation. Before deciding the answer, perhaps it would be useful to review what is meant by the term. For our purposes, evaluation activity has the following characteristics:

1. It is designed and implemented to assess programmatic activity within an institutional context.

2. It is carried on to provide for informed decision making, and in this sense, it has an immediate utility which research may or may not have.

3. It is focused on both process and product dimension of the programmatic activity.

4. It is systematic and objective in its collection and analysis of data.

In teacher education, supervision is carried on within an institutional setting (indeed, within two institutional settings), and it therefore qualifies as a legitimate target of evaluation activity. However, the extent to which it is programmatic and evolving, that is, requires decisions, is somewhat open to question. Undoubtedly some program development is still taking place, but the field does not give the impression of "being alive with bold new ventures." Perhaps, at this point, it would be wise to describe an illustration so that the reader has a bench mark for other references to evaluation.

The Indiana TTT Project (Smith et al., 1974) established a broadly based program of supervision for student teachers enrolled in its Professional-Year Program. Methods instructors from the university and graduate interns working with them offered methods and supervised student teachers through an integrated program. Public school teachers participated in methods and an orientation seminar in order to become more aware of what was expected of their student teachers. A supervisory training program was offered to teachers to upgrade their supervisory skills. Methods classes and almost all of the other activities of the program were carried out in the public schools, and this arrangement permitted a higher degree of communication among the parties involved. Videotape equipment was purchased and place in each school. Taken in combination, these elements constituted the *program of supervision*. Several specific objectives were identified, and evaluation data were collected from all of the parties involved. Data analysis and feedback were used to revise the program. No claim is made here for quality, either of the supervision program or of the evaluation program, but the program clearly does belong in this category.

There are other examples such as the preceding one in the literature, but there are not many. P. Johnson (1968) describes a teaching center at Wayne State University in these terms and reports data which presumably were used in the revision of the program. Lindsey (1968) indicates the need to base decisions in teacher education on empirical data, although her orientation appears to be more like that of a researcher, as I have defined it, than an evaluator.

From the dearth of reports on evaluation in the supervision literature, one can only conclude that it is not a very prevalent activity. Unfortunately, it is difficult to make a case from the absence of evidence. Perhaps I have not been very good at finding it. A quick review of the steps taken will at least indicate the effort made.

1. Of the initial set of 101 references provided to this author by the editors, none contained more than a passing reference to evaluation as it is defined here. It should be noted that the breakdown into research and evaluation categories was made by this author toward the end of the review period. Thus it is unlikely there was any predisposition to select research references.

2. Another set of references, obtained by the author through standard library search procedures, yielded only a minimal number of references to evaluation. The library procedures were not designed specifically to locate references on evaluation but presumably would have uncovered them if they existed in great numbers.

3. Focused search procedures were used to identify specific references to evaluation activity associated with supervisory programs in teacher education.

Taken together, these efforts did yield material in which evaluation was mentioned, but the discussion invariably centered around the evaluation of student teachers, the evaluation of teachers (in school supervision), or the procedures used by teachers (and student teachers) to evaluate pupils. There is remarkably little in the way of plans or efforts to evaluate supervision programs.

If these observations are at all accurate, they raise a question which deserves our attention. Why is it that research appears in the literature but evaluation does not? After all, they both use similar techniques and have evolved from a similar set of scientific values. Since no empirical data exists to answer this question, I shall have to deal with it in a more speculative way and hope that some of my speculations offer leads for future research.

First of all, research can be and is carried out in any context. The world as it exists is sufficient for the researcher, regardless of whether he is interested primarily in individuals or institutions. The evaluator's world is circumscribed by some form of programmatic activity, whether it be a program in compensatory education, early childhood education, teacher education, or a Title III project. Unfortunately, for the evaluator, coherent programs do not appear to exist in supervision. Where they do exist, they have been institutionalized; and evaluation is not likely to be seen as necessary to decision making in institutionalized settings.

The newer supervisory programs generally have not received a great deal of support from funding agencies and hence are not likely to include an evaluation component. Evaluation often does not receive high priority attention from either schools or universities unless it is funded by an outside source. Smith and Coppedge's (1974) study of evaluation in alternative public schools bears this fact out, at least in that context.

Then, too, supervision is likely to be viewed as one component of a teacher education program and, as such, to receive relatively little emphasis in contrast with other components. It may be that an extensive review of teacher education programs would yield a greater incidence of evaluation activities focused on supervision.

Finally, it may be noted that program evaluation has not been considered a very important activity by persons in the field of supervision. We can account for this fact, in part, by the types of personnel involved. Since public school teachers do not see teacher education as their primary task, they can hardly be expected to call for such evaluation. The college supervisors are in many cases a very transient group of graduate students with their own needs and problems. By the time they recognize the need for evaluation, they are ready to move on. Some college and university faculty members are involved, of course, but few are engaged in supervision as their sole responsibility. Furthermore, the pattern of student teacher placement and supervision militates against their thinking in programmatic terms. The only group remaining is largely administrative personnel who coordinate the program of supervision for the university, and administrators have a vested interest in excluding evaluation personnel. For a discussion of points of conflict between administrators and evaluators, Caro's article (1971, pp. 96-104) is very useful.

One reason that is *not* a valid explanation for the paucity of evaluation reports in the supervision literature is the lack of suitable evaluation models. Such models have gained considerable attention in the last ten years in education generally and in teacher education as well. One need only examine the work of Worthern (1968), Stufflebeam (1969), Stake (1967), and Scriven (1967) to be convinced of this fact. However, these precedents have not made an impact on supervision for reasons that have already been discussed.

In summary, evaluation as an activity has been given even a modest degree of attention only in the last ten years. During this time educational and social programs have been on the increase, and funding agencies, particularly governmental agencies, have begun to require evaluation activities in their grants and contracts. As a result, it is not surprising that a highly institutionalized program such as student teaching and supervision has not received the widespread attention of evaluators. Since most of the factors just discussed would have little impact on research activity, it also is not unusual that reports of research would appear frequently in the literature while reports of evaluation would not.

SUMMARY AND CONCLUSIONS

We have examined the literature of teacher education, school supervision, and occasionally other fields to determine the status of supervisory thought and practice in teacher education. This endeavor included a review of research studies, doctoral dissertations, other reviews, opinion articles, textbooks, and more transient materials. It emphasized the literature published during the last ten years. The conclusions which follow roughly approximate the sequential arrangement of material, making it relatively easy for the reader to turn to the earlier discussion for clarification or elaboration.

Two types of relationships provide the anchoring points for supervisory practice in teacher education. The most influential of the two is that between the public school teacher and the student teacher. This relationship appears so well established in the thought and practice of supervision that it has been elevated to the status of a cardinal myth. The mythology is reinforced by empirical research showing that the influence of the supervising teacher is much greater than that of the college supervisor. This finding is hardly surprising, however, when one looks at the physical and psychological factors associated with the two relationships.

The one-on-one relationship has been associated with the dispersed pattern of student placement and supervision since the early 1900s. Although normative data is not available, the dispersed pattern appears to be the mode at the present time. Because the dispersed pattern has met with increasing criticism, a new pattern has been widely adopted in the last ten years. Its rationale is to concentrate large numbers of student teachers in centers that are jointly established by schools and universities in order to provide better services through a more coordinated approach. Even in these centers, the one-on-one relationship continues to be the norm, although a few are experimenting with other approaches. Other patterns are not that prevalent in practice. Apparently few institutions use more than one pattern of placement, and students are afforded little choice in what is widely recognized as a critical period in their training.

The social and psychological implications of the two supervisory relationships have not been sufficiently examined. Studies of the relationship between the public school teacher and the student teacher reveal several factors, some potentially negative, that are worthy of further research. Among them are: (1) the type and extent of influence exerted by the supervisory teacher, (2) openness as an attribute of one or both parties, (3) movement toward autonomy or dependency, (4) the importance of affect, (5) the use or threat of power, and (6) levels of anxiety. Most studies have examined the impact of the teacher upon the student teacher, but possibilities exist in the other direction as well. The relationship with the college supervisor has not been as fully explored, but studies have shown that he is less influential.

There are two distinct points of view in the literature on role expectations. The more serious research studies point to a "teach me" expectation on the part of student teachers. Most of the opinion articles and the more superficial studies identify what might be described as "common courtesy" or "common sense" expectations. For example, student teachers expected teachers to discuss their philosophy of education, to make records of pupils available, and to introduce them gradually to teaching (McConnell, 1960). There is also a heavy component of good human relations in these expectations. At least one study (Kaplan, 1967) revealed a lack of agreement in the expectations of the three parties and a lack of communication that appears to compound the problem.

The value of criticism is particularly cloudy. Many students say they want more criticism than they are getting, while teacher educators (and authors) are cautious about or opposed to its use. Perhaps the laissez-faire model of supervision which appears to be in widespread use has something to do with these differences in response.

Student teachers differentiate very little in their expectations of the two supervisors. Instead of considering differences in roles, responsibilities, physical proximity, and other factors, the student teacher perceives the role of each in relation to his own needs. Unless there is a drastic restructuring of the college supervisor's assignment, there is every likelihood of high dissonance between the expectations of the student teacher and the behavior of the college supervisor. While the student feels the need for observation, feedback, and unconditional regard, the college supervisor is not in frequent or intimate enough contact to provide for these needs. The results on supervisory style are somewhat in conflict with those on expectations. High indirect styles (in Flanders' terms) are generally regarded as more effective, but high direct styles fit into the students' expectations for criticism.

The selection and training of supervisors are two of the most neglected areas in the supervision literature. Where success criteria have been identified, they are more in the nature of common sense items than professional ones. Training requirements are largely formal, minimal, and not rigidly enforced.

There are many discussions of goals and objectives in the supervision literature; but almost without exception, the statements are expressed in terms of the actions and responsibilities of student teachers, apparently on the assumption that this emphasis makes the supervisor more accountable. In this author's view, the failure to tie the work of supervisors to a set of specific objectives which are logically and empirically related to student teacher (and teacher) performance is an oversight of considerable magnitude that in itself weakens the case for accountability.

Teachers and supervisors approve of using observation for analysis of instructional problems. Supervisors (but not teachers) approve of using it for inspection purposes. Teachers also reject the idea that a supervisor is an agent of change. The way teachers supervise student teachers may be a function of the way they are supervised. Since they find criticism and inspection so distasteful, they are not likely to use it with student teachers. Indeed, the laissez-faire model frequently employed by teachers may be a reaction against the kind of supervision practiced with them. While no direct evidence exists on this point, the indirect evidence tends to confirm this observation.

Although a wide variety of instruments have been developed for examining verbal and nonverbal interaction in classroom settings, few are used routinely by large numbers of supervising teachers. Frequent and extensive usage appears to be in the context of special projects or programs that are usually supported by outside funds. The Flanders System of Interaction Analysis and several modifications of it have undoubtedly seen the greatest use. These, like many other instruments, require specialized training in their proper use. The evidence suggests that greater use of instruments should be encouraged since much of the research, particularly on the Flanders and related systems, has yielded positive results.

While the conference is considered by many to be at the heart of the supervisory process, not many normative data exist on the number, type, or utility of such conferences in relation to the different supervisors involved. While the conference has usually been a two-way or three-way affair, experiments have dealt with making it a team or group experience. Most of this experimentation, however, is taking place in school supervision rather than teacher education. Also, the peer model used in teaching clinics needs further exploration in student-teaching settings.

One tool of the conference about which much has been written is the giving of feedback. Although it apparently has been effective with both teachers and student teachers, at least one study (Tuckman & Oliver, 1970) concluded that supervisory feedback added nothing to pupil feedback when the two were combined for analysis. Although Fuller and Manning (1973) and Dussault (1970) identify some of the teacher education literature on feedback, more research on its effectiveness probably has been carried out in group, counseling, and therapy settings than in the context of the supervisory conference. Frankly, this review has only touched the surface of the feedback literature.

It appears that the use of videotape equipment and other technological devices has generally produced positive results. Its more ardent proponents feel it holds considerable promise for examining and perhaps revolutionizing supervisory practice. Although it is widely used on an experimental basis, its routine and regularized use leaves something to be desired. Where it is in use, it is more likely to be employed in the development of teaching skills through microteaching than in the development of supervisory skills.

Formal theories that provide guidance for research and practice in supervision are all but missing from the literature. Dussault's theory (1970) is the one exception, and it has not been given empirical tests.

There are several models of supervision, if one employs the term loosely, but the full implications of each have never been explored. The supervisor-as-teacher model is one of the most widely accepted by both student teachers and their supervisors. The supervisor-as-critic model is not seriously advocated by anyone, but it does appear to be in widespread practice. The findings on this model are conflicting, for students say they want more criticism than they get, but they also respond positively to an indirect style of supervision (in Flanders' terms). Teachers seem to be stronger in their rejection of critical appraisal. Some of the discrepancy between teacher and student teacher responses may be attributed to differences in the role incumbents in each situation. The "professional" teacher, for example, may not feel the principal has much to offer in the way of useful criticism; but the neophyte student teacher may desire all the help he can get. Some writers distinguish between constructive and destructive criticism, although few use the latter term. Much of this distinction appears to be rhetorical since no operational definitions exist. The supervisor-as-counselor (or facilitator) model is advocated in the literature but does not seem to be employed much in actual practice. Finally, the laissez-faire model may be the most widely practiced and least recommended of all.

Except for the laissez-faire model, the most dominant model in any field is apt to be the model that most conforms to the practice of that field. Thus a teaching model would be the dominant one in teacher education and a counseling model in counseling education. As views of teaching have shifted, a similar shift has taken place in views about supervision. Although the model is still rare, the supervisor is much more likely to be seen as a facilitator today than he was fifty years ago.

Whichever one of the several standard means we give to evaluation, it does not seem to be used a great deal in the supervision of student teachers. This observation is particularly meaningful when one attempts to distinguish between research and evaluation. On a comparative basis, there is much more research activity in progress. While the reasons for this fact are not obvious, the following hypotheses are offered. First, evaluation is a relative newcomer to education in general and to teacher education in particular. It has received widespread attention only in the last ten or fifteen years as private and federal funds for programmatic activity have been accompanied by an increasing insistence on accountability. Furthermore, coherent programs do not tend to exist in supervisory practice; and where they do exist, they have been institutionalized. Evaluation is seen as less necessary in such settings. Other factors may be operative as well. Whatever the reasons, a dearth of evaluation plans and results exists in the supervision literature.

Perhaps the best way to conclude this article is to remind the reader of something he already knows: the supervision of student teachers exists in a no-man's-land of responsibility. It is chiefly the responsibility of school teachers, who do not see it as their primary responsibility, and of university supervisors, who have neither the time, the proximity, nor the authority to fulfill the students' expectations of them. If any single conclusion can be drawn from the literature, it is that individual and institutional responsibilities require considerably more in the way of research, thought, and experimentation than they have yet been given.

REFERENCES

Acheson, K. A. The effects of feedback from television recordings and three types of supervisory treatment on selected teacher behaviors. Unpublished doctoral dissertation, Stanford University, 1964.

Allen, D. W. Micro-teaching: A new framework for inservice education. In E. B. Smith, H. C. Olsen, P. J. Johnson, & C. Barbour (Eds.), *Partnership in teacher education.* Washington, D.C.: Association of Colleges for Teacher Education and Association for Student Teaching, 1968.

Allen, D. W., & Young, D. B. Videotape techniques at Stanford University: Television and related media in teacher education. Mimeographed, August 1967.

Amidon, E. J., Kies, K. M., & Palisi, A. T. Group supervision. A technique for improving teaching behavior. In J. E. Heald, L. G. Romano, & N. P. Georgiady (Eds.), *Selected readings on general supervision.* London: Macmillan, 1970.

Anderson, C. C., & Hunda, S. M. Teacher evaluation: Some problems and a proposal. *Harvard Educational Review,* 1963, **33,** 74-95.

Anderson, G. W. *A handbook for student teaching.* Bloomington, Ind.: School of Education, Indiana University, 1973.

Bakalis, M. J. *Action goals for the seventies: An agenda for Illinois education.* Office of the Superintendent of Public Instruction, 1972.

Bandura, A. Influence of models and reinforcement contingencies on the acquisition of imitative responses. *Journal of Personality and Social Psychology,* 1965, **1,** 589-595.

Barbour, C. A study of the change in objectivity of supervising teachers' perceptions about supervising behavior through the use of an observation schedule and conference guide. Unpublished doctoral dissertaiton, Wayne State University, 1968.

Barbour, C. Cognitive aspects in the supervisory conference: An overview. Paper presented at the Association of Teacher Educators' Clinic on Supervision, March 1971.

Barnes, M. W. Building school-university relations in teacher education. In S. Elam (Ed.), *Improving teacher education in the United States.* Bloomington, Ind.: Phi Delta Kappa, 1967.

Berman, L. M., & Usery, M. L. *Personalized supervision.* Washington, D.C.: Association for Supervision and Curriculum Development, 1960.

Blumberg, A. *Supervisors and teachers: A private cold war.* Berkeley, Calif.: McCutchan, 1974.

Blumberg, A. Supervisory behavior and interpersonal relations. Mimeographed, n.d.

Bridges, E. M. Instructional leadership: A concept re-examined. In J. E. Heald, L. G. Romano, & P. Nicholas (Eds.), *Selected readings on general supervision.* New York: Macmillan, 1970.

Brodbeck, M. Models, meaning and theory. In L. Gross (Ed.), *Symposium on sociological theory.* Evanston, Ill.: Row, Peterson, 1959.

Bryan, R. C. *Reactions to teachers by students, parents and administrators.* (U.S. Office of Education, Cooperative Research Project No. 668) Kalamazoo, Mich.: Western Michigan University, 1963.

Buttery, T. J. An exploratory study of verbal behavior patterns of the teaching clinic process in preservice field experiences. Unpublished doctoral dissertation, Indiana University, 1972.

Campbell, N. R. *Physics, the elements.* Cambridge: At the University Press, 1920.

Caro, F. G. Issues in the evaluation of social programs. *Review of Educational Research,* 1971, **41**, 87-114.

Chandler, B. Objectivity of the supervising teachers' perceptions about supervisory behavior through the use of an observation schedule and conference guide. Unpublished doctoral dissertation, Wayne State University, 1968.

Chorny, M., & Storey, A. G. A team approach to student teaching. *Canadian Education and Research Digest,* **5**, 60-65.

Cogan, M. L. *Clinical supervision.* Boston: Houghton-Mifflin, 1973.

Cole, T. J. An experience in teacher training. *Peabody Journal of Teacher Education, 1963,* **41**, 145.

Combs, A. W. *The professional education of teachers.* Boston: Allyn & & Bacon, 1965.

Conant, J. B. *The education of American teachers.* New York: McGraw-Hill, 1963.

Cross, J., & Nagle, J. Supervisory strategies for helping teachers improve students' thinking skills. *Peabody Journal of Education,* 1970, **47,** 208-215.

Curtis, E. L. The college supervisor in a liberal arts college. In R. Pfeiffer (Ed.), *The college supervisor: Conflict and challenge,* Cedar Falls, Iowa: Association for Student Teaching, 1964 (43rd yearbook).

Davis, O. L., & Gregory, T. B. Laboratory components in teacher education. *Peabody Journal of Education,* 1970, **47,** 202-207.

Delaney, D. J., & Moore, J. C. Students' expectations of the role of practicum supervisor. *Counselor Education and Supervision,* 1966, **6,** 11-17.

Dellman, R. A. A follow-up study on the use of interaction analysis in the training of prospective teachers. Unpublished doctoral dissertation, Temple University, 1968.

Dull, L. W. Criteria for evaluating the supervision program in school systems. Unpublished doctoral dissertation, Ohio State University, 1960.

Duncan, J. K., & Hough, J. B. Technical review of the teaching situation reaction test. Mimeographed, 1966.

Dussault, G. *A theory of supervision in teacher education.* New York: Teachers College Press, Columbia University, 1970.

Edelfelt, F. A. (Ed.) *Innovative programs in student teaching.* Baltimore: Maryland State Department of Education, 1969.

Edgar, D. E. Affective relationships in teacher supervision. *Journal of Teacher Education,* 1972, **23,** 169-171.

Edgar, D. E. Warren, R. L., & Brod, R. *Studies in teacher socialization.* Stanford, Calif.: Stanford Center for Research and Development in Teaching, 1970.

Edmund, N. R. & Hemink, L. Ways in which supervisors help student teachers. *Educational Research Bulletin,* 1958, **37,** 57-66.

Educational Research Council of America. *Teacher education in Ohio.* Cleveland: 1970.

Elliott, R. J. Changes in openness of student teachers and cooperating teachers. Unpublished doctoral dissertation, University of Alabama, 1970.

Emmerling, F. C. A study of the relationships between personality characteristics of classroom teachers and pupil perceptions of these teachers. Unpublished doctoral dissertation, University of Alabama, 1963.

Enns, F. Supervision of instruction: A conceptual framework. *Canadian Education and Research Digest,* 1968, **8,** 283-297.

Feigl, H. Principles and problems of theory construction in psychology. In W. Dennis (Ed.), *Current trends in psychological theory.* Pittsburgh: University of Pittsburgh Press, 1951.

Festinger, L. A theory of social comparison processes. *Human Relations,* 1954, **2,** 117-140.

Fiedler, F. E. The concept of an ideal therapeutic relationship. *Journal of Consulting Psychology,* 1950, **14,** 239-245.

Fisher, H. Expectations for leadership. *Educational Leadership,* 1959, **16,** 504.

Flanagan, J. C. The critical incident technique. *Psychological Bulletin,* 1954, **51,** 327-358.

Flanders, N. A. *Teacher influence on pupil attitudes and achievement.* (Final Report, U.S. Office of Education, Cooperative Research Project, No. 397) Minneapolis: University of Minnesota, 1960.

Flanders, N. *Helping teachers change their behavior.* Ann Arbor, Mich.: University of Michigan Press, 1963.

Freeze, C. R. On becoming an open supervisor. *High School Journal,* 1970, **53,** 354-362.

Fuller, F. F., & Manning, B. A. Self-confrontation reviewed: A conceptualization for video playback in teacher education. *Review of Education Research,* 1973, **43,** 469-528.

Garland, C. B. *An exploration of role expectations for student teachers: Views of prospective student teachers, cooperating teachers, and college supervisors.* Rochester, N.Y.: University of Rochester, 1964.

Garner, A. E. The cooperating teacher and human relations. *Education,* 1971, **92,** 99-106.

Gellman, R. A. A follow-up study on the use of interaction analysis in the training of prospective teachers. Unpublished doctoral dissertation, Temple University, 1968.

Glass, G. The growth of evaluation methodology. *AERA Curriculum Monograph Series.* Chicago: Rand McNally, 1971, No. 7.

Goldhammer, R. *Clinical supervision.* New York: Holt, Rinehart, & Winston, 1969.

Goldstein, W. An enlightened approach to supervising teachers. *The Clearing House,* 1972, **47,** 391-394.

Granite, H. Supervising supervisors in an urban school. *Educational Leadership,* 1969, **26,** 382-385.

Gwynn, M. J. *Theory and practice of supervision.* Chapel Hill, N.C.: University of North Carolina Press, 1961.

Haines, A. C. *Concern for the individual in student teaching.* Cedar Falls, Iowa: Association for Student Teaching, 1963. (42nd yearbook).

Hansen, C. W. Principles and criteria for the selection of critic teachers. *Education Administration and Supervision,* 1957, **34,** 403-407.

Harmer, E. W. *Instructional strategies for student teachers.* Belmont, Calif.: Wadsworth Publishing Co., 1969.

Harris, B. M. *Supervisory behavior in education.* Englewood Cliffs, N.J.: Prentice-Hall, 1963.

Harris, B., & Hartgraves, W. R. Supervision effectiveness: A research résumé. *Educational Leadership,* 1972, **30,** 73-75.

Hart, M. A. An investigation of the relationship between the study of Flanders' interaction analysis and changes in the openness of elementary teacher education students. Unpublished doctoral dissertation, University of Rochester, 1964.

Harven, J. D. The supervising teacher: A synthesis of research findings and thought in two volumes. Unpublished doctoral dissertation, Indiana University, 1964.

Hayes, A. P. Effects of college and public school supervisors on student teachers' beliefs, dogmatism and satisfaction with student teaching. Paper presented at the meeting of the American Educational Research Association, Los Angeles, Calif., 1969.

Heald, J. E., Romano, L. G., & Nicholas, P. (Eds.) *Selected readings on general supervision.* New York: Macmillan, 1970.

Henry, J. Culture against man. In J. H. Sanberg (Ed.), *Introduction to the behavioral sciences.* New York: Holt, Rinehart, & Winston, 1969.

Hill, W. H. DBP supervision: A technique for changing teacher behavior. *The Clearing House,* 1968, **43,** 180-183.

Hinckley, W. L. Training of supervising teachers in interview techniques by use of videotaped feedback and modeling procedures. Unpublished doctoral dissertation, Stanford University, 1969.

Hollister, G. E. The group conference of the supervising teacher. *Journal of Educational Research,* 1950, **44,** 54-56.

Iannaccone, L., & Button, W. H. *Function of student teaching and attitude formation and imitation in elementary student teaching.* (Research Report to Office of Education) St. Louis: Washington University, 1964.

Ishler, R. E. An experimental study using Withall's social-emotional climate index to determine the effectiveness of feedback as a means of changing student teachers' verbal behavior. *Journal of Educational Research,* 1967, **61,** 121-123.

Jensen, L. C., & Young, J. I. Effect of televised simulated instruction on subsequent teaching. *Journal of Educational Psychology,* 1972, **63,** 368-373.

Jessee, B. E., & Mocker, D. W. Interpersonal relationships. *School and Community,* 1970, **56,** 33.

Johnson, J. Survey of teacher education practice. Unpublished doctoral dissertation, Northern Illinois University, 1968.

Johnson, P. An assessment of the administrative organization of a cooperative venture. In E. B. Smith, H. C. Olsen, P. J. Johnson, and C. Barbour (Eds.), *Partnership in teacher education.* Washington, D.C.: Association of Colleges for Teacher Education and Association for Student Teaching, 1968.

Johnson, R. J. An investigation of the ability of supervisors to predict responses of their subordinates. Unpublished doctoral dissertation, Purdue University, 1954.

Johnson, W. D., & Knaupp, J. E. Trainee role expectations of the microteaching supervisor. *Journal of Teacher Education,* 1970, **21**, 396-401.

Kaplan, L. An investigation of the role expectation for college supervisors of student teaching as viewed by student teachers, supervising teachers and college supervisors. Unpublished doctoral dissertation, University of Rochester, 1967.

Kline, M. S. *How to do your best as a student teacher.* (Rev. ed.) Trenton, N.J.: Trenton State College, 1972.

Knop, C. Alternatives in student teacher supervision and evaluation. *French Review,* 1972, **46**, 354-359.

Koran, J. J., Koran, M. L., & McDonald, F. Effects of different sources of positive and negative information on observational learning of a teaching skill. *Journal of Educational Psychology,* 1972, **63**, 405-410.

Kracht, C. R. The relationship of scores on the Minnesota teacher attitude inventory and the IPAT anxiety scale questionnaire to evaluation of student teachers' classroom performance. Unpublished doctoral dissertation, Southern Illinois University, 1967.

Krumboltz, J. D., Varenhorst, B. B., & Thoresen, C. E. Non-vocal factors of the effectiveness of models in counseling. *Journal of Counseling Psychology,* 1967, **14**, 412-418.

Kyte, G. C. The effective supervisory conference. *California Journal of Educational Research,* 1962, **13**, 160-168.

Lange, D. N. An application of social learning theory in affecting change in a group of student teachers using video modeling techniques. *Journal of Educational Research,* 1971, **65**, 151-154.

Learned, W. S. *The professional preparation of teachers for American public schools.* New York: Carnegie Foundation for the Advancement of Teaching, 1920.

Legge, W. B., & Asper, L. The effect of videotaped microteaching lessons on the evaluative behavior of pre-student-teachers. *Journal of Teacher Education,* 1972, **23**, 363-366.

Leslie, L. L. Matching student teachers with cooperating teachers: A fruitful effort? *Journal of Teacher Education,* 1971, **22**, 303-309.

Likert, R. *New patterns of management.* New York: McGraw-Hill, 1961.

Lindsey, M. *Speculations on the future of teacher education.* Washington,

D.C.: American Association of Colleges for Teacher Education and Association for Student Teaching, 1968.

Lindsey, M. Professional laboratory experiences in teacher education: 1970. *Inquiry into teaching behavior of supervisors in teacher education laboratories.* New York: Teachers College Press, Columbia University, 1969.

Lindsey, M., & Monahan, T. I. A study of the relationship between congruence of educational attitudes of supervising teachers and their student teachers and evaluation. Unpublished doctoral dissertation, Columbia University, 1968.

Lingren, V. C. The certification of cooperating teachers in student teaching programs. *Journal of Teacher Education,* 1957, **8**, 403-407.

Lohman, E. A. A study of the effect of preservice training in interaction analysis on the verbal behavior of student teachers. Unpublished doctoral dissertation, Ohio State University, 1966.

Maddox, K., Holt, M., Stebbins, T., & Young, K. *Multi-institutional teacher education center.* Charleston, W. Va.: Kanawha Valley Multi-Institutional Teacher Education Center, 1972.

Malikail, J. S. Supervision of student teaching. *Education,* 1970, **91**, 163-165.

Marks, J. R., Stoops, E., & Stoops, J. K. *Handbook of educational supervision: A guide for the practitioner.* Boston: Allyn and Bacon, 1971.

Mason, J., & Blumberg, A. Perceived educational value of the classroom teacher-pupil interpersonal relationships. Mimeographed, Syracuse University, n.d.

May, F. B. Some practical suggestions for developing competency-based independent-study modules for teacher education. *Journal of Teacher Education,* 1972, **22**, 155-160.

McConnell, G. They helped us, but—. *Journal of Teacher Education,* 1960, **11**, 84-86.

McGeoch, D., & Lindsey, M. Supervisory conferences and analysis of teaching at teacher colleges: Columbia University. In D. Corrigan (Ed.), *The study of teaching.* Washington, D.C.: Association for Student Teaching, 1967.

McIntosh, J. A., & Jackson, R. E. *Contemporary practices in secondary mathematics teacher education.* Bloomington, Ind.: Research Center for the Language Sciences, Indiana University, 1973.

McKean, R. C., & Mills, H. H. *The supervisors.* Washington, D.C.: Center for Applied Research in Education, 1964.

Meier, J. H. Rationale for the application of microtraining to improve teaching. *Journal of Teacher Education,* 1968, **19**, 145-157.

Michaelis, J. V. Teacher education: Student teaching and internship. In

C. W. Harris (Ed.), *Encyclopedia of education research.* (3rd ed.) New York: Macmillan, 1960.

Michalak, D. Steps for development of an effective supervisory conference role play. Mimeographed, n.d.

Michalak, D. A. *The teaching clinic handbook.* Bloomington, Ind.: Laboratory for Educational Development, School of Education, Indiana University, n.d.

Milner, E. J. (Ed.) *The supervising teacher. Thirty-eighth yearbook of the association for student teaching.* Dubuque, Iowa: William C. Brown, 1959.

Mitchell, J. V. Education's challenge to psychology: The prediction of behavior from person-environment interactions. *Review of Educational Research,* 1969, **39**, 695-721.

Moffett, G. M. Use of instructional objectives in the supervision of student teachers. Unpublished doctoral dissertation, University of California at Los Angeles, 1966.

Mosher, R. L., & Purpel, D. E. *Supervision: The reluctant profession.* Boston: Houghton-Mifflin, 1972.

Moskowitz, G. Toward human relations in supervision. In J. E. Heald (Ed.), *Selected readings on general supervision.* London: Macmillan, 1970.

Newell, M. A. Contributions to the history of normal schools in the United States. *United States commission of education annual report.* Washington, D.C.: United States Government Printing Office, 1900, **11**, 2447.

O'Hanlon, J. P. Team approach provides variety of student-teaching experience. *Minnesota Journal of Education,* 1967, **47**, 12-14.

Olsen, H. C. Innovation in supervision today. In E. B. Smith, H. C. Olsen, P. Johnson, & B. Chandler (Eds.), *Partnership in teacher education.* Washington, D.C.: American Association of Colleges for Teacher Education and Association for Student Teaching, 1968.

Olsen, H. C., Barbour, C., & Michalak, D. C. *The teaching clinic: A team approach to improved teaching.* Washington, D.C.: Association of Teacher Educators, 1971. Bulletin no. 30.

Osborne, G. S., & Hurlburt, A. S. Credibility gap in supervision. *School and Society,* 1971, **99**, 415-417.

Perrodin, A. An analysis of selected factors in the preparation of secondary supervising teachers in Georgia. Unpublished doctoral dissertation, University of Georgia, 1963.

Price, R. D. The influence of supervising teachers. *Journal of Teacher Education,* 1961, **12**, 471-475.

Prince, O. Q. A study of the Georgia program for educating supervising teachers. Unpublished doctoral dissertation, George Peabody College for Teachers, 1961.

Raby, W. H. An investigation of the use of video-tape recordings as a technique for improving the student teacher's progress. Unpublished doctoral dissertation, University of Missouri, 1968.

Rattis, J., & Lepper, R. R. (Eds.) *The supervisor: Agent for change in teaching.* Washington, D.C.: Association for Supervision and Curriculum Development, 1966.

Raymond, A. The acquisition of nonverbal behaviors by preservice science teachers and their application during student teaching. *Journal of Research in Science Teaching,* 1973, **10**, 13-24.

Readling, J. J., & Blom, M. S. Team supervision: A humanistic approach to accountability. *Journal of Teacher Education,* 1970, **21**, 366-371.

Redfern, G. B. *How to appraise teacher performance.* Columbus, Ohio: School Management Institute, 1963.

Reed, H. M. The college supervisor in a multi-purpose university in a rural setting. In E. Pfeiffer (Ed.), *The college supervisor: Conflict and challenge.* Cedar Falls, Iowa: Association for Student Teaching, 1964. (43rd yearbook).

Richardson, G. C. Student teaching orientation and direction in the cooperative school. Unpublished doctoral dissertation, Illinois State University, 1968.

Robinson, E. W. Teacher self-appraisal: A way to improve instruction. *Journal of Teacher Education,* 1971, **22**, 469-473.

Rogers, C. R. The characteristics of a helping relationship. *Personnel and Guidance Journal,* 1958, **37**, 6-16.

Rogers, C. R. A theory of therapy, personality, and interpersonal relationship, as developed in the client-centered framework. In S. Koch (Ed.), *Psychology: A study of a science.* Vol. 3. *Formulations of the person and the social context.* New York: McGraw-Hill, 1959.

Rogers, C. R. *Freedom to learn.* Columbus, Ohio: Charles E. Merrill Publishing Co., 1969.

Roth, L. H. Selecting supervising teachers. *Journal of Teacher Education,* 1961, **12**, 476-481.

Sandberg, H. H. Beginning teachers' and supervisors' appraisals of selected supervisory techniques. Unpublished doctoral dissertation, Pennsylvania State University, 1963.

Saudals, J. R. Perceptions of supervisors by beginning secondary school teachers on selected schools in Indiana accredited by the North Center Association. Unpublished doctoral dissertation, Indiana University, 1972.

Scholl, R. L. Secondary student teachers' perceptions of effective and ineffective supervisory behavior of the college supervisor. Unpublished doctoral dissertation, Pennsylvania State University, 1966.

Schueler, H., & Gold, M. Video recordings of student teachers: A report of the Hunter College Research Project evaluating the use of kinescopes in preparing student teachers. *Journal of Teacher Education,* 1964, **15,** 358-364.

Scriven, M. The methodology of evaluation. *Perspectives of Curriculum Evaluation: American Educational Research Association Monograph Series on Curriculum and Evaluation.* Chicago: Rand McNally, 1967, No. 1.

Segan, G. B., Jr. Team supervision. In E. B. Smith, H. C. Olsen, P. J. Johnson, & B. Chandler (Eds.) *Partnership in teacher education.* Washington, D.C.: American Association of Colleges for Teacher Education and Association for Student Teaching, 1968.

Seif, E. The significant events: Techniques for supervision in triple T project. Unpublished paper, 1970.

Shaplin, J. T. Practice in teaching. *Journal of Teacher Education,* 1961, **31,** 33-59.

Sibbitt, A. L., Jr. Principals' and teachers' perception of supervisory practices in selected small public high schools of Indiana. Unpublished doctoral dissertation, Indiana University, 1972.

Simon, A., & Boyer, E. G. *Mirrors for behavior.* Philadelphia: Research for Better Schools, 2 vols.

Smith, E. B. The case for the college supervisor. In R. Pfeiffer (Ed.), *The college supervisor: Conflict and challenge.* Cedar Falls, Iowa: Association for Student Teaching, 1964. (43rd yearbook).

Smith, E. B. Needed: New order in student teaching that brings joint accountability for professional development. *Journal of Teacher Education,* 1969, **20,** 29-30.

Smith, E. B., & Johnson, P. (Eds.) School-college relationships in teacher education. *Report of a national survey of cooperative ventures.* Washington, D.C.: American Association of Colleges for Teacher Education, 1964.

Smith, G. R., & Coppedge, F. L. *Evaluation preferences and practices in alternative schools.* Bloomington, Ind.: Division of Teacher Education, Indiana University, 1974. (Forum series).

Smith, G. R., Harste, J. C., Mahan, J. M., Clark, J. M., McGinty, R., & Shimer, S. S. *Stirrings in teacher education.* Bloomington, Ind.: Research Center for the Language Sciences, Indiana University, 1974.

Smith, J. C., & Crump, W. A. An application of instructional development in a state department of education. *Audio Visual Instruction,* 1972, **17,** 18-20.

Snyder, J. F. Techniques and practices for effective supervision of student teachers in music. Unpublished doctoral dissertation, University of Nebraska Teachers College, 1961.

Sorenson, G., & Halpert, R. E. Stress in student teaching. *California Journal of Educational Research,* **19,** 28-33,

Stake, R. E. (Ed.) Toward a technology for the evaluation of educational programs. Perspectives of Curriculum Evaluation. *AERA Monograph Series on Curriculum Evaluation.* Chicago: Rand McNally, 1967. No. 1.

Steeves, F. L. A summary of the literature on the off-campus cooperating teacher. *Educational Administration and Supervision,* 1952, **38,** 129-137.

Stoller, N., & Lesser, G. S. *Phase III: A comparison of methods of observation in pre-service teacher training.* New York: Hunter College, 1963.

Stradley, W. E. *Supervising student teachers.* Danville, Ill.: Interstate, 1968.

Stratemeyer, F., & Lindsey, M. *Working with student teachers.* New York: Bureau of Publications, Teachers College, Columbia University, 1958.

Stufflebeam, D. L. Evaluation as enlightenment for decision making. *Improving educational assessment and an inventory of measures of affective behavior.* Washington, D.C.: Association for Supervision and Curriculum Development, National Educational Association, 1969.

Swineford, E. J. An analysis of teaching-improvement suggestions to student teachers. *Journal of Experimental Research in Education,* 1964, **32,** 299-303.

Switzer, R. L. A comparison of the student-teacher perceptions of supervising teacher behaviors under two student-teaching programs. Unpublished doctoral dissertation, Indiana University, 1971.

Symonds, P. M. The improvement of teaching through counseling of the teacher. *Journal of Teacher Education,* 1955, **6,** 122-127.

Taylor, B. L. An exploratory study of teacher education curriculum and mental health. *Mental Health and Teacher Education.* Cedar Falls, Iowa: Association for Student Teaching, 1967. (46th yearbook)

Taylor, K., & Fields, J. W. Problems confronting the college coordinator in an off-campus student teaching program. *Peabody Journal of Education,* 1964, **41,** 309.

Trimmer, R. L. Student teachers talk back. *Journal of Teacher Education,* 1960, **11,** 537-538.

Trimmer, R. L. Tell us more, student teacher. *Journal of Teacher Education,* 1961, **12,** 229-231.

Tuckman, B., & Oliver, W. F. Effectiveness of feedback to teachers as a function of source. In J. E. Heald, L. G. Romano, & N. P. Georgiady (Eds.), *Selected readings in general supervision.* London: Macmillan, 1970.

Unruh, A., & Turner, H. E. *Supervision for change and innovation.* Boston: Houghton-Mifflin, 1970.

Van Til, W. Supervising computerized instruction. *Educational Leadership,* 1968, **26,** 41.

Webb, D. Teacher sensitivity: Affective impact on students. *Journal of Teacher Education,* 1971, **22,** 244-459.

Werkmeister, W. H. Theory construction and the problem of objectivity. In L. Gross (Ed.). *Symposium on sociological theory.* Evanston, Ill.: Row, Peterson, 1959.

Wilhelms, F. T. Applications in teacher education. In B. L. Taylor (Ed.), *Mental health and teacher education.* Cedar Falls, Iowa: Association for Student Teaching, 1967. (46th yearbook)

Wilson, C. Student teachers adversely affected by super supervision. *The Clearing House,* 1963, **38,** 105-107.

Worthen, B. Toward a taxonomy of evaluation designs. Paper presented at the annual meeting of the American Educational Research Association, Chicago, 1968.

Yarger, S. J., & Leonard, A. J. *A descriptive study of the teacher center movement in American education.* Syracuse, N.Y.: Syracuse Teacher Center Project, Syracuse University, 1974.

Yee, A. A model for the development of teacher education relevant to the '70s. *Journal of Teacher Education,* 1971, **22,** 19-41.

Yoder, W. H. A study of alternatives in secondary student teaching. Unpublished doctoral dissertation, Indiana University, 1971.

Young, D. B. The analysis and modification of teaching behavior using interaction analysis, micro-teaching and video-tape feedback. Paper presented at the National Association of Secondary School Principals' 52nd Annual Convention, Atlantic City, February 1968.

Young, D. B. The effectiveness of self-instruction in teacher education using modeling and video-tape feedback. Paper presented at the American Educational Research Association Annual Meeting, New York, February 1971.

Zahn, R. D. The use of interaction analysis in supervising student teachers. Unpublished doctoral dissertation, Temple University, 1965.

Supervision in Social Work

IONE DUGGER VARGUS

INTRODUCTION

"Why he's only been a caseworker for seven years, and now he's being elevated to a supervisor." Such was the comment twenty years ago when a young man was named to a supervisory position. Elevated he was, for until recently, becoming a supervisor carried with it great status among social workers. Becoming a supervisor was for many a goal, a reward for hard work in the field, and a symbol of high competence in practice. The prime importance of and respect for supervision in social work is noted by Mandell (1973) in her comment that "the most frequently offered lure to social workers in personnel ads of ten years ago was probably competent supervision! [p. 43]"

Today it is no longer necessary to "move up the ladder" to a supervisory position. Young people are being trained in the schools of social work to graduate as supervisors and consultants. As more schools of social work expand their curriculums to include professional training at the bachelor's degree level, attention is being turned to the master's degree curriculum with an eye toward training for supervisory management positions. And as the schools of social work explore new student field placements in areas formerly not developed or available, the graduating student often stays on and becomes the supervisor of new trainees. Kadushin (1974) reports on a follow-up study of recent graduates that reveals that within two years of graduation, many workers with the Master of Social Work degree assume positions as administrators, supervisors, or consultants.

The status involved in being a supervisor may or may not be as important to these younger workers. However, for those who have chosen to be supervisors or who have fallen into these positions without much experience of their own, it has become an educative necessity to gain some insight into social work supervisory practices of the past as well as to gain some foresight into the future. For those new supervisors who have not had the benefit of supervisory role models, or have had a limited number at best, the issues surrounding supervision in social work have once again become timely.

Our purpose here is to review the books and journal articles on supervision published from 1960 to the present. From these works I will: (1) describe the goals, theories, models, and functions of social work supervision and research on supervision as reported in the literature; and (2) suggest ideas for present and future needs in supervision.

It may be useful to point out the limitations of this review of the literature. Methodology, that is, the "how to's" of supervision, was more often a topic in social work articles and books written before 1960 than in those written later. One reason for this fact is that since the 1960s, many broader issues have captured the attention of writers and researchers in social work; supervision methodology as a topic was placed on the back burner. Some might feel that there was simply not that much new to say about supervision. In fact, many of the articles of the 1960s and 1970s carry on debates begun earlier, as shown by bibliographic references which go back to the 1950s or 1940s. Nonetheless, the new issues which do arise, as well as the old ones which continue to inspire comment, serve to point to future trends in this field.

A clarification of terms is necessary here in order to specify a situation that may be unique among applied training practices. In social work, supervision of students in field placements, practica, or internships is generally referred to as field instruction. The literature on working with students has contributed a great deal to the data on supervision of workers. It was easier to demonstrate innovations with students, but it was expected that such innovations would apply to workers in agencies. Thus there is an interchangeability of the literature on worker supervision and student supervision, and the same conceptual model is applied to both. Pettes (1967) does state the difference between staff supervision and student supervision. Specifically,

> The staff supervisor's teaching function is concerned with teaching related to the specific jobs. . . . The student supervisor utilizes the specific job (the student's functioning within the agency), as a base for teaching the knowledge and skills needed generally for professional practice [p. 54].

This distinction is important primarily in the areas of what is taught, perceptions of students, and expectations of students; but it is more a *degree* of difference rather than an alternative supervisory process. For our purposes, then, no differentiation is made between student and worker supervision.

If one were to look at the articles of the 1960s as a whole, one's impression would be that writers were negatively critical about supervisory practice in social work. The necessity of supervision was not challenged; but implicitly and explicitly, the effectiveness of supervision as practiced was called into question. In general, the journal articles show three focuses: (1) criticism of supervision with some suggested changes, (2) development of theory and conceptualizations regarding supervision, and (3) description of some specific techniques.

SUPERVISION AND SOCIAL WORK: A HISTORICAL PERSPECTIVE

Stiles (1963) notes that "it is impossible to describe the development of supervision without referring to the development of casework [p. 19]." This statement is important because the bulk of the articles on social work supervision assume a "casework method" for practice. While the theories behind the casework method differ (for example, the functional school relies on psychology as developed by Otto Rank while the diagnostic school relies on Freudian psychoanalysis), essentially casework involved working with an individual within a psychological or psychiatrically oriented framework. The movement toward casework in practice, then, represented a shift away from the social realities, the need for social justice and the desire to reform society particularly as it affected the poor, which were the historical roots of concern in the profession as practiced by Dorothea Dix and Jane Addams. Thus supervision, when superimposed on the practice of casework, also became a psychologically oriented practice. The supervisor tended to adopt a one-to-one approach similar to that used between caseworker and client. Casework, as a method, dominated the practice of social work for many years; and it remains somewhat influential, as we shall see.

The historical development of supervision is traced to the early practice of the charitable organizations, which found it necessary to train their "visitors." In 1891, the Boston Charitable Organization Society began five training programs each year for agents who worked under the supervision of experienced workers. Other charitable organizations followed suit, and training schools evolved which used the agencies as a field laboratory. Incorporating John Dewey's theory of learning by doing, the training programs established the significance of a supervisor who could teach what to do.

With this background, it was perhaps only natural that the early and primary model for supervision was that of master-apprentice. On a one-to-one basis, the experienced worker could instruct the less experienced worker. Using the worker's written case reports, weekly conferences were held in which the supervisor employed a tutorial approach.

As group work became another method for delivering service, the concept of group supervision came to the fore. Group supervision was described in two ways—supervision of group workers, that is, those who primarily used this method, and supervision of workers in groups. The latter was essentially a supplement to the individual conference.

As we will see, such models as shared supervision and peer supervision have evolved as the result of criticism of the master-apprentice hierarchical approach and the infusion of social science theory into social work and supervision practice.

Social Work Training

Some discussion of the training for social work might also clarify our review of the literature and the section on future issues. As far as the profession was concerned, a true social worker had completed two years of graduate education in an accredited school of social work and had earned an MSW (Master of Social Work) degree. However, it was considered that the two years of graduate education did not produce a full-fledged worker but only a beginning practitioner. Thus upon employment, the worker (now with his master's degree) was expected to continue under regular supervision until he or she became a supervisor. More recently, undergraduate social work programs have proliferated, and the graduate at that level is referred to as a BSW (Bachelor of Social Work). Knowledge and skills once taught to master's degree students are now taught to bachelor's level social workers; and the graduate schools are struggling to establish the role, function, and knowledge base orientations of the MSW trainee.

In addition, some schools of social work and many community colleges conduct training in human services, which calls on social work knowledge for persons at the associate of arts level. While this too is a necessary development growing out of some identified manpower needs in social work, it has further complicated the tasks and objectives for education in social work. Issues concerning supervision as it relates to these developments are raised in the final section.

Social work and subsequently supervision take place in many arenas or fields of service. The settings for practice may be family service agencies, child welfare agencies, medical clinics and hospitals, mental health institutions, mental retardation institutions, correctional facilities, school systems, public housing, and public welfare, to name only a few. The literature seldom makes a distinction among these settings of the supervisory practice, although a few studies may indicate the specifics of content which apply to that field of service.

Social work also consists of a number of methods. While casework dominated the field, group work and community organization are other methods. Social planning incorporates a number of methodological techniques that are different from those used in casework and group work, and it is often accompanied by the term community organization. Administration and/or management is becoming a more prevalent course of study in schools of social work.

Roles and Functions of the Supervisor

Nearly all of the articles describe the roles of the social work supervisor as administrator and educator. At various stages in the development of supervisory practice, it has seemed that one role or the other has been paramount. At times there has been an attempt to further define and differentiate the supervisor's administrative and educative roles. Watson (1973) divides the major responsibilities of each function as follows:

Teaching functions

Although the specifics may vary among agencies, generally the material to be learned can be divided into five areas: (1) social work philosophy and the history and policy of the agency, (2) social work knowledge, techniques, and skills, (3) self-awareness, (4) available resources in the agency and the community, and (5) the priorities of case service and the management of time.

Administrative functions

The administrative component can be broken down into six functions: (1) communications linkage, (2) accountability for performance, (3) evaluation, (4) assignment of cases and distribution of work, (5) emotional support of workers, and (6) utilization by the agency of each worker's experiences [p. 81].

Miller (1971) states that "supervision in social work is essentially an administrative process for getting the work done and maintaining organizational accountability [p. 1494]." Pettes (1967) sees the supervisor as a member of an agency team, all members of which are employed to accomplish the agency's purposes and functions. . . . The supervisor carries responsibility for agency functioning and for staff and/or student development within an allotted segment of the agency [p. 21].

In the 1950s, concern arose over the tendency to regard supervisors as both administrators and teachers. Claiming that there was too much power concentrated in one person, Austin (1963) suggests that these functions should be separated. Devis (1965) demonstrates, using a United States Army setting as an example, that such a separation is possible and effective. Later, the use of labels other than "supervisor" suggests recognition of differing roles. The supervisor, in some cases, came to be called an enabler, a consultant, or a facilitator. Schools of social work began to call the supervisor in charge of students a "field instructor" in order to emphasize the educational components of the role. And at least two programs in one school of social work (management specialists and school-community-pupil specialists at the Jane Addams School of Social Work) further redefined the field instructor with the label of "team leader." This term implies a new function, that of directing the efforts of a mixed social work team.

GOALS AND ACTIVITIES OF SUPERVISION

The articles reviewed here generally mention one of the following three goals of supervision: (1) to assure that the agencies provide adequate service and maintain a standard of service, (2) to help the worker to function to fullest capacity, and (3) to help the worker achieve greater professional independence and autonomy.

Actually, the first and second goals are causally related. The workers' full development is believed to insure adequate agency service. Thus the workers will obtain self-knowledge, gain knowledge of social service, acquire diagnostic skills, become socialized to the agency and the community, develop professional judgment, work within the agency structure, and use supervision adequately.

The literature identified the following activities of the supervisor in carrying out these goals:

Plans and gives assignments
Holds individual conferences
Modifies the worker's use of himself
Introduces the worker to the agency
Tells the worker what he did wrong and what he did right
Assesses the competence of the worker
Teaches skills
Teaches about the agency
Points out rules and regulations in the agency
Evaluates work loads
Evaluates competence of the worker
Suggests alternatives to the worker
Gives emotional support
Creates a learning environment
Mediates the relationship between supervisees and the agency
Inspects the worker's thoughts and actions
Studies the worker's recordings
Controls salary increases and promotions
Opens channels for communication

It is in the pursuit of the third goal, that is, to help the worker achieve greater professional independence and autonomy, that most of the literature of the 1960s is directed. The authors reviewed generally accept the supervisor's functions as those of administrator and teacher but tend to reject the role of the supervisor as a therapist or helper.

The role of therapist, according to many critics, encourages intrapsychic dependency. The supervisor who talks too much about the supervisee's feelings only intensifies existing personality problems. In this type of relationship, the worker fears a supervisor's criticisms and thus fears failure. Eventually the worker becomes afraid to innovate, begins to rebel against the supervisor, or worse yet, avoids the supervisory conference. As a matter of fact, every article or book in this review published after 1950 and detailing the "how-to's" of supervision states that the supervisor should not be a therapist. Why, then, have supervisors continued to be seen in this light? Pettes (1967) indicates that the skills used in casework are similar to those used in supervision, and this similarity causes confusion. This potentially destructive relationship of supervisor as therapist could be avoided, some believe, if supervisors would modify their own perceptions of the role. In her chapter "Casework Related to Supervision," Pettes (1967) teases out the difference between casework with a client and the use of casework knowledge with a student or worker. Her point essentially is that the worker should be regarded as a reasonably capable adult who is different from the supervisor, with different strengths and skills and with different ways of relating. Pettes extends the notion of strength to students, which is a major difference from earlier authors who, in describing the supervisory process, tended to focus on student malfunctioning. Stiles (1963) posed a series of questions which suggest that if a supervisor perceives his or her role as that of an enabler working with a competent person rather than as an overseer of someone who cannot be trusted, more effective supervision is possible. Austin (1963) notes that the profession, in general, is to blame for assuming that a young worker is not fully a professional person.

Austin's contrasts between the assumptions which have led to the traditional system of supervision and the new concepts needed, even though published in 1963, are still valid and are worth presenting in their entirety.

Established System of Belief	*New Concepts*
1. The beginning worker needs a long period of tutorial instruction following his master's degree.	1. The master's degree in social work is the recognized degree of the profession in social work. [The first recognized degree is now the Bachelor of Social Work.]
2. Close supervision is the best medium for teaching workers at any stage of development.	2. The tutorial situation is useful at times in any stage of learning, but the learning that can only come from experience is equally important.

Established System of Belief	*New Concepts*
3. Workers learn and improve their practice in direct relation to the quantity and quality of supervision.	3. Learning and improvement in skill are not necessarily directly related to the quantity and quality of supervision. They may be more closely related to self-motivation and aptitude of the worker.
4. Social work learning and practice arouse personal conflict and anxiety. The worker needs self-awareness in order to he[others, and the supervisor is in the best position to help him gain it.	4. Self-awareness is important in understanding others. If the worker has a problem in the work situation, this must be called to his attention. If he needs therapy, he must seek it outside the agency. Support from a structure that provides incentives that ease strain such as adequate salaries, reasonable leeway in time arrangements, and professional recognition by colleagues will go far in reducing work tensions.
5. The supervisor as administrator is responsible for implementing and interpreting policy to the staff, and for seeing that it is carried out.	5. The professional social worker is capable of understanding and abiding by policy and procedure, and is in a key position to contribute directly to policy-making because of first-hand contact with the clients.
6. The supervisor is accountable for the work of staff members. The supervisor is logically the primary evaluator of the worker because he knows the work of his supervisee intimately.	6. The professional worker can be held accountable for his work. He should be able to recognize the need for an objective evaluation, and to relate to evaluation procedures that respect his internalized ethic of accountability, define criteria and design suitable evaluation [pp. 276-277].

SUPERVISION THEORY AND RESEARCH

With the movement of other disciplines into the helping process, social workers continue to ask the question, "What differentiates us from others?" Boehm (1969) suggests that the focus on social relationships is the distinguishing characteristic of the social work profession. That statement, however, does little to clarify the nature of the word supervision. The problem seems to lie in the absence of a theoretical framework for either the work itself or the supervision of it. Miller (1960) states that the supervision literature had concerned itself with values and commitments but had not advanced a theory on supervision. Theory building in the broader social work journal literature has obviously not been prevalent. Taber and Shapiro (1965) conducted a content analysis of 124 articles covering all of the years of publication through 1963 of three leading social work journals. While there was a sharp decrease in the simple reporting of practice experience and an increase in "references to theories and concepts from the 1920's to the 1950's, the findings could not be interpreted as showing progression toward a 'relatively well-confirmed theory [p. 106].'"

A few articles attempt to deal with this problem. Berl (1960), in his attempt to construct a conceptual framework, identifies four components of supervision—the institutional, the methodological, the educational, and the psychological. As an institutional operation, supervision controls the availability and standards of service. As a methodological operation, the supervisor's responsibilities include the functions of teaching administration. As an educational operation, supervision includes the variables of the situation, the nature of the assignments, and the nature of the relationship between the worker and supervisor. As a psychological operation, supervision requires a sound grasp of psychological theory in order to handle the supervisor-worker relationship.

Spiegal (1962) suggests that role theory be understood for the analysis of the supervisory process. Using the example of the untrained worker in a group service agency, he directs attention to concepts of the worker's role expectations, role enactment, role conflict, and role integration.

Widem (1962) calls on organization and administrative theory to delineate supervisory structure from supervisory process. He discusses four structural aspects of supervision: (1) agency readiness to incorporate a formal structure of supervision, (2) administrative awareness of how structure is essential for process, (3) periodic evaluation of the supervisory structure, and (4) a philosophy of supervision related to agency needs and services.

Foeckler and Deutschberger (1970) compare the research process, social work process, and supervisory process in order to show how all three share the components of study, diagnosis, treatment, and evaluation.

There seem to have been no studies reported during the 1960s on the effectiveness of supervision in social work. A research effort by MacGuffie, Jansen, and McPhee (1970), however, hypothesizes that "as students and field supervisors interact, the expression and perceptions about their interactions will become positive [p. 263]." Their data source was an interaction scale administered to supervisors and their students four times during the academic year. The results showed that after one year of "intensive interaction," the student and the supervisor achieved shared perceptions of their relationship with each other. Questions remain, however, as to what constitutes "intensive interaction" and what other activities the students engaged in during the year.

A study depicting the student point of view of the supervisory relationship was reported by Rose (1965). The Relationship Scale compiled by Rose and J. M. Reinnk is an "instrument developed for the purpose of estimating the intensity of criticism of an individual with respect to another individual to whom he stands in a hierarchically subordinate position [p. 91]." The subjects consisted of 122 undergraduate students in social welfare and 21 graduate students in social work. The hypothesis was that "the intensity of criticism of the supervisor by a student is, in part, a function of the phase of learning in which the student is involved [p. 96]." Some evidence supported the hypothesis; but there was evidence that other factors, such as the quality of supervision, also influenced the intensity of criticism.

A more informative study was conducted by Kadushin (1974), who surveyed 750 supervisors and 750 supervisees. The latter all held the MSW degree which, the author acknowledges, is not entirely representative, for only 30 percent of supervisees have master's degrees in social work. The study was comprehensive in that it investigated the supervisee-supervisor relationship, the roles and functions of the supervisor, and the methodology of supervision. In view of the previously described complaints, it is of interest to note that Kadushin found that the current supervisory situation is satisfactory to the majority of supervisors and supervisees. Seventy-three percent of the supervisors were "extremely satisfied" or "fairly satisfied," and about 60 percent of the supervisees had similar feelings. Other findings from this study help to illuminate the *current* status of supervisory practice. These findings are summarized in the following paragraphs.

Trends in Supervisory Methods

The individual conference remains the principal context for supervision. Supervisors meet with their supervisees in regularly scheduled conferences on the average of three or four times a month for a period of an hour to an hour and a half. Although group supervisory meetings frequently supplement individual conferences, only 14 percent of the supervisors indicated that such meetings were the principal context for supervision.

Evaluation of supervisees is used primarily for the administrative purposes of determining salary increases and retention or separation. The supervisor evaluates almost exclusively on the supervisee's products—written case records, verbal reports of case activity, correspondence, and reports. Information is rarely solicited from the client, and audio- or videotapes are not regularly used to obtain further data on the worker's performance.

Trends in Supervisory Relationships

Supervisors and supervisees are hierarchically oriented in their relationship, although both would like to see the relationship defined as consultant-consultee. Supervisees generally do not complain that the supervisor becomes too involved in personal problems, and in fact they are more willing "to accept the therapeutic intrusions of the supervisor than supervisors are to offer such help [Kadushin,

1974, p. 296]." Supervisors, more than supervisees, see their power as resting almost exclusively in their expertise. Where supervisees are dissatisfied, it tends to be in the areas where the supervisee feels that autonomy and initiative are restricted or where the supervisor does not provide much help in dealing with client's problems.

Trends in Supervisory Roles and Functions

Social science theory began to be used to buttress arguments about whether supervision should be essentially an administrative or educational task, a topic apparently discussed much in the 1950s. Austin (1963) calls on organizational, administrative, role, and communication theory to suggest that there should be a separation of the roles.

Supervisors and supervisees rated the most important function of supervisors as teaching the casework aspects (knowledge, skills, and attitudes) of the job and the second most important function as "case consultation, the analysis and planning of client contacts with supervisees [Kadushin, 1974, p. 293]." While supervisors did not have a high preference for functions concerned with teaching supervisees administrative aspects of the job or for acting as liaison between administrators and supervisees, they reported that they spent most of their time on such activities. These activities are viewed by supervisees as an important supervisory function. Both groups agree that one of the least important objectives is "to insure accountability for the use of public funds [Kadushin, 1974, p. 293]." Finally, 74 percent of the supervisors and 57 percent of the supervisees saw no conflict in the fact that the supervisor carries both administrative and teaching functions.

As we have seen, the Kadushin study is especially helpful in ascertaining the present state of social work supervision. It would seem that the attempt to introduce group supervision as an alternative to the individual conference, or as one which would help to reduce the concern about hierarchy, has not taken hold.

Social workers' traditional belief that authority comes through knowledge seems to persist at the supervisory level if the supervisors interviewed are, indeed, representative spokesmen for their colleagues. This fact could suggest that the social science theory of systems, organizations, and roles as it affects the authority and power of the supervisor has not been accepted or understood. Levy (1973), in recognizing that supervisors do have power, suggests that ethics must be consciously assumed. Furthermore, Kadushin (1968) comments that a supervisor must be willing to risk and deal with supervisee hostility, rejection, and accusations of being bureaucratically oriented.

One personally disturbing outcome of the Kadushin (1974) study is the indication that both supervisors and supervisees feel the least important objective of supervision is "insuring accountability for the use of public funds. [p. 293]." Rating this objective as the least important may simply have been an artifice of the questionnaire design, or it could be that supervisors see this as the function responsibility of some other administrator within the agency. But the fact remains that the demand for accountability is increasing from both governmental and voluntary funding agencies. Slashes in social service programs have occurred at an alarming rate, partially as a result of social work's inability to account to the public for what it does. It is not an easy task to report the nature and effects of this profession's efforts—a profession that is so broad, so varied in its activities, and so complex. However, accountability can be accomplished through sufficient motivation, interest, and understanding. The process, it seems to me, requires that workers and supervisors be involved in the systematic collection of data.

Literature Proposing Alternative Models

From comments about the role, function, and activities of supervision, suggestions for alternative supervisory models have emerged. These alternative models will be discussed in the following paragraphs.

First, a group method of supervision has been proposed by Judd, Kohn, and Schulman (1962) and Getzel, Goldberg, and Salmon (1971). Here the supervisees meet as a group. The focus is on educational issues rather than personalities. The group members help each other by sharing ideas and suggesting alternative courses of action. Help and decisions are lateral rather than hierarchical. The group members feel more united. The supervisee's body of experience is enlarged, and his or her objectivity and perspective grow in relation to the task itself. The supervisees also have more control since they determine what material will be used for the group meeting.

In this method the supervisor is a leader, teacher, listener, and consultant who must be flexible and alert in order to synthesize the diverse thinking within the group. The supervisor should not attempt to apply group therapy.

Second, shared supervision and case consultation are discussed by Leader (1964). This model was developed to go beyond group supervision, which Leader sees as an elaboration of the traditional supervisor-worker relationship. The worker has access to a panel of consultants who serve in an advisory capacity. The worker may choose to discuss a case with any consultant for any purpose and at any time. An administrative supervisor is designated, and through a device called the register, he reviews the trends and patterns in the workers' performances. He also reviews administrative operations such as recording. The review typically takes place once every two months.

Third, let us consider peer supervision. This consultation between peers provides theoretical insights. There is no hierarchical relationship or the automatic assumption of administrative duties by one person.

Finally, Watson (1973) describes six different models of supervision which are used simultaneously in the agency of which he is director. These models encompass all of the ideas and suggestions we have just considered plus additional ones. They are: the tutorial model, case consultation, the supervised group, the peer group, tandem supervision, and the team. Watson explains the differences among models with respect to the experience of the worker, the functions of the supervisory personnel, the regularity of supervision or team meetings, and the kind of interaction which occurs.

For inexperienced workers, Watson advocates the tutorial model, utilizing a one-to-one conference, and the supervisory group model. Case consultation is also conducted on a one-to-one basis, but the experienced worker is not bound by the opinion of the consultant, who is essentially a teacher. The peer group has no designated supervisor. Instead, experienced workers share common areas of competence. Group members meet on a regular basis to discuss cases. Similarly, tandem supervision allows two experienced workers to consult with each other in a collaborative fashion. The team is a varied group which meets regularly with a team leader who guides the team toward effective service delivery.

Watson does not advocate a fixed progression from one model to another. Rather, he feels it is a choice which "depends on the worker, agency, service, need, or time; sometimes a combination may be effective [p. 82]."

Literature Proposing Alternative Techniques

Using a model of supervision which is more appropriate to the method of practice is an alternative technique explored by Miller (1960). Where the supervisees are group workers, the supervisor should not apply a casework model of supervision. A supervisor may give help to a worker by directly observing him and by teaching him skills. This instruction can be given immediately and need not wait for the weekly conference. The supervisor acts as a leader and as a role model.

Another alternative technique involves having the supervisor engage in direct service in addition to his supervisory functions (Patterson & Clayton, 1961; Hallowitz, 1962). This approach would enrich the teaching component of supervision, for the supervisor could more quickly identify with the worker's problems. Yet another alternative technique employs other vehicles in addition to the written case record for supervision purposes. Itzin (1960) suggests that the use of taped interviews allows for more accurate feedback from the interview process. Crawford (1971) suggests transcribing taped interviews and developing a color chart which assigns different colors to various processes that occur in the interview. Also, Leader (1968) questions the accuracy of case records and recommends that supervisors observe interviews directly.

Ryan and Bardill (1964) suggest having the supervisor participate in a joint interview. When two or more clients (for instance, family members) are interviewed together, the field instructor and student could conduct a joint interview. This process would serve as a teaching aid in which "the student gains both an opportunity to observe the treatment process, and to participate in it [p. 474]."

Limiting the time of supervision is an alternative technique suggested by Wax (1963), who emphasizes the educational component rather than the therapeutic component of supervision. Supervision, in this model, lasts for a maximum of two years. It is a planned approach to supervision with learning goals and needs clearly identified and tied to defined stages.

Developing performance criteria and objectives is an alternative advocated by Billig (1971) and Anderson (1974). While these articles are aimed at supervision with students, their authors argue that workers, too, should know what is expected of them. These authors suggest defining specific objectives within specific settings. A final alternative suggested by Murdaugh (1974) involves changing the terminology of supervisor-supervisee to something which more clearly describes the educational component and diminishes the hierarchical status.

Summary of Research Topics

The preceding discussion has involved a review of the literature. The issues that have been highlighted through the research are: (1) issues of power and authority, (2) issues of role and function, (3) issues of attitudes, and (4) issues of the "how-to's" or methods. These are not so much separate issues as they are interlocking ones. Kadushin (1968) emphasizes the interplay of issues in "Games People Play in Supervision" when he notes the number of games workers use to reduce the power disparity between themselves and the supervisor. It is clear that depending on how supervisors use their power, they may either help a worker to grow and develop or they may harm him by encouraging dependency. The authority that is inherent in the supervisor's role is perceived by others, even if the holder wishes to deny it. The denial of power has had nearly the same consequences as the abuse of it, for the denial arouses hostility and confuses the interaction process. The movement toward describing the supervisor as a facilitator and enabler often has not been accompanied by specific behavioral activities, although the notion behind that movement has been that the power disparity would be reduced.

The articles which deal most frankly with the attitude of the supervisor toward the worker are those by Stiles (1963) and Austin (1963), but this concern is also implicit in much of the other literature. Again, one must refer to social work practice to see how the problem in supervisory practice may have evolved. In spite of its idealistic rhetoric, social work has oriented itself toward the deficiencies and pathologies of individuals. Social workers, according to most of the articles reviewed, tend to ignore the strengths that consumers bring to the interview and instead pay attention only to the weaknesses. As Ryan (1971) has so clearly shown, social workers, among others, have "blamed the victims." Since supervisory attitudes and techniques have grown out of the nature of practice itself, this characteristic habit of looking at the deficiencies and incompetence of the worker has also been carried over.

Out of this concern have come suggestions for carrying out supervision in ways which recognize competence but still provide for greater growth. Many of the researchers cited encourage the supervisors to plan their supervisory tactics with the worker, to develop performance objectives which include criteria for measurement, to see their role as teacher rather than therapist, to cease supervision after several years, and to develop a variety of consultative and supervisory styles which take into account the experience and ability of the worker.

Emerging Needs and Issues

During the 1940s and 1950s, it may have been possible to be prescriptive about supervision, for it was based on casework methodology. It is no longer possible. Some of the casework practice principles, particularly those which involve attitudes toward clients, have been attacked. One can easily recognize an urge in the literature written after 1960 for the profession to return to social action, social reform, and social change. Roles are being emphasized. Such roles as advocate, negotiator, broker, agent of change, and outreach worker are being introduced into the curricula of master's degree programs. As the list of social problems becomes longer, the fields of practice expand accordingly, with day care at one end of the continuum and care of the elderly at the other. Poverty has been rediscovered; and amid much embarrassment, social welfare institutions and social work agencies have had to admit their contributions to racism. Some sacrosanct attitudes have been challenged. A speech by William Ryan at the National Conference on Social Welfare in 1971 shocked the profession by confronting it with its participation in "blaming the victim." While intellectually the profession could agree with Ryan, breaking the bonds of habit has not been easy.

While structural changes have actually occurred in some quarters, the literature on supervision does not reflect the recent attention given to new arenas, new issues, and new roles. The attempt to apply this new knowledge to supervision is, at best, very difficult. I will attempt to call attention to these changes by raising questions throughout the rest of this review. The issues of power, roles, methods, and attitudes will be touched on as they apply to questions asked.

SUPERVISION FOR WHOM?

Paraprofessionals

During the 1960s, the social welfare profession began to employ the indigenous nonprofessional worker. These workers are recruited from the target neighborhoods and populations served by social agencies. Prompted by the establishment of the Office of Economic Opportunity, indigenous workers were hired to help the agencies deliver more responsive service, to help the worker himself to gain more self-respect, and to develop new employment opportunities for low income persons. It is undeniable that this move posed many questions to the potential paraprofessional and many challenges to the profession. Yet supervisors tended to plunge in prematurely. The following example is from a conference held several years ago on paraprofessional supervisors.

The three-day inservice training program was directed toward supervisors who were to have their first experience with paraprofessionals or "indigenous aids" as they were then called. During the first two and a half days, the supervisors were taught the methods and tools for supervising paraprofessionals. Not until the third day was a consultant called upon to raise some of the questions and concerns that paraprofessionals might bring with them. How might they feel, for example, about working for the establishment? How might they perceive the supervisor? How would their new roles and new perspectives affect their relationships with their communities? While their indigenous status implies obvious advantages in working in the community, would they not experience conflicting values and loyalties? How might supervisors handle this conflict? Would the supervisors really see the worker as a client? The supervisors were rightly distressed that these issues were left to the end of their training. It was suddenly clear that tools and techniques, when discussed outside the context of real trainees' concerns, are almost useless.

The performance of indigenous workers has proven to be successful, and training programs have been established for them under their new title, paraprofessionals. Still, many workers continue to enter the field with negative attitudes toward social work, attitudes which can make a supervisor uncomfortable. Others continue to feel isolated in their roles and, feeling powerless, wish to move up the ladder. Supervisors need to help paraprofessionals maintain the independence and style which allows them to respond to the community, often more effectively than the professional, while not totally discouraging their desire to become professionals. It is a delicate balancing act.

Social Workers with the Bachelor's Degree

Now that more schools of social work are training social work professionals at the undergraduate level, what should supervisors expect from them? Recognizing that much of the content that former graduate students received is now incorporated at the bachelor's level, should supervisors treat undergraduates as they formerly treated graduate students? What kinds of tasks is it appropriate to assign to them, and how does one see to their professional growth and development? In private conversations, some faculty members have acknowledged that undergraduates in social work training often have more enthusiasm, initiative, and receptiveness to people and ideas than do graduate students in training. Why it is so is not clear. The important question concerns how supervision can help to maintain and support these qualities. Briggs (1973) notes that "the limits placed upon B.S.W. personnel seem to be more a result of professional reservation, than actual lack of competence [p. 3]."

Because graduate schools are now having to devise a different curriculum at the master's degree level, a frequent suggestion is that graduate schools train their students to assume supervisory responsibilities, particularly to supervise the BSW. The controversy surrounding such a move arises from the inevitable concern over the power question. The supervisor who is only slightly older and more experienced cannot, some believe, have much credibility to the supervisee. Perhaps this issue will force a whole restructuring of the traditional concepts, methods, and approaches to supervision.

Minority Practitioners

Until recently, social work was one of the few professions that minorities could enter readily, albeit with the knowledge that discrimination would still occur once the job was secured. Twenty years ago a minority worker might choose to fight the discrimination in an agency by demanding a caseload which included some white clients as well as the all-minority workload that was handed to him. Now, however, the minority worker might *insist* that the supervisor assign him primarily to minority consumers. Once again, the traditional supervisor can anticipate a conflict, for the kinds of problems that the minority worker may wish to deal with and the techniques he might use in dealing with them are often at variance with the agency's sense of purpose and method. Yet it has been, and the literature reveals that it still is, one of the functions of supervisors to orient the worker to function within the structure of the agency. The supervisor is expected to help the worker identify positively with the agency. If the minority worker feels, however, that the minority consumers are not well served, how does the supervisor relate to these concerns? Many supervisors respond by calling the worker oversensitive.

More concerned supervisors, however, are faced with uncomfortable alternatives that are neither easy nor always satisfying. Should the workers be encouraged to approach the administration when appropriate changes can be made? Can the minority worker be helped to sort out the problems which can be solved through different techniques of service from those which require another agency's collaboration? Can supervisors recognize those racial or cultural complaints which may actually be "systems" complaints? Are supervisors aware of their own racism, which may reduce their credibility to the worker? Can the supervisor accept the fact that the black worker may take his direction from an organization such as the Association of Black Social Workers or from such prominent black social scientists as Ladner and Billingsley, who are redefining the problems of and approaches to minority peoples? It would seem that with social work's concern for people and humanity, the profession would not have to be caught up with such questions. Yet the problems mentioned here are all actual ones that have been reported from the field by black MSW graduates (Vargus, 1975). The questions of worker background and identity certainly merit attention from supervisors.

The Supervisor's Professional Image

At social work conferences and in the social work literature, a debate rages concerning the social worker's real identity and what his stance should be. If one were to ask whether supervisors see themselves as maintaining the status quo in society or as leading social change, most would probably give the latter answer. Everyone talks about change today; even the most clinically oriented workers talk about changing individuals and groups.

There is, however, a vast difference between teaching parents how to be more effective with their children (a task so often referred to as a change activity) and confronting an agency with the need to change its policies so that it more effectively delivers services to the poor and neglected. There is also a great difference between the latter (which I refer to as microchange) and bringing about change in national social policy and legislation in such areas as income maintenance and housing (macrochange). Can the supervisor who is oriented toward microchange conduct it through agency practice? Can or should supervisors attempt to influence their employing agencies in terms of policies as they affect the clients' needs?

While it is probable that social work supervisors, through administrative meetings, have had an informal influence on policy, it is interesting to note that such activity is not listed as a formal function of supervisors. Moreover, newer graduate students who have been exposed to the principles of social change often recount the supervisors' resistance to students' suggestions that the agency's policies and services be assessed. As we have seen, the literature on the methodology of supervision stresses helping the worker to accept the rules and regulations of the agency—not to examine them, and clearly not to change them. Perhaps the resistance to change could be reduced if the social work supervisor could see this function not as change for change's sake but as a renewal function which helps the agency to continually improve.

Prior to the recent social change versus individual change debate, the "hottest" issue was that of professional image. One's image was an outgrowth of one's method, whether case work or group work, and a further subclassification of that method. The *Encyclopedia of Social Work* (1971) describes several approaches to social casework as well as to social group work. Casework, the functional approach, the problem-solving approach, the psychosocial approach, and the behavioral approach are different methods of working with individuals. In social group work, the various ways of working with groups include the interactionist approach, the behavioral approach, the developmental approach, and the preventive approach. Several of the approaches are offshoots from some earlier practice, a fragmentation which in itself engendered controversy. Faculties within schools of social work are noticeably split on the methodological and ideological issues. Therefore, finding a school which is like an organic whole and which "implies the same basic philosophy of social work, a like set of values and fundamental purposes and aims that are identified [p. 265]," as Charlotte Towle suggested in 1950, might be more difficult than ever.

However, the diversity that one might find among faculty in values and philosophies can be quite healthy. Not only does diversity characterize the present state of the field, but diversity also provides students with choices of role models. A student can be helped to see that social work in the form of direct service and social work in the form of social reform or institutional change may ultimately embrace the same objectives, although they use different avenues and different methods. Some schools of social work teach an integrated combination of direct service and systems change approaches. The professional image that any social worker identifies with is, in the final analysis, an individual choice. The implication for supervisors, however, is that they must share this image with their workers and students who may be placed in their agencies. Too often, persons accept the supervisory assignment of students because of the status involved without accepting the philosophies and techniques which the students have been taught. It may only be human to attempt to socialize the young worker into one's own tradition; but such attempts, especially when they are covert, can make for hostile relationships. Traditionally, only the biases and attitudes of *workers* have been examined through the supervisory process. We are suggesting that the supervisor also clearly recognize and share his positions and even his ambivalences about professional issues and methods.

A Model for the Present and the Future

The professional model for social work supervision is unquestionably more broadly based today; yet with a few exceptions in group experience, all of the literature reviewed for this study assumes that supervisors are interacting solely with casework practitioners. What happens in the interaction with community organizers, planners, and middle-level management personnel, assuming that they are not supervisors already? If they are, how does one "supervise" them? What about supervision for those in the roles of advocates, brokers, evaluators, and a host of others which the literature in social work generally discusses but which the supervisory literature barely mentions. As Watson (1973) clearly shows, there can be a number of models of supervision even within one method of practice (casework) and within one agency.

One model which definitely calls for differentiation in concepts is that of supervising teams. "Teaming" is a method of delivering a service to consumers whereby a team, consisting of appropriate personnel, works on the resolution of the problem. Medical, correctional, and educational institutions are more likely to use interdisciplinary teams; but social welfare institutions may use teams composed only of social workers.

The person carrying the role of team leader may be equated to a supervisor for semantic purposes; as more agencies take up teaming, former supervisors will be probably be chosen as team leaders. However, just as the team delivers its services differently, so must the team leader redefine behavior. Since a team is basically a small group which engages in decision making, mutual teaching, resource sharing, peer control, and sharing responsibility for outcomes, it might seem that a supervisor is not necessary. Nevertheless, the team leader is a critical member of the team; and his management, administrative, and organizational development skills are particularly useful to the team. Such skills help a team to assess the feasibility and cost effectiveness of approaches, to evaluate processes and outcomes, to coordinate activities, and to "sell" the team concept to other institutions or personnel.

As an adovcate of team supervision which incorporates the ideas of peer and shared supervision, I feel that this model is best suited to answering the questions, concerns, and complaints raised earlier. For example, problems of hierarchical power are reduced. Members of the team, regardless of educational attainment, are recognized according to their performace. Through teaming, it is possible that a paraprofessional, a BSW, and a MSW could work interdependently without losing their sense of individuality or competence. The power which supervisors now seem so reluctant to admit is theirs by virtue of their administrative activities can, in reality, be reduced, for accountability, competency evaluations, and task assignments begin at the level of the team itself.

Teaming also speaks to another concern raised earlier. Vargus (1975b) described the activities of teams in a program in which there was a concern for delivering services on a wider scale and where intervention was required with the many systems that impacted on the consumers of social work services.

Within a team structure, a supervisor who becomes team leader need not throw out all of the previously learned "how-to's" of supervision. Objectives and expectations of workers or students will still need to be clarified. Just as before, a supervisor attempts to give new workers cases which involve some definite service which the client needs. A team leader can help a new team to take on those kinds of problems which can be managed with some potential for success. The team leader, as is true with the traditional supervisor, continues to help a worker build skills. For instance, listening, observing, and communicating are skills which cut across roles and are as appropriate for the team members as for the direct service worker. The team leader, upon assessing the need for skill building, might set the stage by suggesting a role-playing exercise or arranging for videotape.

Self-awareness, which has been a must in social work practice, is still needed by the worker who is a part of a team approach, again regardless of roles. Self-awareness includes the use of self in carrying out one's activities and a recognition of one's biases and attitudes. A team process often highlights these aspects, and the attempt to hide them by the "games people play in supervision" (Kadushin, 1968) is not as easy.

A supervisor from the traditional method offers a great deal to the role of team leader if he is willing to restructure his approach to interacting with the members of the team and is willing to take on a broader base of knowledge which cuts across methods and theory. In fact, team leaders in one demonstration program evaluated this approach to supervision as one which "not only reduced the burden of responsibility on them as field instructors, but helped them to conceptualize problems differently. [Vargus, 1975a, p. 91]."

Of course, not all social work settings are a natural for approaching the delivery of service through teams. But whatever model is used and whatever the title—facilitator, consultant, enabler, or team leader—the effectiveness of the supervision task will greatly depend on a conscious recognition of the supervisor's values, philosophies, and ability in that role.*

REFERENCES

Anderson, R. L. Introducing change in school-community-pupil relationships: Maintaining credibility and accountability. *Journal of Education for Social Work,* 1974. 10(1), 3-8.

Austin, L. The changing role of the supervisor. In H. Parad and R. Miller (Eds.), *Ego-oriented casework,* Family Service Association, 1963.

Barnat, M. R. Student reaction to the first supervisory year: Relationship and resolution. *Journal of Education for Social Work,* 1973, 9(3), 3-8.

Bartlett, H. The widening scope of hospital social work. *Social Casework,* 1963, 44(1), 3-10.

Bartlett, H. M. The place and use of knowledge in social work practice. *Social Work,* 1964, 9(3), 36-46.

---

*The author wishes to acknowledge with appreciation the careful reading and commentary of this article by Lillian Thornton and Audrey Pittman who are faculty members at Temple University with many years of experience in supervision.

Berl, F. An attempt to construct a conceptual framework for supervision. *Social Casework,* 1960, **41**(7), 339-345.

Berl, F. The context and method of supervisory teaching. *Social Casework,* 1963, **44**(9), 516-522.

Billig, S. Some elements in supervisor evaluation of field work students. *Journal of Education,* 1971, **153**(3), 66-72.

Billingsley, A. *Black families in white America.* Englewood Cliffs, N.J.: Prentice-Hall, 1968.

Boehm, W. The nature of social work. In P. Weimberger (Ed.), *Perspectives on social welfare.* N.Y.: Macmillan, 1969.

Briggs, T. L. An overview of social work teams. In D. Brieland, T. Briggs, & P. Leuenberger (Eds.), *The team model of social work practice.* Syracuse, N.Y.: Syracuse University, 1973.

Costin, L., & Vargus, I. *Social work and the public schools.* Bloomington, Ind.: Midwest Center for Planned Change in Pupil Personnel Programs, Indiana University, 1975.

Crawford, B. Use of color charts in supervision. *Social Casework,* 1971, **52**(4), 220-222.

Devis, D. Teaching and administrative functions in supervision. *Social Work,* 1965, **10**(2), 83-89.

Downing, R. Bridging the gap between education and practice. *Social Casework,* 1973, **55**(6), 352-360.

Duncan, M. G. An experiment in applying new methods in field work. *Social Casework,* 1963, **44**(4), 179-184.

Foeckler, M. M., & Deutschberger, P. Growth-oriented supervision. *Public Welfare,* 1970, **28**(3), 297-300.

Getzel, G. R., Goldberg, J., & Salmon, R. Supervising in groups as a model for today. *Social Casework,* 1971, **52**(3), 154-163.

Gordon, W. Knowledge and value: Their distinction and relationship in clarifying social work practice. *Social Work,* 1965, **10**(3), 33-39.

Hallowitz, D. The supervisor as a practitioner. *Social Casework,* 1962, **43**(6) 287-291.

Itzin, F. The use of tape recording in field work. *Social Casework,* 1960, **41**(4), 197-202.

Judd, J., Kohn, R., & Schulman, G. Group supervision: A vehicle for professional development. *Social Work,* 1962, **43**(1), 96-102.

Kadushin, A. Games people play in supervision. *Social Work,* 1968, **13**(3), 23-32.

Kadushin, A. Supervisor-supervisee: A survey. *Social Work,* 1974, **19**(3), 288-297.

Kaslow, F. W. *Issues in human services.* San Francisco: Jossey-Bass, 1972.

Ladner, J. (Ed.). *The death of white sociology.* N.Y.: Random House, 1973.

Leader, A. A new program of case consultation. *Social Casework,* 1964, **16**(2), 86-90.

Leader, A. Supervision and consultation through observed interviewing. *Social Casework,* 1968, **49**(5), 288-293.

Levy, C. Ethics of supervision. *Social Work,* 1973, **18**(2), 14-24.

Leyendecker, G. A family agency reviews its educational program. *Social Casework,* 1963, **44**(4), 185-192.

Lurie, A., & Pinsky, S. Queens Field Instruction Center: A field instruction center for multilevel education in social work. *Journal of Education for Social Work,* 1973, **9**(3), 39-44.

MacGuffie, R., Janzen, F., & McPhee, W. The expression and perception of feelings between students and supervisors in a practicum setting. *Counselor Education and Supervision,* 1970, **9**(4), 263-271.

Mandell, B. The equality revolution and supervision. *Journal of Education for Social Work,* 1973, **9**(1), 43-54.

Miller, I. Distinctive characteristics of supervision in group work. *Social Work,* 1960, **5**(1), 68-76.

Miller, I. Supervision in social work. In R. Morris (Ed.), *Encyclopedia of social work* (16th issue), Vol. 2. New York: National Association of Social Workers, 1971.

Morris, R. (Ed.) *Encyclopedia of social work* (16th issue), Vol. 2. New York: National Association of Social Workers, 1971.

Murdaugh, J. Student supervision unbound. *Social Work,* 1974, **19**(2), 131-132.

National Association of Social Workers, Practice commission. Identifying field of practice in social work. *Social Work,* 1962, **7**(2), 7-14.

Patterson, C. M., & Clayton, W. H. The one-to-one method of field work training. *Social Casework,* 1961, **42**(4), 180-183.

Pettes, D. E. Supervision in social work: A method of student training and staff development. *National Institute for Social Work Training Series.* London: Allen and Unwin, 1967. No. 10.

Rose, S. Students view their supervision: A scale analysis. *Social Work,* 1965, **10**(2), 90-96.

Ryan, F. J., & Bardill, D. P. Joint interviewing by field instructor and student. *Social Casework,* 1964, **45**(8), 471-474.

Ryan, W. The social welfare client: Blaming the victim. *Social Welfare Forum.* National Conference on Social Welfare. New York: Columbia University Press, 1971, 41-54.

Seaberg, J. Case recording by code. *Social Work,* 1965, **10**(4), 92-99.

Shannon, R. Developing a framework for field work instruction in a public assistance agency. *Social Casework,* 1962, **43**(7), 355-359.

Specht, H. The deprofessionalization of social work. *Social Work,* 1972, **17**(2), 3-15.

Spiegal, I. Role behavior and supervision of the untrained worker. *Social Work,* 1962, **7**(3) 69-76.

Stiles, E. Supervision in perspective. *Social Casework,* 1963, **44**(1), 19-25.

Taber, M., & Shapiro, I. Social work and its knowledge base: A content analysis of the periodical literature. *Social Work,* 1965, **10**(4), 100-106.

Towle, C. The contribution of education for social casework to practice. In C. Kassius (Ed.), *Principles and techniques in social casework.* Family Service Association of America, 1950.

Vargus, I. D. *Contemporary social work.* New York: McGraw-Hill, 1975(a).

Vargus, I. D. A team approach to school social work. In D. Kurpius & I. Thomas (Eds.), *Planned change in pupil personnel programs.* Bloomington, Ind.: Indiana University, 1975(b), 87-89.

Walsh, M. Supervisory appraisal of the second-year student in field work. *Social Casework,* 1960, **41**(7), 530-533.

Watson, K. Differential supervision. *Social Work,* 1973, **18**(6), 80-88.

Wax, J. Time-limited supervision. *Social Work,* 1963, **3**(3), 37-43.

Widem, P. Organizational structure for casework supervision. *Social Work,* 1962, **7**(4), 78-85.

Supervision of Renewal Training

C. PATRICK MCGREEVY AND TENNES M. ROSENGREN

INTRODUCTION

A disclaimer must be made at the outset. Other parts of this book have dealt with the nuances of supervision as associated with the services a professional provides to his or her client. The process of providing professional services and of supervising that service has a fairly discrete definition of activity in such circumscribed situations.

However, a chapter on supervision of renewal training lacks clear definition and thus raises many questions. What is meant by renewal training? Who is the client? Who is the professional? What does this professional do and why? And perhaps most important for the purposes of this book, how does one proceed to supervise such an ambiguous activity? While schools serve as the example of an organization in which renewal activities can occur, the reader should extrapolate examples appropriate to his or her employing organization.

Renewal training is both an activity and a state of mind. Broadly speaking, renewal is a process of educational change and decision making which aims to create a self-sustaining reform mechanism throughout an educational system. The approach represents a total and comprehensive effort to redefine schools and their educational goals. The redefinition ought to represent a total plan which goes beyond isolated classrooms and curricula to include the student's total schooling. All members of the school community including parents, students, teachers, and administrators must be represented or must directly participate in defining the school's goals and means of achieving them.

A contrast to the renewal concept is embodied in staff development departments commonly found in large and many smaller school systems. The major task of these staff development departments is providing experiences to the district faculty and staff that contribute to the educational relevance of the school. Usually these efforts boil down to presenting a three-hour course that meets weekly for anywhere from six to sixteen weeks and offers variable credit from a local college or university. This credit, in turn, can be applied to increments on the district salary schedule. At best such courses improve the professional competence of the individual teacher or administrator. At worst the experience is simply one more course which any experienced student can stick out.

The clients of renewal training can be anyone and everyone in the school system, if the decision is made to *rejuvenate* or *restore* the potency of the individual. It is clearly different from traditional inservice efforts which attempt to *improve* or *update* the professional's competencies. Renewal seeks to go beyond the "methods and materials" courses, which are additive in nature, to a more pervasive attitude which speaks to the individual's belief in and even hope for education. The school organization or system then becomes the client.

The professional trainer in renewal may "teach" a specific sequence of materials in a specific area—for example, modern math, oceanography, or affective education. Here the effort is directed toward keeping the professional current with societal needs and aspirations as well as with scientific discoveries and understandings. At the national level, for example, plans have been discussed regarding the establishment of regional teacher centers similar to those in England and Japan at which a professional could "bone up" on current developments in his particular subject area.

Another area toward which renewal training can direct itself is the teacher-student relationship. This area would include training in the use of such new technological aids as video recorders and classroom computers, group dynamics, and peer teaching. It would, in short, focus upon helping teachers become better teachers.

The areas of curricular and instructional methods have received nearly exclusive attention in teacher inservice education. One clear reason for this is the sense of immediacy most teachers feel about their classroom charges. Thirty students, each with his own needs and motives, do much to make any teacher, particularly the novice, feel anxiously inadequate. In such a situation, any solution, however temporary, is often seized.

The traditional emphasis upon individual teaching stations mitigates against one teacher assisting and/or supervising another. In addition, the organizational structure with distinct grade levels leads many educators to believe in a staircase instructional pattern. The availability of the many commercially produced instructional packages, which vary from cassette recordings to student workbooks, also increases the focus upon curriculum and instruction. In this situation it becomes very difficult to develop a strong organizational framework to foster change and encourage collaboration among personnel.

Considerable research and experimentation have taken place in the areas of curriculum and instruction. For a comprehensive review of these areas, the reader is referred to the *Second Handbook of Research on Teaching* edited by Robert Travers. This highly detailed reference reviews the relevant research and writings in teaching and ranges from methods and research on special problem areas to the teaching of the various school subjects.

Organizational Renewal

The dimension of renewal chosen for discussion here in some ways transcends the materials and methods needs of individual professionals. Organizational renewal, long a neglected area, for the most part concerns the interpersonal communication patterns of the adults that staff the school, from custodian to administrator. It also focuses on the authority relationships that exist, for example, between principal and teacher or between teacher and student. It is basically involved in the issue of decision making and in the very purpose and structure of schooling.

Historically, schools have responded to society's demands for change by adding (and seldom by deleting) a new program or course. This patchwork strategy of change is failing. We must learn to deal with schools as organic wholes. Schools must develop and incorporate new norms into the organizational fabric which allows, and even encourages, change to take place as a continuous process. Among the important norms in need of change are those associated with openness of communication, willingness to share and collaborate, and willingness to trust and take risks. The alternative is the continuance of an organizational structure where experimentation and risk taking are threatening and, though needed, become nearly impossible to achieve.

It is the position of the authors that changing a part of a school or school system will not suffice. Such changes, needed as they may be, preclude the broader issue of how an educational organization can develop in a way that allows continued growth of all members of the learning community without getting bogged down in bureaucratic red tape. We must find ways to provide experiences for all— administrators, teachers, and students—so as to minimize that sense of despair that creeps over a person who feels trapped, be it in the first grade or behind the desk in the high school principal's office.

The balance of this review will be devoted to the following points: (1) a review of what has been written over the past few years in the area of renewal, staff development, and organizational change; (2) an examination of prevailing myths or beliefs which seem to impede changing our school organization; and (3) a model for renewal which includes the components and actions thought necessary to implement and maintain a system responsive to external and internal demands for change.

RELATED LITERATURE ON CHANGE

An extensive search of the literature on changing school organization reveals some commonly held views of what should take place but, with notable exceptions, almost nothing in the way of documented research. The following section will present a sampling of the views and, where possible, a review of strategies for change and the results of their use. Discussion focuses on the importance of leadership, collaboration, climate, and interpersonal relationships, along with several specific methods—decentralization, staff development, staff differentiation, role changes, and outside consultants.

A useful framework from which to begin looking at educational renewal is provided by Anderson (1972). He presents basic assumptions regarding the roles of members in the school community and the change process. While his paper is primarily directed toward students, one could as easily argue a similar position for any of the adults in the system.

Several educators have given useful advice on methods of change. Gorman (1972) maintains that "the first requirement of successful change is that its purpose must be clearly stated and thoroughly understood by all who are to have a part in carrying it out [p. 566]." Furthermore, he feels that constructive change replaces what it discards, and that school reform should start with custodial changes (that is, in the cafeteria). Finally, he suggests a design change for all students. In a design to implement Gorman's model, Jones and Stanford (1973) provide the following suggestions. They choose to view the school as a therapeutic community and advocate that the community operate by providing two-way communication, shared responsibility, decision making through consensus, utilization of the abilities of all, and social interaction as a learning process.

Graham (1970) draws upon his experiences as director of the Teacher Corps to offer the following observations on change: (1) there should be clear commitment by all essential parties; (2) the effort must be large enough to be treated seriously; (3) the effort must persist long enough for change to take hold; (4) amendments based on experience should be encouraged; (5) there should be a plan for program continuity (that is, institutionalization); (6) multiple models and techniques for reproduction should be developed; and (7) evaluation should be undertaken to consider alternative means of change and cost effectiveness.

Focusing on organizational change in smaller secondary schools,

Buser and Stuck (1970) provide a taxonomy of major functions and tasks within a school system. They offer the following "shoulds" for change: (1) change should be made for a purpose; (2) all persons affected should be involved; (3) plans should be flexible and simple in scope and design; (4) support from the community should be obtained in advance; and (5) the plan should be practical in terms of economics, the professional staff available, accrediting requirements, and the known research.

Baldridge and Burnham (1975) reported on the results of two research projects which were directed toward the dynamics of organizational change. The analysis revealed three factors associated with educational change. First, the position and role of innovative people in a system was more important than such individual characteristics as sex, age, and personal attitudes. Second, the large and complex system which fosters differentiation seems to produce specialists who innovate solutions to specialized problems. And third, a heterogeneous environment creates situations that come to demand responsive behaviors. The authors added a cautionary note that their research does not replace other interpretations of innovative practices. Rather, they argue that when linked to the structural characteristics of the organization and the environment, a fuller account can be made of much organizational innovation.

Methods for change are best exemplified by actual implementation. A series of articles titled "Profile of a High School" appeared in a 1971 *Phi Delta Kappan* issue. In this series, five staff members of John Adams High School in Portland, Oregon, describe their perceptions of the school and its development. These accounts demonstrate how change can take place and what it takes to bring about this change.

Williamson (1974) presents an organizational model which is designed to transform the school into a community center for both inquiry and self-renewal. His model is applied to the John Adams High School, which conceptually began as a training center for the young people attending the school and as a teacher research and development center. The original design for Adams was based on an analogue of a medical teaching hospital. He presents a careful analysis of the Adams' organizational successes and failures and argues the case for joining the community and school renewal needs.

In reviewing the research findings on organizational goals and the measurement of goal achievement, Coleman (1972) concluded that participative decision making increases organizational effectiveness, if professionals participate in setting the goals. Gregore and Hendrix (1973) cite an earlier study by Herzberg as further support for the contention that participation in decision making increases involvement. They quote Herzberg as reporting that people were more motivated and happy in their work when they (1) provided solutions to problems; (2) received recognition from supervisors, colleagues, peers, and clients; (3) enjoyed the nature of the work itself; (4) were given responsibility for their own work; and (5) felt opportunities were available for change in status or for added responsibility.

A personal account, from a teacher's viewpoint, of what happens in a school that adopts a strategy of organizational change is presented by Lehman (1972). She noted that the faculty, while publicly wanting to share responsibility for decision making, privately had difficulty in maintaining day-to-day involvement. Much effort was necessary to avoid reverting back to the traditional system in which the principal and/or the organization consultants would make the decisions. The teachers' realization that their opinions and decisions do in fact matter, while initially hard to believe, was crucial to the change effort. She notes in closing that

> organizational change itself induces change in people. It is idle and dangerous to suppose that, once we have reorganized a school successfully, things will remain stable. The process of renewing organizations brings about instability. And, though this is a bit disturbing to some people, it is also exciting [p. 54].

In a study conducted in New York State with sixty-five participating districts, Goldman and Moynihan (1975) found the major problems in planning change in these systems involved people and dealt with organizational variables. They noted the paucity of writing and training in educational planning which would help the practitioner to cope with such "human" problems.

Schmuck and others at the Center for Advanced Study of Educational Administration at the University of Oregon have adopted many of the procedures that originally were associated with the National Training Laboratory. They have presented some research evidence to substantiate their model of planned change (Schmuck & Miles, 1971; Schmuck, Runkel, Saturen, Martell, & Derr, 1972).

The group studying change at the University of Michigan's Center for Research on the Utilization of Knowledge has also developed some very helpful materials for educators sponsoring change in their schools. Havelock (1970) has organized a resource book which translates research into plans and activities which practitioners can implement in their day-to-day work. Another "guidebook" developed by Havelock (1973) has a similar format but expanded contents. This is an excellent reference for anyone seeking to implement change in schools. Yet another useful reference for the agent of change was compiled by Fordyce and Weil (1971). This book, which outlines methods of implementing organizational change, includes case studies which are analyzed in detail. The second chapter in a book by Umans (1970) presents a systems study of the problem of planned change in education.

The Role of Leadership

Tye (1970) takes a strong position in describing the role of the building principal in change. He argues that the single school is the basic structure from which to begin implementing change. His second contention is that the principal is the most effective agent of change. Tye proceeds to list nine qualities which he believes the principal should possess. He concludes this highly relevant paper by describing eleven conditions the principal as change agent must create.

Bockman (1971) presents a similar view of the principal as an agent of change. She feels that the principal must demonstrate a consistently positive attitude toward the school staff and faculty. She stresses the need for sharing decision making, thus giving more self-determination to others. Schmuck (1972) also advocates that the leader (the principal or superintendent) share power with those people affected by the decisions. He contends that staff satisfaction is in proportion to their participation in decision making.

Trump (1972) presents a somewhat different view regarding the principal's role in change. While he, too, feels that the principal is the most critical person in any change strategy, he argues that the principal should spend at least three-quarters of his time in the area of instructional improvement. Under such a plan the principal would spend only one-quarter of his time on management matters. If one assumes that organizational change occurs through structural and interpersonal changes of a managerial nature, then it appears that the principal utilizing Trump's model would be shortchanging the renewal strategy in his or her school.

A critical obstacle facing any principal seeking to make his or her school more responsive is all too often the problem of role perception. Sarason (1974) emphasizes the organizational constraints that one experiences when he moves from teacher to principal. A teacher's view of the roles of the principal and the school can severely limit his vision of what could and should be done for children when he assumes his new role as principal. Sarason correctly reasons that the principal is pivotal in any serious school organization change. However, he rather pessimistically notes that too often principals become trapped by their own limited role expectancy and their desire to present a well-ordered system.

Swaab (1972), writing from his perspective as a supervising principal, reasons that the principal sets norms and must model the desired behavior of trust and openness. The process of organization development or planned change offers the most feasible means by which a school staff can determine their educational priorities and take actions to reach their goals. Shared decision making is a crucial step in this process. A similar view of the supervision of teachers by principals is offered by Husarik and Wynkoop (1974) in a paper describing a "collegial" model of supervision that a principal might adopt in his or her relationship with teachers.

The problem of identifying the leadership competencies and functions of an elementary school principal was undertaken in a project jointly sponsored by the Chase Manhattan Bank, the Learning Cooperative of the Board of Education of the City of New York, and the Bank Street College of Education (Klopf, Blake, Scheldon, & Burnes, 1974). The pilot program included the training of twelve principals. Furthermore, it focused attention on the selection, preparation, and development of a taxonomy of seven functions critical to the creation of an optimal learning environment for children.

The Consortium Approach

Several projects with public and private funds have attempted to implement change in a group of schools through developing networks of communication and support. Goodlad (1972) describes the process and assumptions of such a consortium, which was organized by the Institute for Development of Educational Activities (IDEA). The League of Cooperating Schools articulated four guiding premises:

1. The individual school is the largest manageable organic unit for educational change. This assumption is based on the observation that each individual school develops a unique culture which must be carefully considered in any change process (Sarason, 1971).

2. The individual school is not strong enough to overcome the status quo forces that typically exist in the surrounding community.

3. People take risks more willingly when associated with successful organizations or systems (for instance, foundations or universities).

4. A central hub (the Office of the Research Division of IDEA in this case) is necessary for communication and support with other league schools.

Goodlad's paper, beyond describing the league's strategy for change, poses some provocative implications for continuous staff development and for the possible roles of teacher education colleges in renewing local schools.

The National Association of Secondary School Principals Model Schools Project, which involves thirty-four schools, represents another consortium change model (Trump & Georgiades, 1970, 1971, 1973). The authors describe areas that are the most and least easy to change, steps to implement such changes, and threats to the change process.

A consortium project directed toward upgrading principals' capabilities in their role as instructional leaders is described by Anastasiow and Fischler (1969). The project utilized a team teaching model which enabled each principal to develop greater depth in one or two subject areas. They would then consult in one another's schools and would ultimately improve all of their instructional programs.

Another form of the consortium approach to renewal is described by Mack (1975). The school training center is an institution designed to upgrade the skills of the various members of the learning community, from administrator to community representative. The underlying rationale for these centers is that school systems can no longer depend on new teachers to supply innovative ideas and practices. Rather, the existing staff and faculties must begin to shoulder the major effort of renewal.

Feitler and Lippitt (1972) report on a consortium project involving fourteen schools. The project focused upon providing teachers and administrators with planning and organizational problem-solving skills. The purpose of this training was to increase the capabilities of the involved schools in order that they could define and solve their own problems on a continuous basis.

Malcolm (1974) describes a strategy aimed at changing the role of both the training institution (the university) and the consumer institution (the schools). This project was developed and funded by the Bureau of Educational Personnel Development, U.S. Office of Education; and it emphasizes collaborative training between new people, most of whom are minority members, and those who have positions of authority in schools and universities. The focus of the training is upon utilizing present knowledge regarding communication, interpersonal relationships, and organizational change. The respective institutions are also placed in a position of collaborating in order to secure funds. Both institutions are expected to become more responsive to the needs of the broader communities which they serve. An excellent description of one of these seven programs and its progress over three years is presented in a report from the Midwest Center/Satellite Consortium at Indiana University (*Consortium Approach*, 1975).

The Training of Teacher Trainers Program (TTT), also developed and funded by the Bureau of Educational Professions Development of the USOE, is reviewed by Hook (1972). The focus of the program was primarily upon improving the competencies of those persons chiefly responsible for teacher preparation. This very complex and ambitious program attempted to create change in teacher education by collaboratively involving the schools and the supporting community on a parity basis.

A spin-off of the TTT Program is described in an article on "networking" (Merrow, Foster, & Estes, 1974) in which the authors argue that in order to survive in a school system, superintendents must talk to one another regularly. They propose to have superintendents, principals, and community members organize into groups and tap one another as resources. While not radically new, it is promoted as a means of solving day-to-day problems. The concept of networking could work at all levels within schools and school districts as a viable renewal strategy.

In an extensive and highly relevant paper, Wayson (1974) identifies problems and potential solutions in the training and renewing of elementary school principals. Several cautions were offered to those readers considering change. He specifically points to the notions that decay is inherent in all training programs and that constant adaption to continually changing circumstances is most important. He suggests a consortium which would employ regional networks and a national faculty from throughout the country. No certification would be permanent. The proposed curriculum falls into three categories: (1) developing control over one's life and career; (2) learning how to help others develop more effective personal and professional behavior; and (3) learning how to make organizations congruent with educational objectives.

School Climate

Hetzel and Barnard (1973) argue that changes in the educational program, structure, and methodology have failed because of the process used in implementation. They propose that the critical variable in change is the people implementing the change, and they propose a plan for motivating such persons. Basically, they argue for a process climate of mutual respect and involvement achieved through awareness, problem ownership, the generation of alternative solutions, evaluation and closure, and the recognition and reward of efforts. Similarly, Wood (1973) stresses the importance of positive interpersonal relationships in change and cites six characteristics of the climate for change—trust, understanding, support, commitment to goals, open communication, and an emphasis on improving education (over a need for success). He includes "how to" guidelines for producing the desired climate which are specifically aimed at curriculum directors but are applicable to all educators. The guidelines basically operationalize the concepts of open communication, ownership, and involvement.

In a research evaluation of inner-city schools, Owens and Steinhoff (1969) found that even though the achievement level of the control group was no different from the More Effective Schools project group, the atmosphere of the latter group was more supportive, satisfying, and self-actualizing for the staff. Consequently, these schools had fewer absences and lower rates of teacher-turnover. The teachers were also more enthusiastic, interested, and hopeful about the future. Rhodes (1969) takes the importance of climate a step further and argues that the process or pursuit itself produces change. Furthermore, the interactive exchange of information or "linkage" may be both process and product, for "educational improvement and institutional renewal are inseparable. . . . The process is the product [p. 207]."

John Davis (1975), in describing the changes accomplished in the Minneapolis alternative school and desegregation/integration projects, emphasized total staff participation. Such participation must be backed by the local board of education and administrators, thus leading to shared authority and decision making. A related feature of such participatory decision making is the potential for more fully utilizing the personnel resources within the school district. Whitcomb (1975) describes a similar approach being developed for the nineteen campuses of the California State University and Colleges.

Hanson (1971) poses the question of why schools are protected from the forces of change that affect other types of organizations. He suggests three factors differentiating schools from other organizations: (1) the school is a monopoly (as opposed to a competitor) in terms of input, funding, and service acceptability; (2) educational goals are nonoperational, making evaluation of success difficult and/or ambiguous; (3) the school system does not have an "outward looking" adaptive system providing long-range feedback (that is, follow-up studies of graduates).

Administrative Decentralization

A major change method is seen by McDonough (1974) as synonymous with "local leadership" and giving decision-making power to those persons most aware of educational needs—principals, department chairpersons, teachers, and parents. Brownell (1971) believes that both decentralization and centralization have merit in different situations. He does, however, see decentralization as correlated with a belief in people's ability to govern. Jacobs (1974) agrees with the decentralization stance but believes caution should be exercised in its implementation. He contends that the trends toward diversity of educational values and needs, the shifting of more power and influence to the community and the single school, and the move toward accountability will force decentralization. Jacobs states that "without commensurate authority [staff and administration] cannot logically be held accountable for programs over which they have little or no control [p. 16]."

A school system employing the decentralization process is described by Bair (1969). He has proposed three districts instead of one large district, each having its own budget and its own associate superintendent with total responsibility for budget development and for employing, evaluating, promoting, and dismissing personnel. He believes that the decision-making process should be in the hands of the community and members of the teaching profession. He states, "I am convinced [decision making] is essential to the survival of American education [p. 275]."

Rogers and Wolley (1974) describe the process and what happens when a junior high school faculty assumes the administrative and management functions of their school. Judging on the basis of teacher turnover, student and teacher absences, and suspensions and vandalism, the effects are remarkably positive. Again, the point seems to be that decision-making authority and increased performance go hand-in-hand.

Ornstein (1975) surveyed administrative decentralization nationally in seven large school systems. As decentralization occurs there is a tendency for increased community participation which can take the form of either advisory group activity or shared decision making. Ornstein noted that most educators advocate the advisory role, thus leaving their influence over decision making relatively intact.

Personnel Deployment

Staff development or inservice education programs represent other methods for professional and personal self-renewal within the present educational system.

Adams, Sinclair, and Storm (1972) list six components for staff development, all of which must interrelate: renewal centers, renewal seminars, individual school efforts for improvement, exchange programs, leadership education, and evaluation of program effectiveness. For staff renewal programs to be effective, they must be meaningful to the participants in terms of deep involvement and commitment. Lamb (1972) also stresses the need for both professional renewal and personal renewal. Though speaking in the context of the administrator, his words seem applicable for teachers as well: "Renewal is personal in the sense that each administrator must have the opportunity to know himself, to sustain the ability to transcend and extend his personality qualities deep within the persons inside and beyond his organization [p. 84]."

Mattleman (1973) supports a comprehensive staff development program (a "treatment" as opposed to a "band-aid") to train, retool, and support teachers. The nine-point guideline for a staff development program includes needs assessment by participants, contributions by participants, the appreciation of individual differences, positive reinforcements, operational and realistic expectations, and an overall practical time agenda. Finnegan (1972) and Unruh (1972) report detailed case studies of two school systems which have staff development programs that incorporate comprehensive guidelines for personal and professional growth.

Several writers on the topic of inservice training as a change strategy emphasize that in order to insure changes in educational systems, the participants need to be involved in the planning (Hull, 1975; Koble & Gray, 1975; Mohan & Hull, 1975; Cochran, 1975). When teachers and administrators are involved in the planning of programs, their commitment and attitude toward those programs are positively sustained. It seems that no matter how good the training model, if individuals are not made a part of what is to happen to them, nothing in fact will happen.

Staff differentiation is another method or means of change. English (1969) classifies four models of staff differentiation according to emphasis: learning paradigms, teaching paradigms, curricular paradigms, and organizational paradigms. He provides several practical suggestions for implementing staff differentiation. The first roles changed should be at the "middle management" level—that is, principals, coordinators, supervisors, and directors. An assessment of needs by students, teachers, and community should accompany planning for staff changes. Teachers should be involved in all aspects of planning. Instructional support systems must change as the teacher's role changes. The administration should shield innovating schools from public or system pressures and anxiety.

The creation of new roles as a method for change is being advocated by several writers. Mickler (1972) argues for the replacement of the supervisory model by the "teacher educator-evaluator' model. Basically, he calls for a "teacher educator" to act as a facilitator of change, a counselor, a resource person, and a support system. This person would only evaluate teacher performance. The greatest change provided in this model would be in the principal's role; and according to Mickler, "The role of the principal is reduced to its proper context—that of providing the organizational arrangements, conditions, materials, and support necessary for effective learning and teaching [p. 516]."

In providing for professional and organizational improvements, two new roles are suggested by Beckerman (1973). The "training specialist" would design and initiate new programs within a school district and the "extension educational specialist" would stimulate programs from a university base, especially through land grant university extension divisions. These roles would basically fill the void left by school administrators involved only with management-maintenance responsibilities.

The New Providence School District in New Jersey has created a new role for its administrators. Administrative teams have been formed to discuss problems and concerns, to share knowledge and insight, to develop specific individual objectives, and to coordinate efforts. Advantages of the administrative team model, according to Anderson (1973), include complete honesty among team members, relaxed interpersonal relationships, and professional and personal support. The creation of the outside consultant who is a specialist in organizational development represents another change strategy through role differentiation. Gallesich (1973) states that the attitudes, values, and beliefs of an outside consultant or agent of change are crucial to the change process, and he argues for a "multiple perspective" including: (1) an objective outside view of the school, (2) an empathic understanding of life in the school, and (3) a clear view of self in the interactive process. Four areas provide a framework for gathering and organizing data to form an objective outside view. First, external forces and systems—the relationship of an individual school to the hierarchy, the values and climate of the central administration, parent groups, and so forth—should be identified and studied. Second, the internal forces—the formal structure roles, norms, and people—should be clarified. Third, the school's history should be examined, including the trends in status, faculty morale and attrition, educational orientation, and community real estate values. Finally, staff perceptions of the consultant who is gathering this information need clarification.

SCHOOL MYTHOLOGY

Within any organization, there tend to be several assumptions, belief systems, or myths with which the members of that organization operate. These myths represent a kind of collective belief system about the members' aspirations and sense of the possible. Myths can foster growth, maintain the status quo, or contribute to the decline of an organization. In order to have any kind of school renewal, these myths and their contribution to the organization need to be examined. The following myths appear to be needed by most school communities in order to maintain some sense of predictability and security. Yet these same myths or beliefs do much to forestall or prevent the reformulation of the school organization into a viable system capable of change.

The Child-Centered Myth

Since the middle and late 1960s, students have made their concerns heard through methods ranging from protest to involvement. This trend may have started at the college level but by now has descended to the elementary school level. Most programs that are considered innovative have focused upon the student. Such programs involve behavioral objectives, individualized instruction, modular scheduling, new curricula in the behavioral sciences, and open classrooms. All of these programs are designed to involve the students and help them to become what and who they really are. These efforts are certainly commendable and definitely need to be pursued. But what of the teacher? Herein lies the myth! The students may become involved, but too often the teacher is being excluded.

The problem of the child-centered myth is the assumption that schools are for children and need not consider the psychological needs and expectations of the employed personnel. Most teachers are excluded from organizational problem solving, goal setting, and decision making. How can these same teachers be expected to involve students in decision making, individualized programs of study, and classroom rule setting? The model the teachers have to follow is lacking in reinforcement qualities. Many of these teachers were involved in the protests for academic and personal freedom during the 1960s, and it would be rather naïve to think they no longer have some of the same needs and expectations of the school community.

Many teachers feel a keen lack of control over what happens to them. It would seem to follow that if the adults in the system had a sense of contributing to their own future, both personally and professionally, they would be better able to model this feeling for students. It is faulty to assume that schools are only for children and that all events should focus on the children. It is also faulty to assume that the adults in the schools will model responsible behavior if they have no responsibility for or involvement in what happens in the school.

The Control and Order Myth

It appears that most public schools are run for a few members—

those who get out of control. Schools have traditionally assumed they must maintain control over the students, but it does not stop with students. While teachers must control students, the principal must control the teachers, the superintendent must control the principal, the school board must control the superintendent, and the community must control the school board. How many members of any of these groups get out of control? What messages do these groups deliver to one another in the areas of trust and responsibility?

A problem that often results from defining control as an organizational virtue is the impact that it has on individuals. The teacher, the administrator, and the specialist are judged on their control abilities; and in the process of pursuing this valued attribute, these same people often wind up controlling themselves too tightly. We too often fall victim to the organizations which employ us.

Certainly, there are individuals who behave inappropriately, but do they represent the majority? In most schools today the rules and regulations are made to control the entire student body and staff and not just those who abuse rules. It is the fault of the control myth that assumes that all students will act out if they somehow are not controlled by rules and regulations. Similarly, it is wrong to assume that all teachers will become negligent if not controlled, that the principal will automatically engage in radical behavior if left alone, that the superintendent will misdirect the efforts of educating the young if the board does not watch carefully, and that the board of education will not consult the community on school matters.

The excessive need to control people fosters distrust, and it assumes that people are not responsible and will become destructive if left alone. Most school systems set down elaborate goals and objectives that are ostensibly for the growth and development of each individual into a responsible person. One of the basic assumptions of being responsible is that a person can be trusted to behave appropriately. What are we telling students and teachers in a school system about trust if the administration needs to control these groups?

If the people in the school system do not experience trust and responsibility, they will not be very good models of it. Teachers need to be trusted to make decisions, solve problems, and set the goals that affect the school. Any effort in teacher or school renewal must have as one of its ingredients an element of trust. When trust is assumed, there is freedom to move and an opportunity to become responsible for one's own behavior. If becoming a responsible person is a desirable goal, then schools must give up the myth that people need to be controlled.

The Authority Myth

This myth may be better known as "who has the authority" or the familiar "passing the buck" syndrome. The barnyard pecking order in a school system and how that is dealt with will influence any efforts at teacher renewal within that system. It becomes rather routine for many school personnel—from teacher to principal to superintendent—to say they do not have the authority to make something happen. The sense of impotency or powerlessness in some systems seems to pervade all members of the school community.

The authority myth provides a convenient rationalization for some who say they are not allowed to effect changes or who watch another flounder in a move toward changing the system. Someone is always above the next person in the school system pecking order, and this person is viewed as having a little more authority and/or competency.

What has happened since the advent of behavioral objectives, performance criteria, and accountability? Have schools and the people in them really become excited about the opportunity to be accountable for what happens in that school? Have they looked on this as an opportunity to demonstrate that they want the buck to stop with them? The answer to these questions is all too often— simply, no! In many systems people are moving toward panic. They feel someone is going to be observing them at all times. Security is threatened, and even more rigidity is setting in rather than some desired risk taking. Who is going to decide what the criteria are? For what are the teachers in the system going to be held accountable? Is such a decision going to be made by someone higher up? Who is going to hold the higher up accountable? It seems as though the behavioral objective and accountability movement may lend itself to more of the same sort of buck passing if some changes are not made.

The accountability phase of education is being introduced into a system where the persons who will be held accountable have little or no say concerning whether they should or should not be held accountable. The buck is expected to stop with the teacher, and the teacher has very little, if any, input into what that means. How is this situation going to be any different than it has been in the past? Is the teacher going to demand that students be held accountable for their learning and social behavior? Assuming the answer is yes, will the students have an opportunity for input into the accountability criteria if teachers themselves have little?

If any plans for teacher, school, or educational renewal are to be effective, all persons involved need to have an opportunity to engage in the process of deciding what is to happen. The buck will not stop until people feel they have some authority in making the decisions. If teachers have some authority, they then can choose to take responsibility and be held accountable.

The Credential or Competency Myth

The accountability era has brought with it the competency movement. Yet all school personnel need to be certified or credentialed. The credentialing process is one whereby a person, through engaging in certain kinds of behaviors, receives a piece of paper saying he or she can now engage in some other kind of behavior that affects the minds of children and adults. Suppose they demonstrate that they can not engage in something called teaching? Medill Bair (1969), superintendent of a large city school system, proposed that universities and colleges draw up warranties on their graduates. This arrangement would put the certificate of responsibility on the university. If the graduates were not able to carry out the necessary functions within the five-year warranty period, the university would have to take the graduates back and retrain or renew them. As it stands now, certification means that teachers, counselors, or principals have spent some time taking courses at a university, college, or inservice program.

Certification should not represent the end of a process when, in fact, it marks the end of an experience. This ending does not mean the experience, or another like it, will never be engaged in again. Teacher renewal is a process that is continuous. Persons who engage in a renewal process are on a continuum at various points which represent their experience. It would be faulty to assume that all school personnel have the same experience and naïve to think they should all receive the same credential. Similarly, competency in one area at a given time also should not assume permanence. Competencies, like credentials, must be seen as continually in need of renewal.

The New People Myth

This myth has existed for some time in education, but it peaked in the 1960s. During this time the Federal government supported a great deal of training for new people entering education. The assumption was that if new, energetic people with "right" ideas could get into a given school, the school would then change.

The hindsight of the 1970s has shown the fallacy of the new people myth. One fault was that the number of new people was insufficient. In many instances, however, numbers alone were not the crucial variable. The preparation given these people was too often inappropriate for the realities of their work. Too little attention was given to the accommodating qualities of educational organizations. Scant effort was given to concentrating these new people in order to maximize their change efforts and their development of a mutual support system. The schools, for the most part, did not change; they simply altered some practices, adopted the current jargon, and continued business as usual. Today we are faced with the dual problems of an excessive number of professionals, many of whom are ill prepared to deal with educational change, coupled with a future decade of declining school enrollments.

The "if only we could get the right person syndrome" has long been the educator's lament. Many principals believe that if they have the right teachers, everything will be right. Many teachers believe that all they need in order to get things organized is a new principal. Universities seek new deans and presidents in order to promote change. At first glance this idea does not seem so bad. However, these new people soon become old people if something does not happen in the system to make things different. It is a poor assumption, at best, to believe that one or even a few new people in a school are going to have a lasting impact on that school.

The new people myth is easy to believe. Perhaps our "disposable" culture, which favors discarding that which does not or cannot provide instant utility, sustains such a belief. To renew people is a more difficult task. Most people who go to graduate schools of education are seeking to be renewed in some way. They often leave their teaching, counseling, or principal positions in order to get renewed. There most certainly is a message in this migration to graduate schools. It could be because they want to get a raise, meet new people, and gain status; or it could be because something is lacking in the systems they left. Most advanced graduates tend not to go back to the system or school they left. They are looking for a *change*. Members of this group, in effect, become new people and want to go somewhere else.

It appears to become a cyclical process. Intervention in that process is difficult. If intervention is to be made, it must be made at the source, the school. People in the school need to be renewed in the field; they need to be afforded all the experiences that would be given them at a graduate school—for example, the degree they are pursuing, released time, funding, and the opportunity to take risks.

The Money Myth

The belief that money is absolutely essential to effect change has become the most difficult barrier to overcome in changing schools. It is assumed that schools need large amounts of money in order to really educate the community. Many school systems feel that if they could only pay teachers and principals more money, there would be no problems. Educational materials are being produced at a phenomenal rate and are marketed for what often seem to be exorbitant prices. When Fedeal grants terminate, situations at project sites go back to the status quo. The "we ran out of money" message is loud and clear.

It would be foolish to think that money is not an extremely crucial factor in education. The reward system for school personnel in most schools is based on the pay scale. School personnel do not have many other payoffs in their system and want to be compensated for what they do—teach and manage. However, there seems to be some evidence that people work at various occupations for reasons other than money. If none of these "other things" are forthcoming, money becomes the prime motivator. Perhaps the myth is that these "other things" will also cost large amounts of money.

What would the price tag be on an open, problem-solving climate?

One of the requests of many school personnel is to get things out in the open so they can begin to feel a sense of ownership toward what their school is all about. Certainly it can not be very expensive to create a problem-solving climate in which all members of the staff know what is going on and can have input into solving the difficulties. School climate may cost little more than time and a place where staff can gather to share their perceptions of situations that need attention.

It does not seem likely that the development of interpersonal trust, both with colleagues and with supervisors, would be too expensive. Support, both personally and professionally, is needed to keep people from becoming lonely and isolated. It seems that interpersonal trust would promote the exchange of ideas and feelings which, in turn, would enhance the educational process. Trust comes from how people perceive their environment; how a person thinks and feels may have little to do with money.

The expertise one has may have little to do with the position that person holds in the school system. Would it take a large amount of money to activate this process? Leadership and knowledge do not always go with degrees and positions. Throughout any school, experts exist in a variety of areas. The person who has the knowledge and qualities to carry out a particular task should be given the authority to pursue that task. The delegation of authority by expertise costs little more than trust in others, regardless of their positions.

The individual's participation in decision making may become one of his or her most highly valued possessions. Does it cost so much to have all members of a group involved in making decisions? When people are involved in deciding their own futures, a certain amount of commitment and accountability is attached to their decisions. The investment rate becomes higher and, when someone has interests at stake, involvement becomes the ethic. Engagement in the decision-making process in the school system may be the key to keeping the teachers renewed.

In summary, the myths and assumptions under which many schools operate can serve people well in situations where they feel they have very little or no influence. When people are feeling lonely, isolated, and insignificant they give these feelings to the students both verbally and nonverbally. Educational renewal will have to intervene in this process and will have to begin to renew individuals' feelings of significance.

The process of school renewal must address itself to examining the basis of these and other myths. New beliefs or myths must develop, and of prime importance is the belief in the capacity of the individual, the group, and the organization for self-directed growth and development. A truly vibrant educational system may then evolve.

A RENEWAL MODEL

The future of educational renewal, school renewal, or teacher renewal (terms often used synonymously in the literature) will be determined by whether or not renewal can be conceptualized in such a way that it can be made operational. Many programs and projects have and are being developed to renew teachers and other school personnel—for example, inservice training, staff development, special institutes, and consulting programs. Much of what has been done in the areas of teacher and administrative training is, in effect, renewal. However, there seems to be a lack of a way to conceptualize the total renewal process. What are the main elements of educational renewal, and how can they be operationalized and implemented?

One model for conceptualizing the renewal process has three major dimensions—*clients, values,* and *actions.* Each dimension has elements which interact with those elements of the other two dimensions as well as those within the same dimension. An individual involved in a renewal process must simultaneously interact in day-to-day contact with other individuals, various groups, and the total educational organization, be it a single school or a more complex system of schools. Thus the clients become the *individual,* the *groups* of which the individual is a member, and the total *organization* to which they belong. A set of beliefs or myths regarding the purpose and process of renewal needs to be understood, accepted, and operationalized by the clients. The values of *collaboration, ownership,* and *feedback* represent beliefs that the authors feel are necessary to effect renewal. The final dimension, that of actions, involves *assessment and evaluation, planning,* and *implementation.* These three dimensions—clients, values, and actions—comprise a model for conceptualizing and operationalizing educational renewal.

FIGURE 2
A Model for Renewal

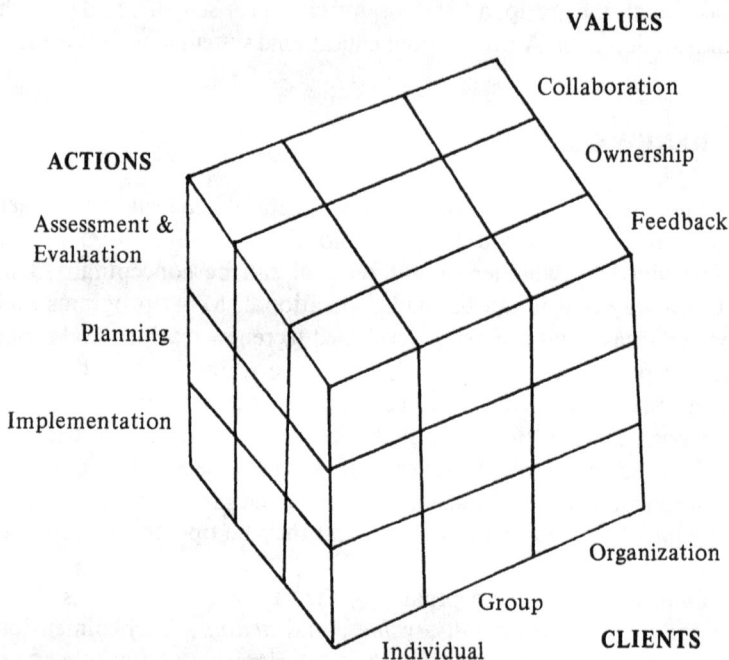

VALUES

Collaboration

ACTIONS   Ownership

Assessment &   Feedback
Evaluation

Planning

Implementation

                                                    Organization

                                        Group

                            Individual   **CLIENTS**

Clients

The clients in the renewal process present themselves as individual clients, group clients, and the organizational client. All individuals in the school community—including teachers, parents, administrators, students, support personnel, and human service personnel—can be influenced or renewed on an individual basis. The individuals, in turn, make up various groups and subgroups—teachers, counselors, staff, departments, families, parent associations, and central administration—which often present a workable unit for renewal training. The total organization, the school or school district, can be viewed as a client; and various interventions can be introduced throughout the system to complete the renewal process.

Values

The values that are necessary in order for renewal to take place have been identified as collaboration, ownership, and feedback. For the renewal process to be effective and continuous, individuals and groups must incorporate these values into their belief systems. Without valuing interdependence, determination of one's own future, and the giving and receiving of precepts and concepts, the renewal process will be little more than a cognitive exercise.

Collaboration is that element needed in order to make and implement a mutually agreed upon decision by two or more people. One person cannot act independently of the other and cannot be completely dependent on the other. It becomes an interdependent relationship in which the individuals or groups function with others in contributing to and carrying out problem-solving efforts. The interpersonal relationships in a group or organization form the basic fabric of the collaborating effort. Members of groups that are interdependent realize they cannot achieve their goals by acting independently of each other. Similarly, individual systems or organizations must develop collaborative relationships with one another and thus extend their capacity for delivering human services. The consortium arrangement between several school systems and/or universities has been shown to increase the individual system's potency as well as to stimulate growth in the total network of systems. Collaboration leads to another value, pluralism, which involves the mutual respect and valuing of each individual's feelings and thoughts.

Ownership is seen as that dimension of belief in which a person feels the group or organization is a direct extension of himself. In such a situation the individual comes to feel personally responsible for the image and activities of the system. It seems this element is necessary if individuals are to feel involvement and commitment within a group or organization. Individuals and groups within organizations need to make an investment in that organization if its goals and objectives are to be realized. The decision-making process is the best means by which people in organizations can feel they have input into what happens to them as people. When individuals or groups contribute to making decisions and solving problems, they can express actions that determine their own destinies. They thus experience more control over their lives. The value of determining one's own future creates a feeling of power and significance. Investment in the organization, involvement in the group(s), and commitment to goals and objectives are ultimately the results of participating in the decision-making process.

Feedback is seen as that element needed in order for individuals, groups, and organizations to maintain congruency with expectations. Without periodic checks or feedback, perspectives and perceptions of individuals, groups, and organizations may remain vague at best and unknown at worst. Personal and group validation comes from some form of feedback between and among individuals and groups. If individuals are to understand their relationships to groups and groups their relationships to the organization, then feedback becomes essential. The process of giving feedback on how the client's behavior is observed and understood builds a self-correcting factor into the system. Monitoring by utilizing feedback protects against a group or individual becoming inconsistent and incongruent with their stated goals. Valuing feedback as a way of validating personal and professional growth is advocated in the renewal process.

Actions

The actions needed to realize educational renewal are closely aligned with the familiar scientific method. The careful collection of data and drawing of hypotheses (assessment), the translating of data into specific goals and alternatives (planning), the application of systematic methods and procedures (implementation), and the process of determining whether goals have been achieved (evaluation) are the essential steps for operationalizing the model.

Assessment is seen as the systematic analysis of the causes of a client's problematic behavior, regardless of whether the client is an individual, a group, or an organization. It is also viewed as a means of determining the developmental, preventive, or remedial needs of these clients. Assessment must produce data to clarify problems and goals and to lead to the development of plans for attaining these goals. Evaluation is seen as the process of determining whether goals have been attained by the clients. Assessment and evaluation go together in the action process and are interrelated. The major difference between assessing and evaluating is one of timing. Assessment defines the initial state or condition. Evaluation assesses whether plans have been formed appropriately and implemented accurately and obviously follows the implementation step. Evaluation can also be seen as the initial step of the second, third, or any future phase because it is both the end and the beginning of the feedback loop.

Planning is seen as the process of taking the assessed data and formulating strategies for achieving the desired goals of the clients. The primary objective of an action plan is to lead to client growth or success. Planning becomes a continuous process based on data and hypotheses drawn from the assessment. Incorporated into any plan or strategy are the various theories and day-to-day knowledge about individuals, groups, and organizations. Drawing upon the knowledge and techniques of theory and the available human resources, plans are created that best meet the needs of the various clients.

Implementation is seen as the systematic application of plans for action. The procedures or methods that are needed to implement a plan are drawn from available or created resources. The implementation of any plan of action requires the most efficient use of all resources. The individual or group (teacher, administrator, parent, or student) with the most expertise in the problem area needs to be involved.

The model in operation is seen as a means of continuously renewing rather than leading to an end product. The individuals, groups, and organization are continuously collaborating on making efforts and decisions and on giving and getting feedback; and the never-ending process of asessment and evaluation, planning, and implementing common goals and objectives moves with time.

At any given time, one or more of the three dimensions may be examined to determine the level of functioning. An individual teacher (client) may want to assess (action) collaborative efforts (beliefs) to determine if needs are being met and goals are being attained through a particular teaching technique. An observational method or another person may be utilized to provide this teacher with feedback (belief) and to evaluate (action) whether this individual's (client) goals are being met. This procedure also is applicable for group and organizational clients. The decision-making process (ownership) can be assessed and evaluated (action) by an individual, any group, or the organization (clients); and a new strategy (planning) to change it can be implemented (action) through the combined efforts (collaboration) of those persons in the system(s) who are affected.

To illustrate further, the organization may want to continuously assess its collaborative efforts, the ownership of decisions, and the feedback that exists within the system. Various plans and strategies may be drawn up and implemented to test certain hypotheses that have been formed from the assessment. In turn various groups may be involved in the assessment, planning, and implementation of these new ideas and goals. Individuals possessing the expertise needed for realizing these goals are given the authority and concomitant responsibility to achieve these goals.

The Role of Conflict

It is obvious that the model described requires an enormous effort on the part of the many clients. It especially requires the present authorities in the system to be secure in themselves as persons and as professionals. One by-product of change which generally is both unexpected and unwanted is conflict.

As channels of communication develop and are opened, people are bound to express and see divergent views and values. This process is individualization. Obviously, the views of the client (individual, group, or organization) can be expected to clash or conflict with those of other clients. It is absolutely essential that the conflict that is bound to accompany change receive both legitimation and a forum for expression.

Conflict in values and beliefs (myths) can be a great source of energy provided an opportunity is given to process the differences. Successful utilization of conflict is difficult; too often we are prone to deny it or resolve it and make it go away. Conflict utilization is necessary in order to begin and then maintain the forces that will insure successful educational renewal.

The Role of Supervision in Teacher Renewal

Supervision as defined here is *control and management of training in an applied setting.* Educational renewal is by definition a renewing process or retraining process in an applied setting. The renewal process as presented in this study is a process of changing. Supervision in educational renewal or teacher renewal could be conceptualized as the control and management of change. If change is to be controlled and managed, what kind of people will be supervising the change?

An existing member of the school organization in the role of renewal supervisor or renewal agent presents the advantage and disadvantage of dealing with his or her perception of the school organization. While that person may "know the territory," he must also deal with his respective history, accumulated through prior interactions within the school. A person whose major allegiance is not with the school can offer a perspective that is broader and more objective. That person, however, faces the credibility issue facing an outsider. A plausible resolution to the membership role issue is, whenever possible, to team the external foreigner with the internal resident. Each can contribute to the other's understanding of the organization, thus allowing more precise judgment.

It would be naïve to think that any one person possesses all the skills necessary to supervise change in individuals, groups, and organizations. If members of the school community are collaborating, making decisions, and giving feedback, then, in effect, the school community becomes its own supervisor. The traditional role of the supervisors in the school, of those who have the authority to supervise because they occupy positions labeled "supervisor," will not be functional in teacher renewal. The teacher renewal supervisor will have authority to supervise not because of position but because of authority by virtue of expertise. He or she will have authority of *idea* rather than authority of *action*.

The creation of a person to fill a nonexistent function allows one to borrow from past knowledge and to speculate about the future appropriateness of the description. In effect this person (or persons) is unknown and must be described in a more general or idealized manner. In our attempt to define the renewal agent, it must be understood that we are trying to describe a real person and not the unattainable "Super Agent."

The role of the supervisor in teacher renewal will involve the management of change through consulting. The consultant is seen as the person with the knowledge, skill, and expertise needed to deliver the most effective feedback in a given situation. When delegated authority comes through expertise, the consulting supervisor could be any number of people within the school organization. Supervision becomes a collaborative effort in which it is conceivable that students may supervise teachers, teachers may consult principals, and principals may give feedback within the school system.

It would be faulty to assume that a school organization could achieve the consultant-supervisory role in a short period of time. Long-range planning would have to be done in order to insure success. The long-range goals of supervision would be those of collaboration and authority by virtue of expertise. The short-range goals would be to demonstrate what supervision is, how it is carried out, and what people who are the most effective are like. This goal may have to be achieved by renewing the present supervisors through utilizing outside consultants. Someone in the system must begin the process of renewal and must be able to demonstrate that process. What should this person be like?

If the role of the supervisor is to control and manage change, then those who supervise should be able to manifest management skills. They need to be viewed as possessing skills that others need and, perhaps most important, to be seen as people who behave in the spirit of collaboration, ownership, and feedback. The supervisors must be perceived as models of high status, models who are intellectually able and socially skilled, people who can put themselves on the line and risk failure as well as achieve success. The supervisors of change will need to be highly skilled facilitators of communication if they are to possess the reinforcing properties needed to become effective models. By demonstrating the renewal process through behavior, the supervisor will become a model for others. The utilization of effective modeling in renewal is suggested as the most efficient way of making changes.

Supervisors in the renewal process will need to be skilled teachers. They will need to be able to engage in the action steps as presented in the renewal model and to demonstrate the values to individuals, groups, and the total organization. Their assessment skills in determining needs and conditions, their ability to form strategies to move from one condition to another, and their modeling behavior in implementing the basic methodology of collaboration, owner-ship, and feedback will result in the renewing of others. They will teach others this process by living the process. Supervision of change must ultimately engage everyone who is involved in the change process. All members of the school com-munity must have an opportunity to teach and learn. If renewal is a collaborative effort where people are interdependent, if renewal is to involve all in decision making, and if feedback is of value, then everyone becomes a supervisor and is, in part, responsible for the control and management of educational renewal.

REFERENCES

Adams, J. A. Sinclair, R., & Storm, H. Staff renewal: Turn it on or give it up. *Theory into Practice,* 1972, **11**(5), 307-313.

Alexander, M. Organizational change and the principal. *Educational Technology,* 1972, **12**(10), 55-57.

Anastasiow, N. J., & Fischler, A. S. Teaming of principals project. *National Elementary Principal,* 1969, **47**(4), 17-23.

Anderson, R. A. A humanized and individualized secondary school program. *Theory into Practice,* 1972, **11**(1), 43-49.

Anderson, R. B. Administrative team in motion. *School Management,* 1973, **17**(3), 19-20.

Anderson, W. Trends, hopes, and needs for self-renewing educational institutions. *Journal of Research and Development in Education,* 1972, **5**(3), 86-93.

Antonelli, G. A. Questions for the innovator. *NASSP Bulletin,* 1973 **57**(370), 9-16.

Bair, M. One superintendent's answer to a city's educational problems. *Phi Delta Kappan,* 1969, **50**(5), 274-279.

Baldridge, J. V., & Burnham, R. A. Organizational innovation: Individual, organizational and environmental imports. *Administrative Science Quarterly,* 1975, **20**, 165-175.

Barger, R. Evaluation and decision making for the classroom. *Theory into Practice,* 1974, **13**, 58-64.

Beckerman, M. M. "Inside-outside" team. *Educational Leadership,* 1973, **30**(6), 530-532.

Belasco, J. A. Organization control strategies and the emergence of trust. *Journal of Educational Administration,* 1972, **10**(1), 34-45.

Berman, L. M. *Supervision staff development and leadership.* Columbus, Ohio: Charles E. Merrill, 1971.

Blumberg, A., & Schmuck, R. Barriers to organizational development training for schools. *Educational Technology,* 1972, **12**(10), 30-34.

Bockman, V. M. The principal as manager of change. *NASSP Bulletin,* 1971, **55**(356), 25-30.

Brownell, S. M. Desirable characteristics of decentralized school systems. *Phi Delta Kappan,* 1971, **52**, 286-288.

Burgess, L. Accelerating change in urban education. *NASSP Bulletin,* 1975, **59**, 74-79.

Buser, R. L., & Stuck, D. Staff organization in the smaller secondary school. *NASSP Bulletin,* 1970, **54**(348), 107-115.

Clothier, G. M. Inner city teachers: A preservice model. *Theory into Practice,* 1972, **11**(4), 252-257.

Cochran, L. H. Inservice education: Passive-complacent-reality. *Theory into Practice,* 1975, **14**, 5-10.

Coleman, P. Organizational effectiveness in education: Its measurement and enhancement. *Interchange,* 1972, **3**(1), 42-52.

Colton, D., Husk, W., Krachniak, S., Kritek, W., & LaPlant, J. Professional development for urban administration. *NASSP Bulletin,* 1975, **59**, 13-20.

Comras, J., & Masterman, R. A rationale for comprehensive in-service programs. *The Clearing House,* 1972, **46**(7), 424-426.

Consortium approach to planned change: A review and evaluation. Midwest Center/Satellite Consortium for Planned Change in Pupil Personnel Programs for Urban Schools. Bloomington, Ind.: Indiana University, School of Education, Department of Counseling and Guidance, 1975.

Cross, R. The administrative team or decentralization? *National Elementary Principal,* 1974, **54**, 80-82.

Cruickshank, D. R. Renewal in graduate teacher education. *Theory into Practice,* 1974, **13**, 149-150.

Davies, D. Reflections on EPDA. *Theory into Practice,* 1974, **13**, 210-217.

Davis, H. L. Preparing principals for action, leadership. *NASSP Bulletin,* 1974, **58**, 29-37.

Davis, J. B. A case study: Change in a big city school district. *Journal of Teacher Education,* 1975, **26**, 47-51.

Doll, R., Love, R., & Levine, D. Systems renewal in a big city school district: The lessons of Louisville. *Phi Delta Kappan,* 1973, **14**(8), 524-534.

Duffin, R. Increasing organization effectiveness. *Training and Development Journal,* 1973, **27**(4), 37-46.

Eberly, D. J. An action-learning program that provides a change. *NASSP Bulletin,* 1974, **58**(380), 30-36.

Engel, M. Practices and pre-requisites in educational change. *Phi Delta Kappan,* 1974, **15**(7), 457-459.

English, F. Teacher may I? Take three giant steps! The differentiated staff. *Phi Delta Kappan,* 1969, **51**(4), 211-214.

Eurich, A. C. Recommendations for changing the urban school. *NASSP Bulletin,* 1971, **57**(351), 185-193.

Feitler, F. C., & Lippitt, L. L. A multi-district organizational development effort. *Educational Technology,* 1972, **12**(10), 34-38.

Felicetti, R. F. Are you communicating internally? *NASSP Bulletin,* 1974, **58**(378), 22-25.

Finkelstein, L. B. Implementation: Essentials for success. *NASSP Bulletin,* 1973, **57**(347), 39-41.

Finnegan, H. Into thy hands . . . : Staff development. *Theory into Practice,* 1972, **11**(4), 215-224.

Flynn, C. W. Management effectiveness by organizational development. *NASSP Bulletin,* 1974, **58**, 135-142,

Fordyce, J. K., & Weil, R. *Managing with people: A manager's handbook of organization development methods.* Reading, Mass.: Addison-Wesley, 1971.

Forter, W. J. Delegation: A needed ingredient for effective administration. *The Clearing House,* 1972, **46**(7), 395-398.

Gallesich, J. Organizational factors influencing consultation in schools. *Journal of School Psychology,* 1973, **11**(1), 57-65.

Goble, N. Planning community involvement in school decision making. *Pennsylvania Educator,* 1972, **3**(6), 4-5.

Goldman, S., & Moynihan, W. J. Problems in educational planning at the school district level. *Educational Technology,* 1975, **15**, 14-19.

Goodlad, J. I. Staff development: The league model. *Theory into Practice,* 1972, **11**(4), 207-214.

Goodlad, J. I. The child—his school in transition. *National Elementary Principal,* 1973, **52**(4), 28-34.

Gorman, B. W. Change in the secondary school: Why and how? *Phi Delta Kappan,* 1972, **53**(9), 565-568.

Graham, R. A. Educational change and the Teacher Corps. *Phi Delta Kappan,* 1970, **51**(6), 305-309.

Gregore, A. F., & Hendrix, D. F. Are turned-off teachers turning off your schools? *School Management,* 1973, **17**(3), 8-9.

Hanson, M. On stability, change and accountability. *NASSP Bulletin,* 1971, **55**(357), 15-24.

Hanson, M. Structural and administrative decentralization in education: A clarification of concepts. *Journal of Educational Administration,* 1972, **10**(1), 95-103.

Hart, L. A. Necessary ingredients for retraining teachers. *NASSP Bulletin,* 1973, **57**(377), 9-18.

Havelock, R. G. *A guide to innovation in education.* Ann Arbor, Mich.: University of Michigan, Center for Research on the Utilization of Knowledge, 1970.

Havelock, R. G. A critique: Has organizational development become a social technology? *Educational Technology,* 1972, **12**(10), 61-62.

Havelock, R. G. *The change agent's guide to innovation education.* Englewood Cliffs, N.J.: Educational Technology Publications, 1973.

Havelock, R., Huber, J., & Zimmerman, S. *Major works on change in education: An annotated bibliography with author and subject indexes.* Ann Arbor, Mich.: University of Michigan, Center for Research and Utilization of Scientific Knowledge, 1969.

Hess, F., & Greenstein, G. Organizational development: An idea whose time has come. *Educational Technology,* 1972, **12**(10), 57-60.

Hetzel, R., & Barnard, D. The human agenda: Critical variable in innovation. *Educational Leadership,* 1973, **30**(6), 526-529.

Hocking, T. K., & Schnier, R. R. Humanizing education by training the faculty. *Personnel and Guidance Journal,* 1974, **52**, 603-608.

Hook, J. N. *One dollar gets you ten: TTT as an educational catalyst.* Durant, Okla.& Southeastern State College Research Foundation, 1972.

Huber, J. Accepting accountability. *The Clearing House,* 1974, **48**, 515-517.

Hull, W. L. Installing innovations via inservice education. *Theory into Practice,* 1975, **14**, 43-48.

Husarik, E. A., & Wynkoop, R. J. A principal's dilemma: Can supervision be collegial? *NASSP Bulletin,* 1974, **58**, 13-19.

Irwin, J. R. Can large schools be humanized through school organization? *NASSP Bulletin,* 1973, **57**(373), 143-145.

Jacobs, J. A model for program development and evaluation. *Theory into Practice,* 1974, **13**(1), 15-21.

Jones, M., & Stanford, G. Transforming schools into learning communities. *Phi Delta Kappan,* 1973, **55**(3), 201-224.

Kier, W. R. Humanizing large schools: One school's experience. *NASSP Bulletin,* 1973, **57**(373), 146-150.

Kinghorn, J. R. Individually guided education: A high school change program. *NASSP Bulletin,* 1974, **58**(380), 24-29.

Klopf, G. J. The principal as an educational leader in the elementary school. *Journal of Research and Development in Education,* 1972, **5**(3), 119-125.

Klopf, G. J., Blake, S. M., Scheldon, E. S., & Burnes, J. C. A taxonomy of educational leadership. *National Elementary Principal,* 1974, **53**, 47-53.

Klotz, J., & Semmann, K. Supervision in today's labor-management crisis. *NASSP Bulletin,* 1974, **58,** 20-25.

Knoepfel, R. W. The politics of planning man in the decision process. *Long Range Planning,* 1973, **6**(1), 17-21.

Koble, D. E., Jr., & Gray, K. E. The planning process as an inservice activity. *Theory into Practice,* 1975, **14,** 34-42.

Lamb, G. Programmed self-renewal. *NASSP Bulletin,* 1972, **56**(362), 84-87.

Leeper, R. R. *Changing supervision for changing times.* Washington, D.C.: Association for Supervision and Curriculum Development, 1969.

Lehman, L. Organizational change and the teacher. *Educational Technology,* 1972, **12**(10), 52-54.

Levine, D. M., Derr, C. B., and Junghans, R. P. Educational planning with organizational development: A people-involving approach to systematic planning. *Educational Technology,* 1972m **12**(10), 14-26.

Mack, F. R. P. Organizational model for a school training center. *Educational Technology,* 1975, **15,** 32-33.

Malcolm, D. D. The center satellite model: Grand strategy for change. *Personnel and Guidance Journal,* 1974, **52**(5), 303-308.

Mattleman, M. S. Staff development: Band-aid or treatment? *Educational Leadership,* 1973, **30**(8), 754-755.

McDonough, P. J. Administration decentralization. *NASSP Bulletin,* 1974, **58**(381), 43-47.

Medway, F. J. A social psychological approach to internally based change in the schools. *Journal of School Psychology,* 1975, **13,** 19-27.

Merrow, J., Foster, R., & Estes, N. Networking: A survival mechanism for urban superintendents. *Phi Delta Kappan,* 1974, **56,** 283-285.

Merullo, E. A. Inservice programs for principals. *NASSP Bulletin,* 1974, **58,** 142-147.

Meyer, J. C. Steps for revitalizing schools. *NASSP Bulletin,* 1974, **58**(379), 89-92.

Mickler, W. A., Jr. New roles can facilitate change. *Educational Leadership,* 1972, **29**(6), 515-517.

Mohan, M., & Hull, R. E. A model for inservice education of teachers. *Educational Technology,* 1975, **15,** 41-44.

Myers, D. A., & Sinclair, R. Improved decision making for school organizations: What and what for. *National Elementary Principal,* 1973, **52**(4), 43-50.

Ogletree, J. R. Changing supervision in a changing era. *Educational Leadership,* 1972, **29**(6), 507-510.

Ornstein, A. C. School decentralization: Descriptions of selected systems. *NASSP Bulletin,* 1975, **59,** 13-20.

Owens, R. G., & Steinhoff, C. R. Strategies for improving inner-city schools. *Phi Delta Kappan*, 1969, **51**(5), 259-263.

Prash, J. New roles for educators. *Educational Leadership*, 1972, **29**(6), 499-502.

Rhodes, L. Linking strategies for change: Process may be the product. *Phi Delta Kappan*, 1969, **51**(4), 204-207.

Rogers, J. W., & Wolley, R. S. Teachers take over and the results are good. *School Management*, 1974, **18**, 36-39.

Sarason, S. B. *The culture of the school and the problem of change*. Boston: Allyn & Bacon, 1971.

Sarason, S. B. The principal and the power to change. *National Elementary Principal*, 1974, **53**, 47-53.

Schmidt, S. M., & Kochan, T. A. Conflict toward conceptual clarity. *Administration Science Quarterly*, 1972, **17**(3), 359-370.

Schmuck, R. Developing collaborative decision-making: The importance of trusting, strong, and skillful leaders. *Educational Technology*, 1972, **12**(10), 43-47.

Schmuck, R. A. Humanizing the school organization. *Catalyst for Change*, 1972, **2**(2), 26-27.

Schmuck, R. A., & Miles, M. B. (Eds.) *Organization development in schools*. Palo Alto, Calif.: National Press Books, 1971.

Schmuck, R. A., Runkel, P., Saturen, S., Martell, R., & Derr, C. B. *Handbook of organization development in schools*. Palo Alto, Calif.: National Press Books, 1972.

Sergiovanni, T. J. Leadership, behavior, and organizational effectiveness. *Journal of Education*, 1973, **4**(1), 15-24.

Sergiovanni, T. J., & Carver, F. D. *Organizations and human behavior: Focus on schools*. New York: McGraw-Hill, 1969.

Sisson, R. L. How did we ever make decisions before the systems approach? *Socio-Economic Planning Sciences*, 1972, **6**(6), 523-539.

Stiles, L. J. Certification and preparation of educational personnel. *Phi Delta Kappan*, 1969, **50**(8), 477-480.

Swaab, A. M. Organizational change and the principal. *Educational Technology*, 1972, **12**(10), 55-57.

Travers, R. M. W. (Ed.) *Second Handbook of Research on Teaching*. Chicago: Rand McNally, 1973.

Trump, J. L. Principal: Most potent factor in determining school excellence. *NASSP Bulletin*, 1972, **56**(362), 4-9.

Trump, J. L., & Georgiades, W. "Doing better with what you have": NASSP model schools project. *NASSP Bulletin*, 1970, **54**(346), 106-133.

Trump, J. L., & Georgiades, W. Which element of school programs are easier to change and which are most difficult and why? *NASSP Bulletin, 1971*, **55**(355), 54-68.

Trump, J. L., & Georgiades, W. Factors that facilitate and limit change. *NASSP Bulletin,* 1973, **57**(373), 93-102.

Tye, K. The principal as a change agent. *National Elementary Principal,* 1970, **49**(4), 41-51.

Tyrrell, R. W. The open middle school: A model for change. *NASSP Bulletin,* 1974, **58**, 62-66.

Umans, S. *The management of education: A systematic design for educational revolution.* Garden City, N.Y.: Doubleday, 1971.

Unruh, G. Staff development in the university city. *Theory into Practice,* 1972, **11**(4), 230-234.

Wayson, W. W. Educating for renewal in urban communities. *National Elementary Principal,* 1972, **51**(61), 6-18.

Wayson, W. W. A proposal to remake the principalship. *National Elementary Principal,* 1974, **54**, 28-44.

Whitcomb, D. B. Renewal in higher education. *Education and Urban Society,* 1975, **7**, 182-186.

Williamson, J. N. The inquiring school: Toward a model of organizational self renewal. *Educational Forum,* 1974, **38**, 393-410.

Wood, F. H. A climate for innovation. *Educational Leadership,* 1973, **30**(6), 516-518.

The Supervision Process: Analysis and Synthesis

DEWAYNE J. KURPIUS AND RONALD D. BAKER

CONCLUSIONS AND SUMMARY

The purpose of the first part of this final chapter is to summarize, integrate, and cross-reference common themes in the preceding reviews and commentaries on the supervision of applied training in counseling, psychotherapy, psychiatry, teacher education, social work, and renewal training. In the second part, the editors will present their observations about various explicit and implicit matters generated by the contributing authors. Hence the theme of review and criticism extends into this summation with the intention of generating questions about supervision in applied training in the socially and behaviorally influencing professions as a whole and as unique enterprises. The wealth of professional tradition, social context, and service domain is largely leveled in the topical summaries in this part. The intent of these summarizations is to identify commonalities and noteworthy differences among the review articles and to point out strengths and deficiencies in literature content. A subject index is given after each summary to assist the reader in quickly locating specific issues discussed and reported by the contributing authors.

The initial part of this chapter is organized around eight topics or subject themes that emerged from the literature as highly significant. They appear in most, if not all, of the reviews. The topics are: (1) goals of supervised training—intended aims and outcomes for supervision; (2) models of supervised training—conceptual frameworks and representations of supervisory processes; (3) supervisory roles—positions and status of individuals in supervisory roles; (4) supervision skills—knowledge, skills, and talents necessary for the supervisor in the conduct of applied training; (5) techniques of supervision—methods, media, and programs employed in the conduct of supervised training; (6) evaluation of supervision—determining the quality of the supervisory process and outcomes; (7) research issues in supervision—problems and deficits in inquiry into supervision; and (8) historical trends in supervision—issues of change in the professions.

First, let us return to the original definition of supervision. *Supervision is the conceptualization, implementation, control, and management of training in applied circumstances and conditions.* It is the extension and transfer of classroom, laboratory, and tutorial instruction into the applied or field setting. Supervision for our purposes pertains to the preparation of individuals for professional status, in-service training for professionals maintaining acquired skills, and renewal training for professionals expanding upon and updating previously acquired skills. Our definition of supervision does not include the supervision of professional workers for purposes of inspecting occupational performance.

Conceptualization is the ideational plan of what supervision should be and the part it should play in the total training or educational program. Subsumed under conceptualization are the philosophy, tradition, and mission of the program; the broad assumptions about people and social values as they relate to the professions; and the assumptions about supervisory roles, tasks, and intended outcomes. Conceptualization refers to the network of guidelines for a departmentally applied training program.

Implementation in supervision is the initiation and effecting of action. Training techniques and procedures must be put into motion or application. Implementation connotes the use of tools and craft. In supervision, various tools or methods are used. The conditions under which they are applied depend upon the conceptual framework from which the supervisor operates.

Control is regulation and restraint. Control in the supervision of training begins with defining the scope of the training task based on its goals and objectives. Once these elements are defined, they become the rules which limit implementation.

Management is the purposeful use of certain means to attain an outcome or aim. Management implies a decision-making dimension for goal achievement. The management function in supervision articulates technique application (implementation) and regulation (control) with a plan of evaluation toward a desired training goal.

Such terms as *control* and *management* portray supervision as a planned, goal-oriented training activity. It cannot be a spontaneous, "fly-by-the-seat-of-the-pants" effort *if* it is to be effective in reaching the intended goals. Even the most existentially or phenomenologically oriented views in the professions directed toward influencing social behaviors exact certain qualities and types of performances from their trainees. Student practitioners are influenced toward a professional model and, even more specifically, toward a value stance within the profession. The effectiveness and efficiency of the influencing process, as in any other training effort, depend upon the coherence of the plan, techniques, execution, and evaluation. Nevertheless, efficient or inefficient, supervisors operate from a plan that dictates the realm and sequence of experiences that will aid their supervisees in approximating a desired professional template.

The eight summaries and indexes introduced earlier follow next. The definition of supervision previously presented applies to each use of "supervision" or "supervision of applied training."

Goals of Supervised Training

Goals are general statements of intent and are often value oriented. They give direction to operations and processes but do not prescribe how the operations are to be mediated. Additionally, goals form the foundation for evaluation and accountability efforts within and between systems of professionals and the public.

In their discussion of supervision in counseling and psychotherapy, Brammer and Wassmer noted that the literature principally contained statements about how supervision was to be conducted and gave little justification or direction for the suggested methods. A general lack of agreement about goals for supervision and inadequately operationalized goal statements characterize the literature of the fields, with perhaps the exception of the social work area.

Kagan and Werner observed in the psychiatric literature not only ambiguous statements of goals but also insufficient definitions of the various facets of supervision. Similarly, in teacher education Smith found scant description of intentions for supervisors' activities but did observe that goals were set for student teachers. Abilities and opportunities to study and evaluate supervisory processes or outcomes suffer in the absence of goal declarations. Consequently, supervisor accountability cannot be assessed.

In social work, Vargus reported three prominent goals concerning standards of agency service, worker effectiveness, and professionalization. She cited a sizable list of operations supervisors must perform to approximate the goals. It appears that the setting for supervision in the social service agency permits, if not demands, goal clarification to facilitate agency missions of public service. Supervisor goals are seemingly agency goals.

The issue of goal specification is addressed by all of the authors. Their observations consistently point toward two themes: goals are either undefined or directed to supervisees' rather than supervisors' performances.

Goals of supervised training are discussed on the following pages:

COUNSELING AND PSYCHOTHERAPY

PSYCHIATRY

Goal attainment scaling method	36
Multiple supervision for multiple goals	24
Objectives within systems approaches	31

RENEWAL TRAINING

Lack of clear definition	183
Long- and short-range goals	214
Measuring organizational goal achievement	189
"Shoulds" for change	188

SOCIAL WORK

Belief systems	161
Goals of supervision	159

TEACHER EDUCATION

Evaluation goals	127
Goals for student teachers, not for supervisors	105
Need for intermediate objectives	105
Professional and personal objectives	105
Purposes of supervisory visits	107

Models of Supervised Training

A model is a representation of an object, event, procedure, or abstraction. It provides a conceptual base for relating factors, variables, events, and roles geared to achieving a desired end. Within the literature of the five fields explored, role and model are occasionally used synonymously, as in "supervisor-as-therapist-model." Role is incorrectly defining a model in this instance. An individual, a supervisor, may function in diverse roles in a given model of supervision. Techniques also are expressed at times as models, again incorrectly. "Team supervision," for example, is a technique for supervising, but it connotes no goal in itself. Models define roles and their interrelationships. Models have goal orientations and seldom prescribe or imply any technique for achieving a goal.

Six models of supervision are expressed directly or implicitly in the reviews and discussions. These models are teaching, counseling, consultation, evaluation, administration, and organizational change. The first five models pertain to supervisory roles and functions with minimal concern for the applied setting; the last centers upon the organizational context and the roles within it.

The most common model described in psychiatry, social work, teacher education, counseling, and psychotherapy is *supervision as teaching* or instruction. Supervision in this mode is an extension of classroom and laboratory instruction into the field or applied setting. There is particular emphasis upon cognitive development of the supervisee in problem identification, problem solving, and information processing. Supervision conveyed by the teaching model dominates teacher education and psychiatry, which also stresses diagnostics and hypothesis generation. The importance of the teaching model in counseling and psychotherapy, however, depends greatly upon the philosophical and conceptual view of behavior change taken by the supervisor or program. For example, those oriented toward psychoanalytic, cognitive, and behavioral therapies or intervention tend to adopt strong teaching modes of supervision.

Consultation is implied or described as perhaps the second most employed approach to supervision. Consultation implies shared problem definition, problem solving, and evaluation between supervisor and supervisee. It is, in short, a collaborative enterprise. There is a suggestion in the literature that consultation becomes a more dominant mode of supervision as the trainee becomes increasingly able and professional in his performance.

In preparing professionals for teaching, counseling, and psychotherapy, a *therapy* model is often applied to effect supervision. Therapeutic supervision centers upon the affective domain of the supervisee and upon the relationship between or among those in the supervisory process. Smith, in teacher education, describes a therapeutic approach to supervision as being seen as desirable to trainees following the previously described instructional supervision. In counseling and psychotherapy, therapy-oriented supervision dominates in existential, phenomenological, and interpersonal process viewpoints.

In addition to teaching and consultative supervision in social work, Vargus describes an *administration* model for supervision.

This model emphasizes social agency case management and service delivery to agency clientele. It is unique to social work and reflects a well-defined public service structure.

Smith, in teacher education, discusses an *evaluation* model of supervision in which critical appraisal of supervisee performance is essentially the goal. The concept of evaluation in this approach is quite narrow; it is noncorrective evaluation or feedback about practice teaching performance. It tends to be negative in content and usually occurs near or at the end of the field training experience. Even though this model is seldom advocated in the literature, it is, Smith notes, widely applied in practice.

McGreevy and Rosengren project a *renewal training* model for organizational change which frames supervision in a complex interaction among clients and client systems. The previously identified models of supervision concern the change or development of trainees in a specified situation. The renewal model has two intents: client change and the management of systems change to maintain sensitivity to consumer needs. Client systems may be a school, a school district, a complex of schools, service agencies, training institutions, *and* the consumer populations (clients) they serve.

Models are discussed on the following pages:

COUNSELING AND PSYCHOTHERAPY

PSYCHIATRY

RENEWAL TRAINING

Supervisory Roles

Role, that is, position and function in a social framework, is defined by the model of operation. The concept of role in relation to a model, as defined in the previous section, speaks to the matter of purposeful social action in a goal-oriented structure. Shaping roles within the social structure are the traditions, rituals, and norms operating in any social unit. It is sufficient to say that in an instructional model of supervision, the supervisor functions as a teacher, in a therapeutic model as a counselor, and so forth. Despite the variety of methods of teaching or counseling, for example (which will be examined in the discussion of techniques), the issue of role focuses on the supervisor's status and authority and the basis for such recognition.

The concept of role status in supervision requires an examination of the equality or relative inequality in social position of the supervisor and supervisee. Excepting the therapeutic and consultative models, the role position of the supervisor is higher than that of the supervisee. The therapeutic and consultative models reflect supervisor-supervisee collaboration for some desired and agreed upon end; consequently, their role positions emerge largely as equal but with different responsibilities.

The supervisor brings to the training scene experience and expertise in a specialty. The supervisee brings a problem to be solved and the capability for its resolution. Their equivalence of role is based upon complementary functions. This equality also includes shared evaluation of performances and training outcomes on clients.

Brammer and Wassmer (counseling and psychotherapy), Smith (teacher education), Vargus (social work), and Kagan and Werner (psychiatry) describe the principal role of the supervisor as that of teacher. Adjunctive roles are also described and are expected by the supervisees. Therapist roles are frequent in counseling, psychotherapy, and psychiatry; and administrative roles are prominent in social work. McGreevy and Rosengren describe an organizational intervention and problem-solving role necessary for renewal purposes.

The effects of the supervisory roles upon the supervisees are evident in educational and personal dimensions. Through supervision, learning acquired in classroom and laboratory settings is transferred into the field setting. The demands of the applied setting not only require integration of diverse experiences and knowledge from earlier situations but also promote new or continued education beyond the lecture hall. A major reported effect is in the personal development and self-understanding experienced by supervisees in the course of their field training. Kagan and Werner and Vargus cite additionally the effect of the supervisor as a professional role model; but they suggest that although this is a common element of supervision, it is not formally structured into the supervisory activity. Supervision is the primary avenue for professionalization and socialization into a field of service. Unfortunately, the supervisee may not be able to distinguish between the supervisor as a trainer and the supervisor as a practitioner with a personal style and value orientation.

Although the literatures of the professions report different roles taken by supervisors in the course of their work, they uniformly fail to identify the conditions or criteria for performing different roles—teacher, therapist, consultant, and so forth—in the sequence experienced by supervisees. How and when it comes about is unspecified.

Supervisory roles are discussed on the following pages:

Supervisory Skills

Skill is technical proficiency, the ability to use one's knowledge effectively in performance. Skills necessary for supervisors seemingly would be linked directly to the models of applied training which they employ or which are integrated in the training program. The literatures suggest and describe some important supervisor skills but do not relate them to any particular model.

Some commonly identified skills needed by supervisors are those of: (1) an observer—a necessary first step in orienting students to critical events in training, in detecting student strengths and weaknesses, and in formulating instructional sequences; (2) a diagnostician of symptoms and problem situations; (3) a problem solver— interrelated with diagnosis, problem conceptualization, hypothesis generation, intervention application, and prognostication; and (4) a model of professional competence and manner. Additionally, and only alluded to, the supervisor needs a knowledge base and ability as a teacher in order to facilitate the primary supervisory role. There is an expressed desire on behalf of the supervisees that the supervisor also be skilled in recognizing their needs as individuals in the professionalization change process.

Other specific requirements have been noted. In social work and psychiatry, case management skills are required. Case management involves different skills in the two areas, the delivery of medical-psychotherapeutic treatment versus the delivery of social services. In addition, agency administration skills are usually needed by supervisors in the social work field.

Three important issues are not discussed in the professional literatures. First, the criteria for determining acceptable or minimal supervisor abilities are undefined. Supervisors, it seems, come to their applied training roles by credential and position more than by competency. Second, abilities of a supervisor emanating from personal style and social competence (unlikely to be trained abilities) are not distinguished from trained professional abilities. This condition breeds further problems in specifying acceptable levels of supervisor competency. Third, the effects of supervisor skill levels and applications stand unevaluated. What makes a "good supervisor" is still ambiguous. Consequently, planned training of supervisors and criteria for selecting supervisors are unexplored or at least unreported themes.

Supervisory skills are discussed on the following pages:

COUNSELING AND PSYCHOTHERAPY

Facilitative conditions	48
Levels of supervisor functioning	51
Qualifications and preparation of supervisors	81
Supervisor-supervisee relationship	60

PSYCHIATRY

Altering attitudes	17
Attitudes and traits	17
Enduring attributes of medical practice	14
Consultation in nonmedical settings	13
Coping with anxiety, identity, and guilt	18
Core skills and functions	19
Multidimensional supervision	15
Preventing dehumanizaiton	17
Psychiatrists and non-psychiatric physicians	13

RENEWAL TRAINING

Leadership	190
Principal as norm setter and model	191

SOCIAL WORK

Importance of positive attitudes toward workers and clients	170

TEACHER EDUCATION

Attitudinal and personality factors	98
Interpersonal relationships	98
Style	102

Techniques of Supervision

The techniques, methods, and strategies of supervision in applied training are directed toward instructional aims of skill and knowledge acquisition. Although attitudinal and value development occur in the training process, little is reported about systematic efforts to influence them.

The dominant approach to applied training across all of the professions is a didactic one. Direct instruction by an expert to one or a small cluster of students is the current and traditional mode of training. The didactic process is the matrix in which more specific techniques are embedded. Uses of texts, journals, and other literature resources are classified under this process. Experiential events in field training tend to be incorporated into the didactic approach to further instructional aims. Face-to-face experience with clients and patients provides a medium for: (1) the development of observational and diagnostic skills, (2) the supervised application of intervention or service strategies, and (3) the feedback of evaluative information about applied performances. The aim of such experiences is to further the *supervisor's* instructional objectives.

In counseling and psychotherapy, Brammer and Wassmer discuss experiential training to promote student self-understanding in the self- and phenomenologically-oriented therapies and counseling approaches. Although the process may pertain to reaching program goals of self-awareness for the trainee, it is adjunctive to the field experiences and is seen only as a necessary condition for advancing the student's abilities with clients. The specific impact of such experiences cannot be predicted for any particular student learner, and the purposes of the experiences can only be stated in a broad and nebulous fashion. Smith, in teacher education, and Vargus, social work, describe student interest in having more self-oriented experiences, especially in later training stages. In psychiatry, Kagan and Werner provide evidence of increased needs for self and interpersonal process experiences in the medical profession as a whole but do not describe the process.

Specific techniques to augment the teaching process are described in all of the literatures. The case study method pervades psychiatry, social work, counseling, and psychotherapy. Modeling, demonstration, and simulation also are common to all the professions.

Relatively recent developments in film and video-mediated instruction appear as innovations. Models and simulations are readily conveyed by these media and can serve to standardize instruction over a period of time and across training sites. Particularly important developments reported in teacher education, counseling, and psychiatry are microinstruction and interpersonal process feedback techniques. These techniques sequentially develop communication, teaching, and self-awareness skills through trial-and-feedback strategies. They capitalize on the best features of film and video-tape for realism and immediacy of information feedback.

Although the one-to-one or individual conference approach to supervision remains as the most common method of didactic or experiential interaction, group methods are increasingly reported; that is, one supervisor and several supervisees meet as a group. Variations on the group theme include peer supervision and multiple supervisor procedures, much like a staffing for a supervisee. Evaluation of group procedures is lacking, but seemingly this technique has the potential for providing the supervisee with multiple conceptual perspectives and sources of feedback about his performance.

Techniques of supervision are discussed on the following pages:

Demonstration	108
Feedback	115
Interaction analysis	110
Microinstruction	112
Observation	107
Technical innovations	111
Visits	106

Evaluation of Supervision

Of the various topics reviewed and discussed throughout this book, perhaps the least amount of space is given to the evaluation of supervision. The literatures are remarkably lacking in this area. Evaluation is the process of measuring and judging the effects of actions and processes within a program or structure relative to specific objectives, goals, or purposes. The intent is to describe to what extent and how well program aims are approximated and attained. The evaluation intent is not a research intent to establish new facts or to define principles and interrelationships among principles. Information acquired in evaluation is not intended to be generalized across programs, settings, populations, or problem themes. It is an accountability effort within a program. A sizable array of evaluation model exist. Their use, however, has scarcely penetrated the applied training facets of the professions examined in this text.

Proper evaluation begins with assessment geared to definitive goal statements. Such statements, as expressed in an earlier section, are rarely explicated for supervision purposes. in the absence of clear or integrated sets of goals for supervisory acts, evaluation of the process as a whole and of the effects of that process, however conducted, is minimal.

Evaluations that do occur concern (1) the effects of specific technique applications to the performances of the supervisees or (2) some global estimate of the quality of supervisee performance in the field site. Supervision and the effect of the supervisor as a source of influence are not evaluated. Rather, pieces of the total effort are assessed and judged. The focus of evaluation is upon the supervisee, not upon the supervisor or the client. In teacher education, psychiatry, counseling, and psychotherapy, evaluation largely is directed to examining changes in supervisee skill levels. These evaluative studies demonstrate the effects of such previously investigated training innovations as video-mediated interpersonal process relationship training, microinstruction, or systematic feedback procedures. In social work as well as in the aforementioned areas, evaluation also takes on the meaning of a broad judgment of professional conduct. Often this type of evaluation is impressionistic and is based upon evidences of professional attitudes and biases, social conduct and personal appearance, and relationships with supervisors. Proficiency in skill and service delivery may constitute a portion of the evaluation, but rarely is the client or patient consulted in this style of evaluation. The supervisor evaluates the supervisee, *not* his own supervisory performance or his and his supervisee's effect on the client. Certain supervisory modes, such as those of therapist and consultant, portray the supervisor as collaborative and nonevaluative. This contradictory condition can produce a guarded performance on the part of the supervisee and can place the supervisor in awkward positions.

The evaluation of supervision is discussed on the following pages:

COUNSELING AND PSYCHOTHERAPY

TEACHER EDUCATION

Research Issues in Supervision

The content of this overview of the articles on research in supervision has been prefaced in the section on goals of supervision. The general absence of defined goals for supervision in any of the fields is evidenced in the quality and breadth of research in supervision and applied training. Given the broadest definition of research—inquiry to discover facts, to show relationships among facts or events, and to apply principles to practical conditions—the literature of the reviewed fields is remarkably lacking. Research methods tend to be limited to case studies, surveys, and correlational investigations. Such designs can be satisfactory for hypothesis generation and can serve as a base for more extensive study but cannot assist practitioners in understanding the effects of the application of specific variables and procedures on outcomes. Consequently, in the absence of interaction studies or experiments, educators and supervisors cannot refine their models, strategies, and outcome assessments. Multivariate designs necessary to contend with recognized complexities of supervisory situations do not appear in research reports.

The inquiries that are available center around professional attitudes, roles, and role expectations in survey modes, and around relationships among personality and social variables and intraining processes in the correlational mode. The small number of experiments or quasi- experiments principally have been directed toward supervisory techniques. Yet the relationship between any particular technique and an encompassing model or theory of supervision is rarely declared. Research in supervision is about training processes—or "how-to-do-it." Outcome studies, that is, examinations of the effects of some supervisory process on the client or patient, are virtually nonexistent. The literature also lacks studies of supervisory research methods and designs.

Instrumentation for the purposes of assessing changes resulting from supervisory intervention is weak. Most assessment procedures are tailored to narrowly defined populations and situations and hence are not easy to generalize for application. Efforts to establish reliability of assessment instruments or procedures are negligible, and demonstrations of validity for outcome or prediction purposes are nonexistent.

Research in supervision suffers from small numbers of subjects in treatment or observational groups. The consequent limitations on statistical inference further restrict the generalizability of the results.

Finally, it is apparent that training sites are not organized for inquiry. Programs tend not to include research as an integral part of the total educational experience. Research is an appendage to applied training and is performed by a handful of practitioners.

Research issues are discussed on the following pages:

COUNSELING AND PSYCHOTHERAPY

Gap between research and practice	43
Lack of outcome research	82
Preexperimental work	80
Research needs	80

PSYCHIATRY

Lack of outcome studies	35
Methodological problems	35
Research in psychotherapy	23

TEACHER EDUCATION

Correlational and factor analytic studies	130
Experimental studies	130
Other research	130
Surveys	130

Historical Trends in Supervision

Supervision has reflected traditions, styles, conceptualizations of problems or issues, technology, and complexities of social institutions across the decades of definable periods. The contributing authors have sketched some historical perspective in their articles, most notably those about social work, teacher preparation, and psychiatry. These fields have represented strong professional traditions and identities since their inceptions.

Trends have been described in terms of models and supervision and techniques of supervision. Vargus in social work and Kagan and Werner in psychiatry explore changing models of supervision concomitant with changing views of problem origins and maintaining factors. These fields in particular were influenced by the influx of psychological and psychotherapeutic concepts and theories which strongly affected the biologically based practices of early psychiatry and the character of the service perspectives in social work. Brammer and Wassmer do not discuss historical events in counseling and psychotherapy per se but do describe the multiplicity of counseling models which have been generated in the past and have affected training within the professions in a manner analogous to psychiatry. The emergence of new models and technical innovations have promoted trends within the professions. Historical trends have been shaped by intraprofessional events rather than by changes in social or public needs.

Techniques of supervision have progressed along similar lines despite the diversity of the professions. Apprenticeship has been the most common approach to field training in the past and present. "Learning by doing" or copying a master practitioner historically has dominated technique. More recent trends in technique have depended upon technological innovations—greater accessibility to publications, electronic communications media, and simulations, for example. And in the medical area, developments in pharmacology have given different dimensions to treatment and consequently to applied training.

The present-to-future orientation of the McGreevy and Rosengren article on renewal training complements the historical perspectives given by the other authors. It differs, however, in its description of the relationship between the professional and the consumer (the client public). Changes in the delivery of professional services depend upon changes in conceptualization and in the base upon which consumer needs influence professional opinions about proper training and service. McGreevy and Rosengren point to the present and future roles of supervisors as increasingly those of environmental interveners and managers. As the context of professional activities is altered, so shall the activities themselves change.

Historical trends are discussed on the following pages:

PSYCHIATRY

RENEWAL TRAINING

SOCIAL WORK

TEACHER EDUCATION

TOWARD A PLANNING MODEL

It seems evident that the study of applied training is in an early developmental phase. Counseling, psychotherapy, psychiatry, teaching, and social work practitioners claim to be searching for more effective, efficient, and relevant ways in which to help their clients. As trainers of new professionals, they also seek more effective training methods. The literature of applied training tells us, however, that the search for more effective educational procedures is usually limited by the traditions in any given profession. As a result, graduates influenced by a particular training program enter the field and try to adjust their clientele to the idealized conceptual framework they learned in training. They are inclined to provide services to people and organizations with little awareness of the true needs of that client or client system and even less awareness of what to utilize from professional history in order to address the present and plan future conditions.

How do we decide how we should prepare our trainees? There appear to be three common practices used to answer this question. One is *task analysis*. This process suggests that we assess the practices of professionals already practicing (counselors, teachers, and psychiatrists, for example) and assume that because they are in the field where all the action is, they know best what is needed for their clients. Consequently, all that trainers need to know is what these practitioners do and then proceed to prepare trainees to do the same things. This approach has some merit because it provides a partial reality check between so-called theory and practice, but what it does not provide is a reality check between client needs and practitioner services. One never knows if the practitioner is adjusting his approach to client needs or if he is adjusting client needs to his approach.

A second way to determine the type of training program is to *assess client needs*. Once a target client or consumer population is identified for a specific institutional program, service needs are defined *with* representatives of that population. Training programs are then developed to help address the consumer needs.

The third approach is to rely on *theory* or theory and philosophy as the base in preparing professionals to deliver client services. This approach is the one most commonly practiced by training institutions. It fits neatly into the traditional practices referred to earlier. The theoretical (or philosophical) viewpoints generally are sufficiently broad or so vaguely defined that individual practitioners and trainers can find great latitude in which to establish their personal styles as models for training and practice. At times personal style and belief determine what viewpoint the professional will choose. Consequently, all he need do is to select a theoretical base which fits his own personal style, select the research literature which supports his beliefs, and begin preparing trainees to perform accordingly. Occasionally, a given training institution will deviate from a theory-based practice, but seldom does it continue this practice. The reasons are many:

1. Conducting needs assessments and task analyses is a complex and demanding process, and most training institutions do not provide adequate resources to carry out these functions.

2. Training personnel have little experience in engaging with practitioners and their clients; and therefore, the interface appears difficult.

3. Training institutions do not reward such creative and futuristic activity because their personnel tend not to understand the need for synergistic practices.

4. Professional organizations (American Medical Association, American Personnel and Guidance Association, and American Psychological Association) tend to be organized around a collegial framework which is a traditional approach to change. This approach is extremely slow to change and is insulated from the outside world.

5. Practitioners have not had the time, energy, or power to influence training institutions to modify their programs.

6. Clients (society) must rely chiefly on political and legislative mechanisms to interact with training institutions to influence change.

7. Future studies, while making great gains, remain very philosophical and lack sophisticated methodologies to impact training programs.

8. Lifelong credentialing is still proposed by professional organizations, universities, and state departments of education as the license to practice and/or train.

9. Continuing and renewed education is still to come; we are at best on the first rung of the ladder.

10. Most organizations are self-maintaining and self-protective. Only a few are concerned with continuous evaluation and development.

This list represents the commonly known practice of catharsis; it is temporarily helpful and generates security through stability. Catharsis is unlikely to promote change. Here we have attempted to propose a framework which will assist in developing an approach to supervision which will interact with task analysis, needs assessment, and theory. We intend only to suggest a framework to stimulate inquiry, which will in turn influence individualized operational definitions of supervision.

Three modes of training which encompass both traditional and more futuristic practices were developed in the literature. These models are summarized and schematically presented, and following Table 2 is an expanded description of the content within each cell.

The models of supervision which are displayed across the chart—teaching, consultative, and therapeutic approaches to supervision—are the dominant modes of training controls and influence in applied areas. For the purpose of illustrating differences and similarities among these training approaches, the three modes are represented as being distinct. In fact and in application, there is likely to be some mixing of modalities—some teaching in consultation, some therapy in teaching, and so forth. Therefore, the boundaries separating the teaching, consulting, and therapy models are not firm barriers but are irregular, "dashed" lines.

The result of comparing the major models in this fashion is that the reader can readily recognize the primary influences and controls within supervisory systems. No value judgments are intended in the sharpening of differences among these approaches. The descriptions within the cells have been distilled from the literature reviewed previously and from future literature. Some assumed differences, including those between therapeutic and instructional approaches to the supervision, cannot be substantiated. Despite the intentions of a therapeutically oriented supervisor in clinical psychology or counseling, for example, the supervisee has no choice in participating in that scheme. The therapeutic model, then, differs little from the teaching model in most conditions.

Teaching, as it is represented in Table 2 and by the literature, is a conventional didactic activity resembling classroom or tutorial instruction. Regardless of media variations, this model implies a controller or manager of information and experiences and a recipient

TABLE 2

Three Modalities of Training

Models Oriented Toward:	Teaching Approach	Consultative Approach	Therapeutic Approach
Goals and Purposes Set by:	Profession/Program/ Supervisor (1)	Profession/Program/ Supervisor/Supervisee (2)	Profession/Program/ Supervisor (3)
Assumptions about Training and Education Held by:	Profession/Program/ Supervisor (4)	Profession/Program/ Supervisor (5)	Profession/Program/ Supervisor (6)
Supervisor Entry Performance Levels and Role Defined by:	Credentials/Position (7)	Expertise/Position (8)	Credentials/Position (9)
Supervisee Entry Performance Levels and Role Defined by:	Credentials/Course Prerequisites (10)	Position/Competence Level (11)	Course Prerequisites (12)
Outcome Objectives for Supervisee Determined by:	Prescription (Per Program and Supervisor) (13)	Negotiation/Prescription (per Program and Supervisor) (14)	Prescription (Per Therapy Approach) (15)
Process Objectives Established by:	Prescription (Per Program and Supervisor) (16)	Negotiation/Prescription (Per Program and Supervisor) (17)	Prescription (Per Therapy Approach) (18)
Process Objectives Influenced by:			
Relationship Style	Task-Oriented	Task-Oriented/Interpersonal-Oriented	Interpersonal-Oriented
Communication Style	Supervisor-Directed	Interactive	Supervisor Initiated
Learning Emphasis	Cognitive	Cognitive/Affective	Affective
Evaluation Control	Supervisor	Shared	Supervisor/Supervisee Self-realization
Power	Position (19)	Expertise (20)	Position/Relationship (21)
Evaluation Based upon:	Program Goals/ Normative Data (22)	Program Goals/ Normative Data/ Criterion Reference/ Supervisee Goals (23)	Program Goals/Supervisor Goals (Per Therapeutic Approach)/Supervisee Goals (Conditional upon Supervisor's Approach) (24)

of such controls and activities. The social relationship is largely governed by the institutional setting and program.

Therapy as a supervisory mode appears principally in the fields of counseling, clinical psychology, and psychiatry. It is not the sole approach to supervision in these professions, but when therapeutic supervision is applied, it is in programs which advocate psychodynamic and self-oriented viewpoints. One major assumption is that a supervisee who understands his own dynamics or self-development can better facilitate change in a client than can a supervisee who does not have this understanding.

Consultation is a blend of the teaching and therapeutic modes plus some unique features. Consultation appears in the literature as a more collaborative, information-based effort between the supervisor and supervisee. The supervisee has responsibilities for generating or expressing training objectives pertinent to his needs and goals. The supervisor as a resource agent may address the supervisee's needs and at the same time direct the supervisee to program objectives or personal objectives based largely on his expertise and specialization.

The following brief descriptions of each cell presented in Table 2 are provided to summarize the great amount of information expressed and implied in supervisory literature.

Cell 1 (teaching): Training goals for the supervisor are interpreted by the supervisor in the light of his professional identity (counseling, teaching, social work, or psychiatry). Program goals are directly linked to professional goals, and it is expected that the learners will internalize these goals as their own during the applied training phase as well as in future practice. There is little reliance on task analysis or needs assessment methodologies for determining learner needs.

Cell 2 (consultative): Training goals for the supervisor are determined through a multidimensional process. That is, program goals have been determined through a process which integrates professional organization goals, practitioner performance (task analysis), client needs (client needs assessment), learner needs (learner needs assessment), and certain theoretical positions which are systematically determined as appropriate.

Cell 3 (therapeutic): Goals are established by selected professional traditions and public missions, by institutional or departmental intentions, but mostly by the supervisor's theoretical approaches to interpersonal change (therapy). The trainees' goals are prescribed by the supervisor according to the theory which he teaches.

Cell 4 (teaching): Certain assumptions about training are held as the most significant. Included are the beliefs that: (1) the knowledge and skills required by the trainee are already known, and the challenge of the trainer is to impart these facts and skills; (2) learner performance is best assessed by the supervisor; and (3) interpersonal skills are less important performance criteria than are those specific facts to be known.

Cell 5 (Consultative): Certain assumptions about training are held as the most significant. First, it is important to understand past practices as we experience the present and plan for the future. Second, training goals are directly related to training outcome. If we do not include the knowledge held by practitioners (task analysis) and if we do not respond to the needs of society (client needs assessment), we will be encouraging clients to follow outdated problem-solving practices. Finally, given a learning culture made up of inquiry norms, problem-solving norms, collaboration norms, and support norms, the learner will achieve the appropriate knowledge, skills, and attitudes to help clients solve their problems.

Cell 6 (therapeutic): Three assumptions about training are held as the most significant. First, interpersonal skill is the single most important competence required of the learner. Second, transfer of training from supervisor and trainer to trainee and client is natural and reliable. Finally, it is unnecessary to prepare the trainee to differentially determine the problem and then to develop a differential plan to solve the problem. All problems can be solved with one theoretical model.

Cell 7 (teaching): Supervisors enter the field of supervision by way of a standard professional and academic credential for that profession. Once entry into the training role is completed, the supervisor operates from the position and authority associated with that position.

Cell 8 (consultative): The supervisor entry performance level is also defined by organizational (institutional) roles and positions, but subsequently competence or expertise in the associated applied field or specialty is required if one is to remain a trainer or supervisor. This competence is determined by reliance on the inquiry approaches used to focus on the past, present, and future methodologies which are assessed as most significant to the trainees and their clients.

Cell 9 (therapeutic): Supervisor entry performance is, once again, based on professional and academic credentials. However, the most important criterion is the supervisor's ability to influence trainees to transfer the therapy model used in training to the clients they are attempting to help. Hence if the training model requires confrontation as a learning strategy, so should a trainee's treatment model.

Cell 10 (teaching): Supervisee entry performance is assumed as normative based on program goals and course prerequisites. Consequently, all trainees receive approximately the same type and amount of supervision.

Cell 11 (consultative): Supervisee entry performance carries some normative data due to the explication of program goals. However, the criteria which will be used to determine successful completion of the experience are used to establish the base rate for trainees who are entering the applied training phase. The difference between the performance expected at the completion of training and the present performance level will determine the primary area of focus for each trainee.

Cell 12 (therapeutic): The supervisee entry performance and role are immediately defined by the supervisor through the constructs of the therapeutic approach used for training. Regardless of the interpersonal skills possessed by the trainees upon entry, each trainee will follow the same supervision sequence.

Cell 13 (teaching): Outcome objectives for the supervisee are prescribed by the supervisor. It is assumed that these objectives are directly related to trainee needs upon entry into applied training and professional requirements upon completion of the training.

Cell 14 (consultative): Outcome objectives are negotiated but are directly related to: (1) program goals which have been validated by practitioner task analysis, client needs assessment, and program concept analysis; (2) trainee goals based upon the future position desired; and (3) trainee needs based upon the entry level of performance and upon supervisor objectives related to his values and beliefs about applied training.

Cell 15 (therapeutic): Supervisee outcome objectives are prescribed by the supervisor and are based primarily upon the supervisor's theory of counseling or therapy. Supervision in this mode relies heavily upon modeling and reinforcement strategies. The therapy theory and model used by the trainer becomes the model for the trainee to develop and demonstrate. As the trainee approximates that model to the supervisor, positive reinforcement begins and increases as the approximations increase.

Cell 16 (teaching): Process objectives closely follow the outcomes prescribed by the supervisor. Most processes are predetermined (for example, each trainee will develop and critique five micro-counseling sessions) by the supervisor.

Cell 17 (consultative): Process objectives are identified and agreed upon by the supervisor and supervisee following a clear definition and acceptance of the outcome expected.

Cell 18 (therapeutic): Process objectives are dictated by the counseling or therapy approach followed by the supervisor. It is expected that the trainee will adjust to these processes and begin to demonstrate the impact of the processes.

Cell 19 (teaching): Process objectives are influenced by five factors. Included are: (1) a relationship style which focuses on tasks to be performed by the trainee; (2) a communication pattern which is directed by the supervisor; (3) a learning pattern with emphasis on cognitive development; (4) evaluation which is controlled by the supervisor; and (5) a power base which is legitimated by the supervisor's position.

Cell 20 (consultative): Process objectives are influenced by five factors. These are: a supervisor-supervisee relationship which establishes a balance between tasks to be performed and the interpersonal elements necessary to understand each other and to work collaboratively to reach the outcome objectives previously stated; (2) a communication pattern which is synergistic; (3) a learning pattern emphasizing both cognitive and affective development with the phases being negotiated; (4) evaluation which is clearly defined and equally shared; and (5) the supervisor's power which is mostly based on expertise and not position. Some relationship power may exist, but it is equally distributed and controlled by both the supervisor and supervisee.

Cell 21 (therapeutic): Process objectives are influenced by five factors. Included are: (1) a relationship style which is interpersonally oriented; (2) a communication style prescribed by the supervisor; (3) emphasis on learning about the affective domain; (4) evaluation approaches which are implicitly expressed by the supervisor; and (5) a supervisor power base which relies heavily upon the supervisor's position and the supervisee's ability to develop a satisfactory relationship with the supervisor.

Cell 22 (teaching): Evaluation of the final product is directly linked to the supervisor's interpretation of the goals of the program as related to the tasks which trainees should perform. Most assessment is norm referenced according to other trainees in the program.

Cell 23 (consultative): Evaluation of the final product is based on several factors. First, did the trainee meet the criterion level stated upon entry into the training? Second, has the trainee developed an evaluation model appropriate for evaluating not only his present performance but also his future performances? Third, does the evaluation model used account for both cognitive and affective variables? Fourth, do the supervisor and supervisee agree on the final evaluation of the trainee? And finally, have trainee, supervisor, program, and professional goals been met?

Cell 24 (therapeutic): Evaluation of the final product is based upon the trainee's ability to fit into the supervisor's therapeutic model. At this final stage, the supervisor expects the trainee to be able to assess himself accurately while following the guidelines provided by the therapy model which has been followed.

Scant mention is made in the professional literatures about the application of multiple models of supervision within any given training context. Writers tend to portray training models as fixed over the duration of applied experiences for any student. That is, it may be implied that the same teaching model is used from the time a student is accepted into field experience training until he graduates into the ranks of the profession. In fact, observation of training shows that there is increased use of a consultative mode of supervision as the student moves further into the applied track.

As the student becomes increasingly proficient, according to whatever standards are being used, his supervisor will be more likely to take a collaborative role.

Each of the substantive chapters in this book contains observations by the authors about the lack of research and evaluation in the supervisory processes regardless of the field. What inquiry does exist is limited to methods of implementing philosophical or conceptual precepts and does not involve questioning the precepts themselves. The consequence is that professional traditions and precedents are the guidelines for supervision. The manner in which the profession is practiced upon the public clientele is also the method of supervision. In counseling, for example, Ryan, Baker, Hosford, and Fitzpatrick (1969) made a national survey of counselor educators and found that counselors train and supervise students largely in the same manner in which they treat clients. They apply their models of counseling to their approaches to field training. This condition is understandable. An accomplished practitioner is likely to apply what he knows best about behavioral, attitudinal, and cognitive change to any change-demanding situation. Few practitioners in any of the professions reviewed here are trained in educational methods. Lacking such training themselves, but having at hand well-developed models for effecting human change, practitioners tend to rely upon personal experiences, case examples, professional standards, and institutional regulations or objectives to determine how and to what end they supervise field training. Hansen, Pound and Petro (1976) reinforce the need for more comprehensive research in an article titled "Review of Research on Practicum Supervision" with the statement "current research that is not based on a thorough review of past works or that fails to replicate the experimental conditions becomes an isolated entity, at best accidently relevant" (p. 114).

This approach to supervision is a traditional one: the passing on of information, values, and customs by word of mouth and personal example from seniors in the profession to neophytes. Traditions are hard to modify. They provide a strong value system and security to those who participate in them. Data which may be gathered within the context of the tradition tends to fortify and strengthen the position. Inquiry and data gathering is bound by the dimensions and values of the tradition and is often highly subjective in nature. In many instances, it simply does not meet sound research standards.

The traditional approach to training and supervision is a closed system. It begins, as it were, with a belief, and all activities within the training system reflect back upon that belief. Information external to the belief system is either interpreted (or reinterpreted) in terms compatible to the system or is rejected. Traditions and beliefs cannot be "researched" away. One accepts or rejects the assumptions of a traditional system on faith. As de Bono (1970) observes, "General agreement about an assumption is no guarantee that it is correct. It is historical continuity that maintains most assumptions—not a repeated assessment of their validity [p. 91]."

In order to approximate the suggested research and evaluation goals recommended by the contributing authors, we need a plan which will open those areas, at least, to closer professional and public scrutiny. An alternative to the traditional system of applied supervision has been described sketchily. For purposes of identification it may be called a data-based system. The data base for this approach to training is developed from needs assessments of practitioners and their clientele, task analyses of practitioners' performance demands and expectations, and competency levels determined by program developers and supervisors. A traditional approach may also have a data base, but it is an informational system related to the processes which support or are supposed to implement the viewpoint, values, and assumptions of the tradition. Consequently, the collection of information about supervisee performance and the establishment of standards for such performance are internal to the tradition. They are, in short, process oriented. In contrast, the data-based approach to training centers primarily on the outcome effects of supervisee performances upon the client population. This approach incorpoates client population needs and social trends into the determination of training procedures.

The differences between the two approaches may be stated in the following manner. The traditional approach asks what the supervisee must know and do in order to apply effectively System X. (System X is presumed to be good for clients.) The data-based approach asks what the supervisee must know and do in order to meet clientele needs and consequent performance competencies. The latter approach permits greater opportunity for the training program and the supervisory methods to be influenced by public wants and by research from fields outside the profession in question. Data-based training may also anticipate future public needs and social trends, while traditional training tends to be exclusively reflective of historical methods and values.

It is important to note that we are not condemning all traditions in the human and social service professions. We are challenging, however, the tendency within traditional systems to disregard self-evaluation, examination of assumptions and methods, and maintenance of accountability for services and practices within training and clientele populations. Similarly, we are not suggesting that client needs assessment alone should provide the data base for applied training and services. Such a system would tend toward following fads or satisfying temporary social trends and local needs.

A reasonable, if not ideal, system of applied training would simultaneously accommodate professional values and ethics, trainee and clientele needs, and sound inquiry or evaluative procedures.

The amount of literature providing guidelines for the data-based approach to supervision is negligible. The approach as a whole offers some appealing directions for remedying some of the complaints of the reviewers about the dearth of inquiry and evaluation in the supervisory arena. We suggest a plan for generating a data-based approach to applied training drawn from a work by Worthen and Sanders (1973). We have modified their presentation considerably. We believe, however, that this scheme can aid developers of applied training programs to establish self-correcting, accountable training procedures. At the same time, this plan can assist those participating in ongoing training programs to begin inspection and perhaps modification efforts within their systems.

The plan may be realized in three general stages: *preparation to develop a training program, implementation of a training program,* and *renewal or adjustment of a training program.* These are developmental stages involving a time continuum. Each stage has four activity components—*setting goals or intentions, conducting observations of goal-related events, setting assessment standards,* and *evaluating efforts to achieve the goals.* Strategies for attaining goals are purposely not discussed. Techniques and programming ventures must be considered in relation to specific training demands, student and client population characteristics, facilities, institutional resources, and so on. It would be presumptuous to expound upon strategy selection, for it should be based upon inquiry into and evaluation of the technique(s) involved. This process should occur among the final steps in programming. It should be emphasized, however, that in traditional training systems, strategy selection usually takes place at the outset of program planning. The training medium is a given element in the training problem. Other programming activities are shaped according to technique selection. At some point, reasons may have been given for a particular course of action. (For example, "Because our practitioners work closely with their fellow human beings, they should be aware of their personal values, beliefs, and psychodynamics.") But as the traditional approach becomes removed in time from its origins, the procedures or strategies themselves become the "intentions" and are construed as goals. (For instance, "We require that our interns undergo psychoanalysis. As a result, they will understand their own personality dynamics and motivations.") Table 3 shows how the developmental and activity parameters can be arranged.

TABLE 3

**Training Program Planning Scheme Relating Programming
Activities to Stages of Program Development**

	Intention	Observation	Assessment	Evaluation
Stage I Preparation				
Stage II Implementation	*DESCRIPTIVE ACTIVITIES*		*JUDGMENTAL ACTIVITIES*	
Stage III Revision/ Renewal				

The classes of activity are cast as descriptive (intentions and observations) or judgmental (assessment standards and evaluation). Descriptive elements concern the specific events to be contained in a training program. These may be program content units or sequences as well as trainee performances. Judgmental elements concern decisions about standards of trainee performance, qualities of program events, and decisions about the degree of adequacy of measured performances and events.

The first stage is the preparatory level for program planning. It contains the broad, general descriptions of program goals, dimensions, and decision parameters. (See Table 4.)

TABLE 4

Activities at the Stage I Level of Program Planning

	Intention	Observation	Assessment	Evaluation
Stage I Program Preparation	Global Goals	Performance Classifications	Parameters of Performance Standards	Decisions about Adequacy of Stage I Features

Superordinate philosophies, values, and wishes frame the intentions (goals) at this level. From these statements are deduced the performance categories expected of the idealized trainee. Standards for anticipated performances would then be established or conjectured. Finally, decisions would be made regarding likely program adequacy and feasibility. The design stage is intended to bring forth the expectations of the program planners and to convert those expectations, values, and so forth into eventually observable, measurable training events. At the first stage, different ideational inputs are desirable, especially in the evaluative efforts. Planners may call upon other professionals or may inspect other programs to gain perspective about their own training and educational projections.

The second stage represents the conversion of wishes and ideals into specific institutional reality. The plans from the first stage are tempered by institutional resources, budgets, personnel, client characteristics, and so forth. (See Table 5.)

TABLE 5

Activities at the Stage II Level of Program Implementation

	Intention	Observation	Assessment	Evaluation
Stage II Program Implementation	Specific Program Goals	Performances and Program Events	Criterion Measurement	Decisions about Adequacy of Measured Performance

Distilled from the global goals of the first stage are the program goals for a specific training effort. Program goals may not address the entire array of desired goals, but they must be appropriate to them. They may not suggest directions contrary to the intentions of the first stage. Trainee performances and training program events are defined according to the training goals. Criterion standards are set, and once performances have been measured, their adequacy is judged.

The first two stages are rather standard expressions of long-standing educational planning and implementation schemes. Most training plans end with the second stage evaluation, if evaluation is attempted on a programmatic basis. The third stage, on the other hand, represents a direction which is necessary if applied training is to be brought into the arena of ongoing social and behavioral research and if programs are to be self-evaluating and self-revising. (See Table 6.)

The intentions of the third stage center upon inquiry goals which lead to program renewal and revision. Deliberate program inspection for modification purposes requires guidelines for implementation in the same way instructional program activation requires guidelines. Very few existing professional training programs have goals for self-inspection and renewal. Sources of information which may facilitate the modification goals must be generated. These sources may include, aside from trainee performance data, reports from program graduates and research findings from other programs.

TABLE 6

Activities at the Stage III Level of Program Modification

	Intention	Observation	Assessment	Evaluation
Stage III Revision/ Renewal	Goals for Modification	Sources of Information	Reliability and Validity of Sources	Decisions about Utility of Information

The reliability and validity of these sources must be assessed according to a specific training curriculum. Ultimately, the utility of the information or data must be determined, again as it may pertain to a given program. Lacking the third stage, which opens a training system to more "public" inspection, the first two stages become involuted, and another "tradition" is established.

It is important to recognize that these stages are conceptual conveniences. Discussion of them is facilitated by examining them discretely. In actuality they are *continuous* processes. The intentions of the first stage permeate all cells of the scheme to some degree. Training efforts (Stage II) and inquiry (Stage III) are, or should be, intermixed. In turn, the third stage may influence revisions in the first stage. This is a highly dynamic system. It is useful because it enables trainers, supervisors, and program directors to identify their current situations and planning needs. It is a vehicle for aiding in the inspection of program status.

We have demonstrated a deficit in research and evaluation in applied training. Through our summarizations of the literature findings we have illustrated similarities and differences among the principal supervisory processes. Earlier we noted that evaluation models abound in social and behavioral sciences but that the professions under study have scarcely used any of them. We believe that the planning model presented, even in such brevity, offers much heuristic value. It is uncluttered by technical verbiage, and it may be applied to ongoing training programs as well as to those at incipient stages.

REFERENCES

De Bono, E. *Lateral thinking.* New York: Harper and Row, 1970.

Hansen, J., Pound, R., & Petro, C. Review of research on practicum supervision. *Counselor Education and Supervision,* 1976, **16**(2), 107-116.

Ryan, T., Baker, R., Hosford, R., & Fitzpatrick, G. Report of a National Survey by the ACES Committee on Counselor Effectiveness. The Annual Meeting of the American Personnel and Guidance Association. Las Vegas, Nevada, March 1969.

Worthen, B. R., & Sanders, J. R. *Educational evaluation: Theory and practice.* Worthington, Ohio: Charles A. Jones, 1973.

Glossary of Terms

Affective disorders. Mental disorders in which a disturbance of affect or feeling tone is predominant. Examples include depressive neurosis, manic depressive psychosis, involutional melancholia, and psychotic depression.*

Bachelor of Social Work. A person who holds a degree from an accredited undergraduate department of social work. The BSW is recognized as the first professional degree in social work.

Case consultation. The worker discusses a case with a consultant but is not bound by the consultant's opinion.

Casework. A method in social work which calls for interventive work with clients on a one-to-one basis.

Caseworker. A social worker who uses the casework method but with a psychological or psychiatric theoretical frame of reference. The use of the term in this sense is distinguished from the person who holds the title of caseworker in many settings but who has not been trained in social work.

Clinical supervision. A method of supervision which emerged from and reflects the use of "clinical" in the field of medicine.

---

*The American Psychiatric Association has given permission to use some definitions from their *Psychiatric Glossary* (4th ed.), published in 1975.

Clinical professor. A school-based coordinator who has a dual appointment from a school and a college or university.

Community psychiatry. That branch of psychiatry concerned with the provision and delivery of a coordinated program of mental health care to a specified population. Implicit in the concept is acceptance of continuing responsibility for all the mental health needs of the community.

Community organization. A method of intervention whereby individuals, groups, and organizations engage in planned action to influence social problems.

Community organizer. The worker who helps individuals, groups, or organizations to engage in social action.

Diagnostic school. Casework practice which relies on Freudian analysis of client behavior.

Feedback. Objective and subjective data from an outside source concerning how one is doing in relation to that one hopes to do.

Field instruction. The supervision of students in a field placement, practicum, or internship.

Field placement. The setting in which a student applies in practice the concepts and methods learned in the classroom. A minimum of four hundred and fifty hours in graduate training and three hundred hours in undergraduate training are required of all students in social work education.

Functional school. Casework practiced using the psychological theory of Otto Rank.

Group supervision. Workers are supervised in a group.

Group work. A method in social work which calls for intervention with individuals through the vehicle of groups.

Indigenous worker. A person, paid as an employee, who has similar social, cultural, and economic characteristics to the client group being served.

Master of Social Work. A person who has had the equivalent of two years of graduate education in an accredited school of social work.

Paraprofessional. A person who does not have a baccalaureate or equivalent degree of certification but who directly assists persons in the performance of social service duties.

Peer supervision. A form of supervision utilizing the student's equals in the supervisory role. It is argued that student teachers acquire evaluation skills in the process.

Primary care physician. The physician who provides basic general health care to an individual or family and who is usually the person the patient turns to first for care. Family practitioners, internists, and pediatricians usually function as primary care physicians.

Psychiatrist. A licensed physician who specialized in the diagnosis, treatment, and prevention of mental and emotional disorders. Training usually encompasses a premedical university education, medical school, and further training including three or more years of approved residency training.

Psychodynamics. The systematized knowledge and theory of human behavior and its motivation, the study of which depends largely upon the functional significance of emotion. It recognizes the role of unconscious motivation and assumes that a person's makeup and probable reactions are the product of past interactions between his specific genetic endowment and the environment in which he has lived.

Psychotherapy. A generic term for the treatment of mental and emotional disorders based primarily upon verbal and/or nonverbal communication with the patient.

Renewal. A process of organizational change and decision making which seeks to create a self-sustaining reform mechanism throughout the system.

Resident. A physician who is in graduate training to qualify as a specialist in a particular field of medicine.

School climate. The "feeling" one gains of a school as an organization. This feeling is seen as permeating all of the formal and informal operations of the school.

School supervision. Supervision which includes the responsibility of the principals, department heads, and other supervisory personnel in the school system for maintaining and improving the instructional program of the schools. Teacher evaluation is one aspect of this responsibility.

Social planning. The use of rational problem solving for program development in major social welfare institutions.

Somatic treatment. A diverse group of treatment methods for

mental disorders which makes use of physical interventions as opposed to using psychotherapy. Medication and shock treatment are examples of somatic treatments.

Tandem supervision. Two experienced workers consult with each other in a collaborative fashion.

Teacher center. Locations where student teachers are concentrated. These centers were created to reduce the gap between the university classroom and the public schools.

Team supervision. A method used in teaching clinics in which professional peers observe and analyze one another's teaching performances.

Teams. A group of workers who divide the tasks and responsibilities of solving a problem.

Tutorial supervision. Supervision on a one-to-one model. The supervisor tutors the worker.

Index

About the Editors

DeWayne J. Kurpius and Ronald D. Baker, associate professors of education at Indiana University, and Irene D. Thomas, associate professor of English Education and English at California State University at Fullerton, have been deeply involved in the area of applied training and have written numerous articles on the topic.